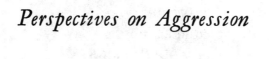

Perspectives on Aggression

CONTRIBUTORS

ROBERT BOICE

H. A. DENGERINK

EDWARD DONNERSTEIN

MARCIA DONNERSTEIN

RUSSELL G. GEEN

PETER J. McDONALD

ANDREW R. NESDALE

EDGAR C. O'NEAL

MICHAEL B. QUANTY

BRENDAN GAIL RULE

DAVID M. STONNER

Perspectives on Aggression

EDITED BY

RUSSELL G. GEEN

Department of Psychology
University of Missouri
Columbia, Missouri

EDGAR C. O'NEAL

Department of Psychology
Newcomb College of
Tulane University
New Orleans, Louisiana

ACADEMIC PRESS New York San Francisco London **1976**
A Subsidiary of Harcourt Brace Jovanovich, Publishers

Dedicated to Leonard Berkowitz

ACADEMIC PRESS, INC.
111 Fifth Avenue, New York, New York 10003

United Kingdom Edition published by
ACADEMIC PRESS, INC. (LONDON) LTD.
24/28 Oval Road, London NW1

Library of Congress Cataloging in Publication Data

Main entry under title:

Perspectives on aggression.

     Bibliography: p.
     1.   Aggressiveness (Psychology)   I.   Geen, Russel G.,
Date   II.   O'Neal, Edgar C.   [DNLM: 1.   Aggression.
BF575.A3 P467]
BF575.A3P47   152.4'2   75-19643
ISBN 0-12-278850-8

Contents

v

List of Contributors

Numbers in parentheses indicate the pages on which the authors' contributions begin.

Robert Boice (11), Department of Psychology, University of Missouri, Columbia, Missouri

H. A. Dengerink (61), Department of Psychology, Washington State University, Pullman, Washington

Edward Donnerstein (133), Department of Psychology, Iowa State University, Ames, Iowa

Marcia Donnerstein (133), Department of Psychology, Iowa State University, Ames, Iowa

Russell G. Geen (1, 193), Department of Psychology, University of Missouri, Columbia, Missouri

Peter J. McDonald (169), Department of Psychology, Tulane University, New Orleans, Louisiana

Andrew R. Nesdale (37), Department of Psychology, University of Alberta, Edmonton, Alberta, Canada

Edgar C. O'Neal (169), Department of Psychology, Newcomb College of Tulane University, New Orleans, Louisiana

Michael B. Quanty (99), Department of Psychology, Johnson County Community College, Overland Park, Kansas

Brendan Gail Rule (37), Department of Psychology, University of Alberta, Edmonton, Alberta, Canada

David M. Stonner (235), Department of Psychology, Oakland University, Rochester, Michigan

Preface

Books on human aggression are generally of two types. They are either monographs in which the writer adopts a fairly precise theory of aggression or collections emanating from symposia and conferences. The latter are usually specific in content and limited to a number of topics defined by the purpose of the meetings. This book fits neither category. It is not the product of a symposium nor is it an attempt by either editor to subsume the varieties of human aggression under a unitary theoretical heading. The points of view expressed in it are many, and the emphasis throughout is on the relationship of theory to the data of empirical investigations. The contributors have all conducted extensive research on aggression or related topics, and all work within the framework of experimental psychology. The book, accordingly, is primarily a review of current experimental research on human aggression, organized along lines that reflect the areas of current research.

Although the material reviewed in the book is heavily weighted in the direction of "pure" research conducted for the purpose of understanding the psychology of aggression, the chapters may also be conceptually grouped into two sets: One has obvious and particular relevance for contemporary social issues, and the applied value of the other is somewhat less obvious. In particular, Chapters 6, 7, and 8, which refer, respectively, to interracial aggression, environmental factors in aggression, and the role of the mass media in violence, touch upon three matters of clear social implication. Although the remaining chapters certainly have strong implications for applied psychology, they deal with subjects in which application is, for the moment, less clear-cut.

Credits

Figures

Figure 1, p. 67. From Borden, R. J. Witnessed aggression: Influence of an observer's sex and values on aggressive responding. *Journal of Personality and Social Psychology,* 1975, *31.* 567–573, Figure 1. Copyright 1975 by the American Psychological Assocition. Reprinted by permission.

Figure 3, p. 86. From Hartemink, J. H. *Physical aggression in schizophrenia.* Unpublished doctoral dissertation, Kent State University, 1971. Courtesy of the author.

Figure 4, p. 88. From Baron, R. A. Threatened retaliation from the victim as an inhibitor of physical aggression. *Journal of Research in Personality,* 1973, *7,* 103–115.

Figure 5, p. 91. From Dengerink, H. A., O'Leary, M. R., & Kasner, K. H. Individual differences in aggressive responses to attack: Internal-external locus of control and field dependence-independence. *Journal of Research in Personality,* 1975, *9,* 191–199.

Figures 1, 2, 3, 4, pp. 138, 139, 141–142. From Donnerstein, M., Simon, S., & Ditrichs, R. Variables in interracial aggression: Anonymity, expected retaliation, and a riot. *Journal of Personality and Social Psychology,* 1972, *22,* 236–245. Copyright 1972 by the American Psychological Association. Reprinted by permission.

Figures 5, 6, pp. 144, 145. From Donnerstein, E., & Donnerstein, M. White rewarding behavior as a function of the potential for black retaliation. *Journal of Personality and Social Psychology,* 1972, *24,* 327–333. Copyright 1972 by the American Psychological Association. Reprinted by permission.

Figure 7, 8, 9, pp. 146, 147, 148. From Donnerstein, E., & Donnerstein, M. Variables in interracial aggression: Potential ingroup censure.

Tables

The Study of Aggression

RUSSELL G. GEEN

Introduction

The 1960s was a watershed decade for theory and research on human aggression. Over that 10-year span, most of the theoretical positions that continue to enlighten and guide aggression research to the present time were formulated. The important work of Bandura, Berkowitz, Buss, Feshbach, and others of the period is reflected in the many citations with which the chapters of this volume are dotted. Most of the work by these investigators consisted of carefully controlled experiments, based on hypotheses derived from some theory of aggression and designed to study some limited aspect of that theory. The reviews in this volume, most of which are devoted to critical summaries of relatively recent research, almost uniformly reveal the theoretical and experimental heritage of the 1960s. The major purpose of the chapters that follow is to provide an updated summary of research findings on topics of current importance, to relate these findings to the theoretical bases on which they were built, and to make some guesses as to the future of theory and research in human aggression.

Ideally, a book on aggression would begin with a general definition of the term that would be more or less satisfactory to all students of the

1

problem and would then attempt to subsume the available empirical evidence under that definition. As will be readily evident from even a casual perusal, the present volume is not being offered as an example of such an ideal. None of the writers proposes to offer a general definition of aggression, and the term is accordingly used to refer to a variety of discriminably different behaviors. In this respect, it is typical of most contemporary writing on the subject. The word "aggression" is most often used in a broadly descriptive sense and in reference to many functionally different behaviors; attempts to formulate a precise overall definition generally founder on a host of conceptual problems (cf. Kaufmann, 1970). To a great extent, our confusion over the meaning of aggression arises from the fact that psychologists have taken the word from everyday language and tried to invest it with scientific precision. However, there is undoubtedly no such thing as "aggression," as a unitary phenomenon, either in the laboratory or in the world at large. Even laymen vary in what they mean by the term, as Rule and Nesdale indicate in their chapter "Moral Judgment of Aggressive Behavior"; it is small wonder, therefore, that psychologists have been driven to recognize such subclasses of aggression as "angry," "instrumental," "impulsive," and so forth, in order to continue applying the word to such widely diverse phenomena. Nor is it obvious what would be gained were we to follow the advice of some investigators (e.g., Tedeschi, Smith, & Brown, 1974) and reverse the definitional process, in effect adopting the definition of aggression used in the common tongue. Aggression is not a simple matter, no matter whose definition is followed.

Confusion and disagreement over definition is paralleled, or perhaps reflected, in a multiplicity of measures. Little of the massive amount of research that has been done on aggression has been addressed to a search for valid dependent measures, although the problem has not been entirely ignored (e.g., Hartmann, 1970; Knott, 1970). The more common practice is to adopt an operational definition of aggression (number or intensity of electric shocks delivered, hostility of verbal ratings, and so on) and to attempt to show that such measures are systematically related to antecedent variables in a way stated in some hypothesis. The dependent measures themselves most often have face validity and little else.

Variables in Aggression Research

Antecedent Variables

Most research on human aggression has been addressed to three sets of variables, which may be labeled as "antecedent," "intervening," and "outcome." Chief among antecedents, in terms of the number of experiments conducted, are variables concerned with provocation. Frustration, physical attack, verbal harassment, and insult are common experimental treatments that effectively serve as stimuli to aggression. In the following chapters, these variables are examined, in various contexts, by Rule and Nesdale, "Moral Judgment of Aggressive Behavior," Dengerink, "Personality Variables as Mediators of Attack-instigated Aggression", and Donnerstein and Donnerstein, "Research in the Control of Interracial Aggression." Rule and Nesdale discuss the characteristics of provocation that lead normal observers to render moral judgments on it, thereby creating not only definitions of the act but also predispositions to respond to it. The Donnersteins are concerned mainly with the effects that the race of the provocateur and that of the victim have upon the latter's reaction to provocation. Dengerink, while describing mainly intraorganismic conditions that follow provocation, nevertheless touches upon the features of the provocation itself that are most likely to elicit aggression, such as, for example, the intentions of the antagonist.

A second class of antecedent variables that has stimulated considerable research involves stimuli related to violence emanating from the person's environment. These stimuli may be related to aggression in several ways: as cues for previously acquired aggressive responses (Berkowitz, 1974), as sources of imitative aggression (Bandura, 1973), as information that produces a lowering of restraints against previously instigated violence (Bandura, 1973; Geen, 1975), or as the cause of increased emotional arousal (Zillmann, 1972). Geen discusses these matters in detail in his chapter, "Observing Violence in the Mass Media: Implications of Basic Research."

Recently some attention has been given to environmental variables that may be antecedents of aggression. To date relatively little has been reported on the role of environmental stressors, such as noise, heat, and population density, on human aggression, but the emphasis being placed on such variables in other contexts (e.g., Glass & Singer, 1972) compels us to conclude that this will be an area of growing interest. In their chapter "The Environmental Psychology of Aggression," O'Neal and McDonald summarize the current state of knowledge on the effects of such conditions.

Intervening Variables

Intervening variables in aggression research may be classified into two types: those that presumably mediate aggressive behavior and those that inhibit it. Among the former are emotional states, such as anger, hostility, and generalized arousal; among the latter are anxiety, guilt, and fear. In Dengerink's chapter, he discusses these variables in detail. Two aspects of the mediator-type variables have been of particular interest to current aggression researchers. One aspect is the role of cognitive attribution processes in the relationship of antecedent conditions and aggression. Attributions regarding the cause of provocation, the identity and intentions of the agent, and the individual's own emotional response to being provoked have all been shown to have an influence on aggression, as Dengerink also shows in his chapter. Furthermore, as Geen points out, the meaning that the observer attributes to aggressive stimuli also profoundly influences the amount of aggression associated with them. Such findings are, of course, thoroughly consistent with data from studies on problems other than aggression which also reveal the importance of cognitive attributions in behavior (this will be discussed later).

The second problem of interest concerning intervening variables in aggression deals with the nature of the emotional reaction to provocation. Two basic positions may be discerned. The "aggressive drive" theory states that provocations, such as attacks or insults, create a behavior-specific drive state that motivates aggressive counterresponding. A corollary to this notion is the idea that aggression reduces the intensity of this drive state and produces a "catharsis" that makes further aggression less probable. This latter notion will be further discussed. The social learning theory adopts an alternative viewpoint to that of aggressive drive (Bandura, 1973). According to this theory, provocation generates a state of increased general arousal. Such arousal, when it occurs, is not response-specific but may instead activate behaviors other than aggression if they happen to be relatively dominant for the individual (cf. Berkowitz, 1969, 1971). Such a hypothesis is especially valuable in accounting for the role of environmental stressors in aggression (see O'Neal and McDonald's chapter): If the main function of provocation is to create arousal, which activates aggression, then arousal arising from other sources may do the same.

One of the more interesting questions that remains to be answered is under which exact conditions do environmental stimuli facilitate aggression and under which conditions do they inhibit it. Such conditions may, in other words, serve as antecedents for either mediating intervening variables or inhibitory ones. At some times and under certain conditions, they may activate aggression responses, by summating or interacting with aggression-relevant arousal, whereas, at other times, they may elicit or energize responses that are incompatible with aggression.

An example may be seen in studies on the effects of sexual arousal on aggression. Jaffe, Malamuth, Feingold, and Feshbach (1974) have shown that sexual arousal induced by the reading of erotic literature elicits greater aggressiveness (in presumably nonangered subjects) than does the reading of science fiction. Such a finding would be consistent with the notion that aggressive responses can be energized by general arousal. Baron (1974), however, has shown that if the subject has been instigated to aggression before being exposed to erotica, the outcome is a level of aggression lower than that shown by subjects who were not sexually aroused. Zillmann (1971), however, showed that if the instigation to aggression follows the exposure to sexually exciting stimuli, no such decrease in aggressiveness occurs. These three studies exemplify the complexity of effects that irrelevant environmental stimuli may have on aggression. Baron (1974) has argued that such stimuli, when they precede instigation to aggression, may elicit arousal that is labeled as anger, which, in turn, summates with attack-relevant anger, whereas, when the stimuli follow the instigation, they may serve primarily to interfere with anger-related behavior. Thus the mere existence of environmental sources of arousal may be less important for aggression than the precise ways in which they interact with more direct provocation.

Outcome Variables

What we are here calling outcome variables do not refer to the aggressive acts themselves but to conditions that follow aggression, such as rewards and punishments. The instrumental reward value of aggression in the attainment of goals has been a matter of prime concern to such investigators as Buss (1971) and Patterson (Patterson & Cobb, 1971). That rewarding aggression enhances the probability of even more aggression is a cultural truism that has haunted American diplomats since the Munich crisis of 1938, often with disastrous results. On a somewhat more prosaic level, the same idea is reflected in parental injunctions against letting their children be rewarded for fighting and in the maxim usually attributed to the American gangster Al Capone: "You get more with a kind word and a gun than with a kind word alone."

Research on the effects of punishing aggression has generally concluded that punishment, especially when physical and of high intensity, is usually associated with subsequent increases in aggression rather than decreases. The work of Taylor and his associates (Pisano & Taylor, 1971), reviewed by Dengerink, may be interpreted in this way. In general, these studies have shown that aggression is more effectively controlled by a rational strategy of measured retaliation than by the administration of intense punishment. Furthermore, as Eron and his associates have shown in their studies with children, physical punishment may enhance aggressiveness both by provoking the recipient and by providing a model for aggressive behavior (Eron, Walder, & Lefkowitz, 1971).

In recent years, we have witnessed a renewal of interest in another supposed outcome of aggression: hostility catharsis. Catharsis refers to a hypothesized reduction in aggressive motivation that follows either the direct expression of aggression, some vicarious experience, such as observing violence in others, or indirect aggression manifested in such high-magnitude activities as vigorous sports. In one or another of these forms, the idea of catharsis goes back to antiquity, although in its more modern form it is usually traced to Sigmund Freud. As Quanty points out in his chapter "Aggression Catharsis: Experimental Investigations and Implications," there are few studies that qualify as adequate tests of the catharsis hypothesis, despite the large volume of literature supposedly directed at the problem. In adopting a stringent definition of catharsis, Quanty shows that most experiments fail to provide an adequate test for the hypothesis that a decrease in aggressive motivation follows aggressive or aggression-substitute behavior, and those which do fail to support the idea of catharsis.

In differentiating among antecedent, intervening, and outcome variables in aggression research, we do not wish to imply that there is no overlap between these categories. Antecedents can often be linked meaningfully to aggression only by assuming the existence of intervening states that serve as mediators. The alternative "general arousal" and "aggressive drive" constructs mentioned earlier are examples of specific conditions that presumably follow frustration, insult, or attack and allow us to conclude that the latter are preconditions for aggression. What we have called outcome variables may also feed back to the class we have labeled antecedents: For example, as we have seen, punishment for aggression may be a frustration that elicits more aggression. Outcomes may also determine intervening conditions: Being rewarded for aggression, for instance, can promote reduced restraints against further violence, and so forth.

Other Topics

Two final matters deserve mention because they represent areas of current interest in aggression that are dealt with in this book. The first is the role of cognition in the arousal and control of aggression. In recent years, theorizing on social motivation in general has emphasized more

and more the importance of the individual's judgments and interpretations of the situation in which he finds himself (London & Nisbett,
1974; Weiner, 1972). An important part of the interpretative process involves attributing motives, intentions, and other such nonobservables to
individuals on the basis of observed behaviors. In aggression research,
attention is now being turned toward cognitive-attributional processes at
both the antecedent and intervening levels. As Dengerink, Rule and
Nesdale, and Geen point out, individuals do not react simply to objective conditions that may appear to be preconditions for aggression.
People judge attacks to be more or less justified, for example, on the
basis of what they perceive to be certain salient characteristics of the
act, the victim, the aggressor, and the overall situation. Furthermore,
the perceived intent of an attacker often appears to be a more powerful
determinant of counterattack than the amount of harm or injury suf-
fered. On the level of intervening variables, an individual's reactions to
provocation will, as Dengerink shows, depend not only on how aroused
he has become, but also on how he interprets that arousal and whether
he labels it as hostility or anger.

The second matter touched upon in this volume is the role of animal
studies in aggression research. As Boice points out in his chapter, "In
the Shadow of Darwin," animal aggression research has followed two
general lines.[1] One line is the instinctivist–ethological, which is known
to most Americans through its "pop-psych" counterpart in the writings
of Lorenz (1966), Ardrey (1966), and Morris (1967). The other tradition
is the behavioristic one. Whereas the popularized instinct approach has
made more of an impact on the general public, the behaviorists have
probably attracted more attention from investigators of human aggression. The work of Azrin and his associates (Azrin, Hake, &
Hutchinson, 1965; Hutchinson, 1973) is the best known of this type; it
attempts to show a functional relationship between aversive stimulation
(such as electric shock and frustrative nonreward) and attack behavior
in animals. Boice takes a highly critical approach to both lines of
animal research, criticizing their theoretical assumptions and, where applicable, their methodology; his conclusion, perhaps not a popular one,
is that animal research on aggression has contributed little to our understanding of aggression in humans.

The book concludes with an overview chapter by Stonner, "The
Study of Aggression: Conclusions and Prospects for the Future," in
which some comments are made on current trends in aggression re-

[1] In the present context, we are referring primarily to behavioral studies of aggression
and not to physiological and endocrinological research, which is beyond the scope of this
book.

search (some of which are mentioned in this brief introduction), and some speculations offered concerning future directions that human aggression research will take. Stonner foresees increasing pressure on psychology to investigate aggression as a social problem and to recommend means of control over violent behavior. Nevertheless, he concludes that the best future course will be one in which psychologists continue to study the problem empirically and primarily experimentally. Only in this way can controls be found that are effective without being worse than the violence they replace. If we imagine the primary task of psychologists to be the continuation of controlled research into the nature of aggression, and not social engineering, then the material covered in this book assumes considerable importance as the empirical foundation upon which future research, hopefully, will build.

REFERENCES

Ardrey, R. *The territorial imperative,* New York: Athaneum, 1966.
Azrin, N. H., Hake, D. F., & Hutchinson, R. R. Elicitation of aggression by a physical blow. *Journal of the Experimental Analysis of Behavior,* 1965, *8,* 55–57.
Bandura, A. *Aggression: A social learning analysis.* Englewood Cliffs, New Jersey: Prentice-Hall, 1973.
Baron, R. A. The aggression-inhibiting influence of heightened sexual arousal. *Journal of Personality and Social Psychology,* 1974, *30,* 318–322.
Berkowitz, L. The frustration-aggression hypothesis revisited. In L. Berkowitz (Ed.), *Roots of aggression: A re-examination of the frustration-aggression hypothesis.* New York: Atherton Press, 1969. Pp. 1–28.
Berkowitz, L. The contagion of violence: A S-R mediational analysis of some effects of observed aggression. In W. J. Arnold & M. M. Page (Eds.), *Nebraska symposium on motivation,* 1970. Lincoln, Nebraska: Univ. of Nebraska Press, 1971. Pp. 95–135.
Berkowitz, L. Some determinants of impulsive aggression: The role of mediated associations with reinforcements for aggression. *Psychological Review,* 1974, *81,* 165–176.
Buss, A. H. Aggression pays. In J. E. Singer (Ed.), *The control of aggression and violence.* New York: Academic Press, 1971. Pp. 7–18.
Eron, L. D., Walder, L. O., & Lefkowitz, M. M. *The learning of aggression in children.* Boston: Little-Brown, 1971.
Geen, R. G. Some effects of observing violence upon the behavior of the observer. In B. A. Maher (Ed.), *Progress in experimental personality research,* Vol. 8. New York: Academic Press, 1975, in press.
Glass, D. C., & Singer, J. E. *Urban stress.* New York: Academic Press, 1972.
Hartmann, D. P. Comments on the choice of a dependent variable in laboratory investigations of human aggression. Paper delivered at Annual Convention of the American Psychological Association, 1970.
Hutchinson, R. R. The environmental causes of aggression. In J. K. Cole & D. J. Jensen (Eds.), *Nebraska symposium on motivation,* 1972. Lincoln, Nebraska: Univ. of Nebraska Press, 1973. Pp. 155–181.
Jaffe, Y., Malamuth, N., Feingold, J., & Feshbach, S. Sexual arousal and behavioral aggression. *Journal of Personality and Social Psychology,* 1974, *30,* 759–764.

Kaufmann, H. *Aggression and altruism.* New York: Holt, 1970.

Knott, P. D. A further methodological study of the measurement of interpersonal aggression. *Psychological Reports,* 1970, *26,* 807–809.

London, H., & Nisbett, R. E. (Eds.) *Thought and feeling.* Chicago: Aldine, 1974.

Lorenz, K. *On aggression.* New York: Harcourt, 1966.

Morris, D. *The naked ape.* New York: McGraw-Hill, 1967.

Patterson, G. R., & Cobb, J. A. A dyadic analysis of "aggressive" behaviors: An additional step toward a theory of aggression. In J. P. Hill (Ed.), *Minnesota symposium on child psychology,* Vol. 5. Minneapolis: Univ. of Minnesota Press, 1971. Pp. 72–129.

Pisano, R., & Taylor, S. P. Reduction of physical aggression: The effects of four strategies. *Journal of Personality and Social Psychology,* 1971, *19,* 237–242.

Tedeschi, R. E., Smith, R. C., & Brown, R. C. A reinterpretation of research on aggression. *Psychological Bulletin,* 1974, *81,* 540–562.

Weiner, B. *Theories of motivation.* Chicago: Markham, 1972.

Zillmann, D. Excitation transfer in communication-mediated aggressive behavior. *Journal of Experimental Social Psychology,* 1971, *7,* 119–434.

Zillmann, D. The role of excitation in aggressive behavior. Proceedings of the Seventeenth International Congress of Applied Psychology, 1971. Brussels: Editest, 1972.

In the Shadow of Darwin

ROBERT BOICE

Introduction

Psychologists often preface other considerations with one on man in his original state of innocence. Just as Thomas Aquinas began his section on psychology in *Summa Theologica* with the six days of creation, contemporary psychologists often start with considerations of primitive man or of animals.

There is an undeniable curiosity in many of us concerning the recapitulation of human aggression from primitive man and even from evolutionary roots in other animals. Scott (1974) emphasizes that "we cannot avoid the question of man's primitive nature, if for no other reason than that people are fascinated by their ancestors and frequently use bad guesses concerning them to excuse bad behavior [p. 430]." Moreover, there is undeniable fun in manufacturing fictions about man's links with nature. Medieval bestiaries featured animals with human components, notably the seductive mermaid, and modern-day college students are infatuated with spacemen who presumably impregnated our ancestors with human qualities.

The real advantage of the tradition of recapitulating man's aggressive nature should lie in empirical research. Increasingly, social

11

psychologists are becoming involved in research on animal behavior. For instance, Zajonc (1969; 1972) is something of a leader in the detailed study of sociality in animals, including insects; he contends that such analysis may eventually generate universal laws of behavior. Consider his notion that we can build these laws with classic discoveries from animal behavior research, such as Schneirla's (1959) idea that weak stimulation elicits approach behavior whereas strong stimulation elicits avoidance; Tinbergen's (1953) idea that elements of approach and aggression are conflicting elements in mating behavior; and Lack's (1954) proposal that regulation of population densities is the essence of many social behaviors. One problem, of course, is whether these generalities extend meaningfully to humans.

An indication of the importance ascribed to recapitulations is their presence in the *Handbook of Social Psychology*. Hebb and Thompson (1969) encyclopedically detail topics including animal intelligence, early environment, social behavior of insects, cooperation, and methods of recording behavior. Scott's (1969) chapter on the social psychology of animals is equally impressive. His premise is that, since precultural man no longer exists, the bases of human behavior, such as aggression, can only be inferred from indirect lines of evidence in the animal kingdom. Scott's forte is a behavioral taxonomy of systems, such as allelomimetic (contagious), epimeletic (care-giving), and even elimina-tive behaviors. These are ordered against phyletic levels including protozoa, porifera, platyhelminthes, mollusca, and chordata. The result is seen as an orderly increase in the scope of behavioral systems as one ascends the scale to vertebrates. Whatever else, chapters such as this add an aura of science to social psychology and the study of aggression.

For all its antiquity and recent growth, the tradition of recapitulation has yet to be taken seriously by most social scientists. Animal considerations may be fun, and the parallels in human behavior may be curious, but not many social psychologists train their students in animal behavior research techniques. The result is that animal chapters in social psychology have an apologetic tone in common. Attempts to convince readers that animal psychology is valuable usually include some of the following rationales:

1. Animal research keeps us honest (i.e., less anthropocentric) in the study of human behavior.
2. If one is interested in nature, animals are important because they are part of nature.
3. Animals show some obvious continuities with humans; thus, the evolution of behavioral bases can be discerned.

4. Animals are interesting, and intellectual curiosity is sufficient justification for any pursuit in psychology.
5. It is impractical to impose genetic, painful, and surgical manipulations on man but not upon animals.
6. Animal research may provide useful hypotheses for human research.

As reasonable as these rationales seem, they are apparently not effective. Why else is there a continued need for their emphasis? I would suggest that researchers on aggression are largely justified in their ambivalence toward animal research; accordingly, this animal chapter is meant to break with some of the aforementioned traditions. The intention is to show that the divisive nature of animal research has contributed significantly to the ambivalence of others toward it by promoting three sources of limitation. The effect of these limitations has been to isolate animal researchers into separate camps and, overall, to present the external appearance of superficiality. The sources can be characterized as: first, Darwinism, the tradition of behaviorism, and the traditional emphasis on learning research in American psychology at the expense of research on aggression; second, Darwinism and the disparate inspirations of functional versus causative views of animal aggression; and third, Darwinism and belief in natural scales of hierarchical evolution that link man and animals in naive fashion.

Though Darwin was admirably objective and innovative (Ghiselin, 1972), these inspirations persist beyond his apparent intentions. As a result, animal psychology has moved into the shadow of Darwin. The suggestion here is that these three sources of limitation and confusion, to be shortly developed, have rendered research on animal aggression far less valuable than is usually admitted by an animal researcher.

There is nothing new in criticizing animal research in the behavioral sciences. Wundt (1894), admittedly no friend of animals, must have enjoyed emphasizing that the reason animals cannot talk is that they have nothing to say. Humanists are equally blatant in their denigration of animal research. Allport (1955) was typical in complaining of a psychology too heavily founded "upon the behavior of captive and desperate rats [p. 18]." What *is* relatively new is a trend of criticism within animal psychology. In this case, criticism is constructive and is intended to broaden the scope and application of animal psychology by emphasizing new combinations of simple approaches (see Hailman, 1969; Hess, 1972). Much the same attitude is presented here, especially as it pertains to showing the narrowness of research on animal aggression.

Darwinism   and   the   Exclusion   of   Aggression   Research   in America

Darwinian evolution was the inspiration for Europeans to study instincts, social signaling, aggression, and fixed patterns of adaptation to the environment. Darwin also inspired Americans to emphasize the study of learning as an adaptation to the environment. Not surprisingly, the different directions are based on appropriate animal preparations; birds, fish, and insects excel in stereotyped behaviors while Norway rats, as commensals of civilized men, are superb learners.

In the American case, continuity of mentality (but not of aggression) became the issue, and Romanes became the prod to a new comparative psychology (Carter, 1899). Animal mind eventually became less mentalistic, but assumptions that intelligence is rooted in evolution have continued to be basic. Even with the ascendancy of American behaviorism, this premise was accepted, although covertly so. This tradition grew at the expense of interest in animal behaviors other than intelligence, including aggression. Its development is viewed here, somewhat simplistically, in three distinct stages with James, Thorndike, and Watson as exemplars.

James and Symptom

The idea that learning is obviously the symptom of mentality properly belongs to Romanes, although James (1890) popularized it as the rationale for studying animal learning. Given this idea, proof of continuity between animal and human intelligence awaited studies of animal learning: *"The pursuance of future ends and the choice of means for their attainment are thus the mark and criterion of the presence of mentality* in a phenomenon [p. 8, italics original]." So ability to make a choice became the criterion of consciousness, and choice behavior in animals was obviously demonstrated in discrimination learning. This was probably the most important impetus for animal learning research in psychology. It is interesting to speculate now about the possible result had these early behaviorists decided to look for evolutionary continuity in aggression instead of in learning ability.

This era in the history of animal learning was more anecdotal than experimental (Petronovich, 1973). Anecdotes were supplied as the only proof of mentality (Romanes, 1904); an overreaction against mentalism and subjectivism was inevitable.

Thorndike and Utility

Thorndike (1911), who described his method as the first deliberate and extensively experimental approach in animal learning research, was an early behaviorist. Learning, to him, was important and worth studying because of its great utility (Burnham, 1972). To Thorndike, associations, not instincts, spelled success in nature and were the chief factor in the supremacy of mammals. The inspiration remained Darwinian since the emphasis was still on successful adaptations to environments, that is, on viewing learning ability as an adaptive entity. Mentalism was now fading from the picture. Aggression, even though seemingly adaptive in evolution, was faring no better as a subject of interest in American psychology.

Thorndike was the first in a long tradition of psychologists caught up in the joy of building clever apparatus for tests of animal learning. This feeling was sometimes accompanied by a self-righteous belief in the powers of objectivism:

> Our method gives some very important results which are quite uninfluenced by *any* personal factor in any way. The curves showing the progress of the formation of associations . . . are absolute, and whatever can be deduced from them is sure [Thorndike, 1911, p. 28].

Two things should be noted concerning this attitude. It helped perpetuate the emphasis on animal learning, on behaviors amenable to objective control. It also helped continue the exclusion of research on aggression in American animal psychology; not until a half-century later did behaviorists devise laboratory techniques which afforded equivalently easy control of aggression (Ulrich, 1966).

Watson and Control

Watson (1914), too, saw animal learning as the most important aspect in the study of behavior. His rationale for the study of learning was as simple and assertively honest as behaviorism. It was, in a word, control. The behaviorist should emphasize learning "since by habit formation he finds the most direct way of controlling animal activity [p. 45]."

Here the interest in evolution (or genetics) was no longer explicit; the rationale for studying learning became implicit as it evolved. Nonetheless, the old Darwinian ideas are still with us. For example, Skinner (1972) uses the rationale of evolution by natural selection as the cornerstone of his schemes in *Beyond Freedom and Dignity*. Consider how he emphasizes the environment as an often inconspicuous but powerful selector of genotypes over generations and of behavior in daily life. He is unparalleled in stating the orthodox position of behaviorism: Darwin's great insight was seeing the subtle power of the environment in determining the character of animals over generations; thus, there was no "act of creation." Skinner's great insight, he feels, was seeing the equally subtle power of the environment in shaping behavior on a day-to-day basis; thus there is no act of creation (again, in the sense of spontaneity) in behavior. At least two beliefs follow from this scheme: All behavior is determined (by environmental shaping), and operant conditioning must have evolved as an adaptive means of surviving the selection pressures of the environment.

Behaviorists continue to emphasize the study of behavioral control and manipulation of learned behaviors. In doing so, they have generally ignored social behaviors, such as aggression. Only recently has the laboratory rat begun to lose its reputation as an asocial creature, largely through the efforts of social psychologists, such as Latané (1969). Indeed, behaviorists have typically shown little interest in their animals beyond their ability to perform in a learning apparatus. Thorndike (1936) noted that he chose animals despite his indifference to them because they offered new research territory. Thus, one of the results of this Darwinian inspiration for the study of mental continuity has been to discourage views of laboratory animals as social, aggressive beings. In a related way, behaviorism has often had effects beyond simple indifference. It has also helped to suppress the idea that behaviors, such as aggression, have important, instinctive components. A case in point is that of the famous social psychologist MacDougall.

MacDougall and Instincts

As Herrnstein (1972) notes, origins and concepts of instincts are largely uncommunicated in American psychology. His analysis shows that the treatment of instinct in American psychology has passed from disrepute, to disuse, to, finally, disguise. The power of behaviorism was in making a straw man of instincts and then destroying them. Instincts were defined by behaviorists as concatenated reflexes, differing from ordinary reflexes only in degree of complexity. In Watson's usage, instincts became integrated movements after a good deal of learning (and only rarely as a direct result of inheritance).

MacDougall came from the European tradition of interpreting Darwinism by emphasizing the adaptiveness of unlearned behaviors. He openly advocated instincts as unlearned entities. Instincts were striving or motivation; they were the urge to action, modifiable on efferent and afferent sides, but with an invariant core. So learning was not excluded. Nor was the seemingly critical biological predisposition. Herrnstein demonstrates that behaviorists never really listened to MacDougall, choosing instead to consider instincts as rigid stereotyped behaviors which can be shown to be almost nonexistent in laboratory rats or in civilized humans.

Despite the antagonism of behaviorists toward MacDougall (see Watson & MacDougall, 1929), they are now incorporating some ideas similar to his but labeling them as motivation (Herrnstein, 1972). The loss for aggression research is that behaviorism continues to ignore questions of inheritance or genetics (Hirsch, 1967), even though a key to critical insights into aggression may lie in the understanding of the distortion of genetic systems of aggression (Scott, 1974).

Darwinism and Functional versus Causative Views

Thus, the first way in which Darwinian inspirations limited animal research on aggression was by emphasizing learning paradigms to the exclusion of most social behaviors. The second kind of Darwinian inspiration is equally pervasive; it concerns the way in which animal behavior is studied and evaluated. It often results in separation and exaggeration of efforts with little effective communication between two disparate approaches. Again, the two views are basically European versus American where animal research is concerned. The former is more likely to value the functional (i.e., adaptive) bases of a behavior such as aggression; the latter is characterized by interest in the control of behaviors such as instrumental responding. Actually the two can be simplified as field versus laboratory approaches. Revusky (1974) has further characterized functional versus causative styles in terms of Aristotelian and Platonic thinking: "Aristotelians organize knowledge according to the way things are, while Platonists, their opposites, organize knowledge through considerations of ideal situations which elucidate general processes [p. 693]."

Dispositions toward field versus laboratory approaches are not strictly the result of Darwinian influence, but have an interesting history of their own (Jaynes, 1969). In brief, the functional and causative views were convenient ways of reacting to Darwinism. Americans were more interested in the evolution of mentality, and so they opted for the control and contrivance of laboratory study. Tinbergen (see Hall, 1974) asserts that American animal researchers were destined to adopt the causative view since Americans have a heritage of interest in conquering nature: "You can only master nature when you understand causation [p. 66]." In any case, the new methods of animal testing devised by Thorndike aroused the admiration of American psychologists. Only a small minority of field oriented behaviorists protested his contrivances; for example, Mills (1899) saw irony in placing animals in confined puzzle boxes and then expecting natural behaviors.

European animal behaviorists, who typically call themselves ethologists, were inspired to unobtrusive, field studies of adaptive behaviors, such as territoriality. Johnsgard (1967) repeats a facetious but telling view of the difference between ethologists and comparative psychologists:

> The ethologist attempts to leave the animal as unrestricted as possible to study its "normal" behavior, and therefore tolerates any necessary discomforts while enclosing himself in a blind. The psychologist, in attempting to reduce the external variables, places the blind around the animal, thereby making it uncomfortable [p. vii].

Two Views of Aggression

Ethologists study the adaptiveness of aggression, ideally by unobtrusively watching its spontaneous appearance in a natural setting. In this way, they hope to discern the function of aggression. Comparative psychologists have only recently begun extensive research on aggression. For them, as for Watson, control and modification of aggression are emphasized. As a rule, they care little for the natural history of aggression, as long as they can bring it under stimulus control. Moreover, comparative psychologists are generally disinclined to abandon the control of the laboratory and to wait patiently for aggression to occur in natural settings. Both approaches have distinct advantages, however: witness the success of van Lawick-Goodall's (1968) field research of the social behaviors of chimpanzees or of the Harlows' (Harlow & Harlow, 1966) laboratory research with affectional systems of rhesus monkeys. Still, where research on aggression is concerned, both views tend to the kind of extremism that limits the contribution of animal study.

Perhaps, because ethologists genuinely enjoy the animals they study and that enthusiasm spreads to generalizations about human behavior, ethology often produces reports that offend psychologists. The offense arises from, among other things, speculation, oversimplification, positing of instincts, and pessimistic ascription of biological bases to human behavior. In addition, ethologists write more entertainingly than psychologists:

> The enlarged female breasts are usually thought of primarily as maternal rather than sexual developments, but there seems to be little evidence for this. . . . The evolution

of protruding breasts of a characteristic shape appears to be yet another example of sexual signalling . . . they also serve to concentrate visual attention to the nipples and to make the nipple erection that accompanies sexual arousal more conspicuous [Morris, 1967, p. 70].

Where research on aggression is concerned, the methods of ethology often seem casual, the results too descriptive, and the application to human behavior fanciful at best. Consider the offerings of Lorenz (1966). His accounts of animal behavior include few numerical data or indications of reliability. These seeming flaws are compounded by generalizations:

Sporting contests between nations are beneficial not only because they provide an outlet for the collective militant enthusiasm of nations [p. 282] . . . [but, he continues] I think we must face the fact that militant enthusiasm has evolved from the hackle-raising and chin-protruding communal defense instinct of our prehuman ancestors [p. 284].

Thus, the potential contribution of ethological research on aggression is greatly diminished by this type of approach and reporting. The problem is accentuated by the opposite biases of psychologists and other environmentalists; they are often less than objective in evaluating ethological writing. Reactions are well known and run a gamut from assertive denials—"War is not in our genes" insists Carrigher (in Montagu, 1968), who claims that belief in a genetic basis of aggression will prolong man's fighting behavior more than anything else—to attacks by otherwise pacific psychologists—such as "That old-time aggression" by J. P. Scott (also in Montagu, 1968). Scott describes Lorenz as a narrow man who reads little beyond his narrow specialty of birds.

It is principally Ulrich (1966) who has popularized objective and controlled laboratory research on animal aggression. The result is an extremism as offensive to ethologists as is the aforementioned offense to psychologists. Ulrich has resurrected a forgotten technique in which agonistic behaviors appear when proximate pairs of animals (often rats) are painfully stimulated (usually with electric shock). One appeal of this research is its amenability to control; as defined, the behavior is nicely specific to a number of variables, such as intensity, duration, and frequency of shock.

This contrived "fighting" response is easily and reliably recorded. Just as Thorndike believed that such qualities made the value of objectivism absolute, researchers in this area sometimes posit a great applicability of this narrow research to the overall understanding of aggression. A basic problem, however, lies in the assumption that there is a simple, characteristic pattern of elicited "fighting" in animals which represents aggression. Less structured approaches to the study of animal aggression show that it is far more complex than the criterion posture of sparring used by behaviorists (Ulrich, 1966; cf. Grant & Mackintosh, 1963). Postures and their sequences are myriad even in the confines of an elicited aggression apparatus, if one simply observes (Turner, Boice, & Powers, 1973). For example, rather than being the essence of aggression, sparring is often only a prelude to fighting and is only one of several threat postures that can avert aggression (Logan & Boice, 1969). Moreover, sparring may be judged as defensive, rather than really aggressive, behavior (Reynierse, 1971) or may be complicated by attempts to escape shock.

To further implement precision, some behaviorists have eliminated the presence of the second animal as a confounding variable. Thus, pain-elicited aggression toward an inanimate object can be measured automatically without the inconvenience of direct observation by the experimenter (Azrin, Rubin, & Hutchinson, 1968). Imagine the incredulity of an ethologist when informed that the social presence of the second animal confounds research on aggression. To add further offense, inform him that genetics can profitably be removed from aggression research: "Use of a docile animal (the albino rat) also eliminates complications due to genetically determined tendencies to fight [Ulrich, 1966, p. 644]."

Tinbergen and Skinner

The clearest picture of the gulf between functional and causative styles of animal study can be seen in the writings of its most prominent leaders, Tinbergen and Skinner.

Early in his career, Tinbergen abandoned a valuable professorship at Leiden for a lectureship at Oxford because his goal was to evangelize ethology to the English-speaking world. His success began with his classic textbook of ethology, *Study of Instinct* (1951); this contained one of the first appeals for a human ethology. It was based on the kind of support which has become a trademark of ethology; he used demonstrational evidence which he claimed to be about equivalent in value to the data from experiments. So to show a maternal instinct in humans, for example, Tinbergen noted that:

1. Children's dolls, with relatively large heads and other infantile characteristics, are adapted to meet the demands of an innate releasing mechanism.
2. The film industry has developed an optimal baby.
3. Childless women select substitutes for babies in their pets.

In the foreword to the reissue of this classic in 1969, Tinbergen states that human ethology had failed to make greater progress because psychology persists in overemphasizing studies of causation. Apparently, he is unconcerned that speculation of the sort just listed has also been injurious to his cause.

Tinbergen's popularity with the public began with his *Curious Naturalist* (1958) and the *Herring Gull's World* (1967). Here he expressed the joy and wonderment of naturalism. He emphasized the interesting diversity of life patterns and of ways of coping with survival and, most important, how slowly insight into the meaning of observation grows. Consistent with the European tradition of observing without manipulating and controlling, Tinbergen attributed his insights to concentration and an open interest. Another prominent European, Freud, labeled the equivalent technique, free-floating attention (Ellenberger, 1970). In his years of patient observation, Tinbergen concluded that psychologists have had an insufficient understanding of natural law; for example, they have failed to realize that nature has developed what is necessary and nothing more. This is another way of saying that studying the adaptive function of behavior in its natural surrounds is sufficient. There is a growing realization in America that bringing behavior into the laboratory where it is controlled and distorted can be a mistake (Hailman, 1969; Hess, 1972).

A decade later, Tinbergen's views "On War and Peace in Animals and Man" (1968) appeared in a prominent medium. Initial emphasis concerned man's resistance to scrutiny as an animal; this was seen as an obstacle to the communication of ethology. He saw evidence of change in the sudden popularity of "admirable" books on the animal roots of human behavior by Lorenz and Morris. For Tinbergen, the real value of ethology lay in its biological approach to questions of survival and evolution; again, the emphasis was on function, not on the causation valued by "short-sighted psychologists."

As befits an article so ambitiously titled, he offers a clue to the main problem of understanding aggression. To appreciate why man alone is a mass-murderer, it is necessary to realize the importance of fear. Tinbergen bases his argument on the classic ethological observation that aggression is approach behavior countered by the adaptive tendency to withdraw. As a result, animals have the advantages of aggression without many disadvantages: They can use aggression to maintain adaptive spacing while resorting to bloodless devices such as threatening or withdrawal when conflict comes near. The problem for man, and the reason he goes to war, is that civilization has upset the balance between fear and aggression. People are taught to persist in nonadaptive fighting rather than be labeled cowards. In addition, he claims, the use of long-range weaponry obviates any adaptiveness in appeasement gestures by the victims.

For the sake of brevity, only two problems inherent in Tinbergen's arguments are discussed here. First, his explanation of man's warlike nature, rests on Morris's assumption that man is a social ape turned carnivore; thus, man as a social, hunting ape acquired group territories which today unite us in war when outside danger appears. Scott (1974), in contrast, claims that our remote ancestors were small, slight creatures with omnivorous teeth and jaws like ours and better equipped to run than to fight or prey: "Therefore, the argument that man kills man because he is a bloodthirsty carnivore has nothing to support it [p. 430]." Second, Tinbergen's notion that perceived appeasement would mollify warlike behavior is inconsistent with conclusions that the animal counterpart of war is xenophobic aggression (Southwick, Siddiqi, Farooqui, & Pal, 1974). Xenophobic aggression is a fearful reaction against strangers characteristic of most mammals living in closed societies (Holloway, 1974). A unique feature of this form of aggression is that appeasement gestures by the stranger are not always effective. If war is like xenophobic aggression, then appeasement will not be especially adaptive as was demonstrated in the Viet Nam massacres recently publicized.

These are, of course, the kinds of problems in the research on animals that make researchers in human aggression rather uneasy. The very abstract nature of animal research, its tradition of polemics, and its contradictions when communicating to the public, all strain the sense of immediacy seemingly needed in work on aggression. Sometimes animal researchers seem to forget that "aggressive behavior is generally viewed in the prejorative sense; we wish to make it stop, and live in a society where we will not be prey to it [Holloway, 1974, p. 3]."

Concerning the advancement of understanding of aggression, Skinner's views are no more promising than Tinbergen's. Moreover, neither view shows promise of change. In his latest article, Skinner (1975) reaffirms the irrelevance of biology to the immediate description of behavior. So, to use what he considers a dominant analogy, we should no more question the internal workings of a computer that apparently simulates human thinking than we should investigate our own apparent thinking. What counts are behavioral characteristics and their contingencies (i.e., causation) and not their functional qualities.

The equivalent to Tinbergen's (1968) paper, "On War and Peace in Animals," is Skinner's (1966) on "The Phylogeny and Ontogeny of Behavior." Although the title suggests that Skinner discusses both genetic and experiential bases (or provenances, Segal, 1972) of behavior, he merely dismisses the former provenance as irrelevant or confusing. Thus the tradition of isolationism continues; there is no real attempt on Skinner's part to incorporate the virtues of functional views. His paper begins with an appeal to recognize the importance of both phylogenic and ontogenic (notice the omission of the common suffix, *genetic*) contingencies in behavior. Soon after, however, he argues that the two are difficult to distinguish: "Behavior is behavior whether learned or unlearned; it is only the controlling variables which make a difference. The difference is not always important [p. 1210]."

Next, Skinner suggests that the phylogenic provenance can never really be known because the contingencies lie in antiquity. The solution, he argues, is to ignore or minimize phylogenic factors by minimizing species differences with operant techniques and by using domesticated animals. Among the problems in this argument is his conclusion that species-specific behavior of domesticated animals is extinguished because of the relaxed contingencies under which they live. There is *no* good evidence that domestication eliminates formerly adaptive behaviors (Boice, 1973). In one of the rare direct tests of this question, laboratory rats, even after hundreds of generations of life in wire cages, still dug burrows in dirt, indistinguishable from those of wild Norway rats (Boice, 1974).

One way in which behaviorism restricts the scope of animal behavior research is by excusing its disinterest in field research. Here is Skinner's (1966) defense in which he refers to an ethologist as a "behavioral taxonomist":

> The behavioral taxonomist may also argue that the contrived environment of the laboratory is defective since it does not evoke characteristic phylogenic behavior.
> But in what sense is this behavior not "natural"? If there is a natural phylogenic environment, it must be the environment in which a given kind of behavior evolved. But the phylogenic contingencies responsible for current behavior lie in the distant past.
> Current environments are almost as "unnatural" as a laboratory [p. 1211].

He continues the same defense in his famous book about freedom (1972). For example, he argues that the operant behaviors of pigeons in the laboratory are undoubtedly identical to the behavior of organisms in nature. As a result we are assured that the variable-ratio schedule which works so well in the laboratory is the "natural schedule." Thus readers are advised that there is no serious difference between contrived and natural conditions [p. 151].

Not much is said about aggression although Skinner concludes that man's genetics support his tendency to struggle against aversive or aggressive treatment. This tendency, he claims, has an evolutionary advantage which is easily demonstrated. The proof comes solely from the research on elicited aggression criticized above (and assumed by Skinnerians to be unconfounded by genetic variables). Ironically, the first chapter of *Beyond Freedom and Dignity* carries a strong admonition against speculating on effects of evolution because of the ease of making inferences where few facts exist [p. 11].

Darwinism and Natural Scales of Evolution

The third way in which Darwinism has limited research on animal aggression involves American psychology and natural scales of evolution. Today there is a sudden, widespread awareness that the traditional belief in these *Scala naturae* is probably a mistake (Hodos & Campbell, 1969). The argument, briefly, is that comparative psychology has erred in its assumption that evolution is linear and that animals can be hierarchically arranged by complexity in natural scales. So, the warning goes, there is no evidence in modern biology that man evolved directly from dogs, rats, turtles, and fish, in that order. For the moment, the paper by Hodos and Campbell and others like it are an inspiration to the young generation of animal researchers. Those who ignore it are taken to task (e.g., Zimmerman & Geist, 1974), and arguments in support of tradition are rare (e.g., Revusky, 1974).

There is nothing new in warnings of problems in natural scales. Such warnings have been, in fact, rather persistent, as a sample of the literature at roughly 20–25 year intervals shows:

1. Beach (1950) gave clear warning of *"Scala Natura,"* noting that pertinent arguments are too often speculative, and that related concepts have been uncritically accepted into psychology as part of the Darwinian movement.

2. Kantor (1935) warned against grand scales formulated without tracing the concrete factors in evolution, whereby animal behavior is erroneously viewed as a generalized quality with a progressive tendency toward complexity and betterment.

3. Holmes (1916) made the now popular point (see Lockard, 1971) that animal behavior evolved "not once, merely, but several times along different lines of descent [p. 123]."

4. Morgan (1896) presaged Tinbergen in arguing that animal behavior is no more elaborate than the demands of the natural niche. He

too presaged Seligman's (1970) popular notion that animal mind is not a generalized kind of ability.

Leaders in animal psychology, such as Hebb (1974), admonish young psychologists not to overlook or forget these classics, but they do. Perhaps what matters is that now the *Zeitgeist* is favorable for the consideration of criticisms of natural scales.

Even if the problems of traditional beliefs in *Scala naturae* are actually remedied, the tradition will still have had a generally detrimental effect on research on animal aggression. Two examples of such an effect are presented in the next sections.

Psychosocial versus Biosocial Behaviors

In Dethier and Stellar's (1970) *Animal Behavior,* types of animals are arranged in a linear scale: invertebrates, fish, amphibia, reptiles, birds, lower mammals, lower primates, up to, of course, man. These are aligned against levels of behavior, also ranked in terms of complexity: taxes, reflexes, instincts, learning, and reasoning. This is a classic example of a natural scale. Accordingly, it invokes assumptions that higher (again meaning more complex) modes of behaving characterize higher animals. Conversely, lower animals are expected to use simple modes as adaptive behaviors.

By the same logic, animal psychologists may expect that only higher animals show "real" social behaviors. So it is that Hebb and Thompson (1969) reiterate Schneirla's famous distinction between biosocial and psychosocial behaviors. Only the latter are considered real. In contrast, biosocial acts typically result from lower animals incapable of the complexity of truly social animals. Presumably, biosocial acts are stimulus dependent and are unlike social behaviors in which purpose and ideation are critical. Biosocial acts are merely sense dominated; they can be identified by their very simplicity, stereotypy, and predictability (defined by Hebb and Thompson as opposites of purpose and ideation). Old Jesuit texts (e.g., Wasmann, 1903) had a similar tone as we were assured that animal actions are not to be considered intelligent in that they "do not transcend the realm of sense perceptions [p.76]."

As a result of this aspect of belief in natural scales, research on social behavior is conducted with "lower" animals in the face of great negative bias. Consider the example of studies with cold blooded animals such as turtles, frogs, and toads. Authors must take great pains to prove that biting and wrestling behaviors are not merely mistaken attempts at feeding. Similar demands for proof would rarely be considered in the case of mammals such as rats. In one instance (Boice, Quanty, & Williams, 1974) precautions included the following: (*1*) controls and tests for misdirected feeding aimed at conspecifics, (*2*) daily testing for over a year, and (*3*) correlated observations of conspecifics living in the wild. Even so, one anonymous reviewer could not resist suggesting that if this were really aggressive behavior, some attentive zoologist would already have noticed it.

Of course, it can easily be argued that research on nonmammalians is of limited value in any case, but to do so is to deny much of a legitimate evolutionary rationale. To the extent that aggression has evolutionary bases, to the extent that it shows different evolutionary strategies, these animals should be given more consideration. The fact that they have not is another limitation of animal psychology.

Adaptiveness

A second problem with natural scales is less obvious because it relates to a concept highly unfamiliar to psychology: domestication. Even though domestication was a key to Darwin's innovative thinking (e.g., Darwin, 1868) and continues to be important in zoology (e.g., Hafez, 1975), its influence in psychology has been minimal except when the term is mistakenly used to malign the laboratory rat (Boice, 1973). Its relation to natural scales and to limitations in animal psychology will become apparent as some aspects of domestication are considered.

Domestication can be defined as the changes occurring when animals are removed from the selection pressures indigenous to their niche in nature and are subjected, over generations, to new selection pressures. Usually, these new selection pressures are most obviously a result of intentional confinement, protection, and selective breeding by humans (Ratner & Boice, 1975). Domestication can be a surprisingly powerful and quick agent of change (Zeuner, 1963).

Effects of domestication are not, as yet, widely documented, but they suggest interesting leads for the study of animal aggression (Boice, 1972):

1. Wild rats usually maintain larger personal spaces, threaten more, and fight less often than laboratory rats.

2. When wild rats threaten each other, postures are more dynamic and numerous than in laboratory rats. When wild rats fight, the action is more vigorous and injuries, even death, are more likely to occur.

3. When laboratory rats are sufficiently stressed, however, they will show all these wild-type tendencies. This suggests that domestication

has changed the thresholds for aggression and related behaviors without having eliminated these adaptive responses.

At least two kinds of insights can come from research on domestication: One suggests a criticism of natural scales, especially the corollary assumption that evolutionary links are direct and unaffected by conditions such as captivity. Captive, domestic animals *are* different in some important ways from their wild counterparts. Information from domestic animals does not necessarily represent behavior of undomesticated animals in their proper niche. Assumptions by psychologists to the contrary have long been a source of irritation to ethologists. In ignoring domestication, comparative psychologists may be overlooking an important common characteristic in many of the animals they study.

The second insight is that domestication operates as an analog of what we might call education in humans. Hebb and Thompson (1969) noted that the essence of education seems to be the rendering of less reactive, quieter people. Similarly, Bruner (1972) describes the ability of civilized man to abstract himself from a situation and to be less specifically reactive to it. Thus it seems that, in humans at least, progress and protection from many natural selection pressures, such as predation, have produced boredom, a propensity to learn for the sake of learning, and the possibly adaptive quality of nonreactiveness to some situations. If this is true, extensive education and its resultant tendencies to abstraction should produce quieter, less reactive, and less aggressive humans. This is an apparently untested notion among social psychologists who typically study college students to the exclusion of less educated people. A curious suggestion of the validity of this idea is seen in reports of Medieval magnetizers who easily hypnotized uneducated peasants but not the presumably less reactive nobles (Ellenberger, 1970). The temptation to follow Tinbergen's example of overgeneralization is difficult to resist. It would be fun to suppose that behavior is organized on genetic templates, some of which are more modifiable than others. For instance, facial expressions in humans show remarkable continuity to those in other primates; some of these appear to be relatively resistant to cultural influence (Ekman, 1973).

The point, however, is to use the descriptions of effects of human education as an inspiration for thinking on domestication and animals. Domestication does seem to inhibit intense aggression up to a point, and seems to be clearly intertwined with effects of education. A number of studies suggest that both domestication and enriched environments produce less reactive adults, while other studies show domestic rats to be better, more flexible performers in learning situations (Boice, 1973).

Perhaps, in the tradition of MacDougall, animal psychologists should consider both the biologic core and the modifiable exterior of processes such as aggression.

To properly evaluate the evolutionary cores of behaviors, animal psychologists should include some study of their animals in field situations. Traditionally, they have done little of this. It seems remarkable, for instance, that psychologists have almost no information about animal learning outside the laboratory. In the rare cases where learning has been observed in nature, it is often the result of protective intervention by man, itself a form of domestication. A famous instance is that of the Japanese monkeys who acquired and culturally transmitted a potato-washing habit; it occured only after humans provisioned the animals with a large supply of food.

We know almost nothing about learning under truly natural conditions yet psychologists typically assume that learning ability, because it seems obviously adaptive, must have evolved in response to natural selection pressures. Without empirical evidence from natural settings, it becomes necessary to ask the sort of question suggested by Harlow (1958):

> I have long been puzzled by the fact that the study of animals under laboratory conditions reveals many learning capabilities whose existence is hard to understand in terms of survival value [p. 273].
> The observational accounts of these animals make it quite clear that problems of this level of complexity are never solved, indeed they are never met, in the natural environment. It is superficially difficult to see how a trait which was never used gave to an organism some slight selective advantage over another organism which did not use the trait because it did not have it [p. 274].

Until there is evidence from naturalistic observation that complex learning ability is adaptive in nature, it is equally logical to suppose that it is largely an artifact of laboratory conditions. This is not a novel idea to ethologists who surmise that conditions of domestication bring boredom, increased playfulness, exploration, and a propensity to learn (Hediger, 1964; Thorpe, 1963). Hailman (1969), after comparing behaviors in and out of the laboratory, concluded that psychologists often produce unnatural learning by artifactually elaborating simple perceptual processes into complex learning.

Thus simplistic notions of natural scales have limited the potential contribution of animal research. In one instance it has surreptitiously discouraged research on aggression in animals other than mammals. In the other, it has encouraged the exclusion of naturalistic study while perpetuating the emphasis on animal intelligence. Both these factors reinforce the limitations discussed earlier; there is clear indication of an American animal psychology which narrows its scope and misses much of its potential in naturalism, in elucidating evolutionary bases of aggression, and in communication with an equally narrow ethology. Still, there should be numerous generalizations to human behavior of potential value to aggression researchers. The next section is a brief attempt to generalize from a particularly promising area of animal research.

Do Sex Role Differences Generalize from other Primates to Humans?

Concern over sex role differences is as timely as its rhetoric is speculative. It is refreshing, then, to discover a relatively new area of primate research in which the results are clear and remarkably suggestive of gender differences in humans. At first glance, they support the belief that males are naturally more aggressive.

Poirer (1974) offers a concise review of this interesting research in the socialization process. His presentation is abstracted here:

1.   Rhesus mothers threaten and punish male infants earlier and more often than female infants. The latter are retrieved and protected more than male infants who are subtly reinforced for rough play by their mothers' behaviors toward them.

2.   Early in life, male infants interact mostly with male peers and are avoided by the closely knit group of females which includes their mothers and sisters.

3.   The less aboreal a primate species is, the greater is the sexual dimorphism, the bigger the males, and the greater the need for elaborating gender differences so that males can aggressively ward off terrestrial predators.

This information suggests an evolutionary basis for sex role differences in humans. But what real value does it offer to the researcher in human aggression who is already skeptical of animal research?

For the investigator who simply wishes to know that such maternal behaviors exist, the animal research offers nothing unique. Insofar as the patterns are similar in humans, they could be observed in humans with equally careful study. It is even debatable whether or not the animals are less expensive or more convenient to study than humans.

Next the skeptic can seize upon the obvious limitations of assuming an evolutionary link. Contemporary primate researchers (who insist on the validity of evolutionary approaches) readily admit that human aggression is unique in that it can be internalized, delayed, and even controlled (Holloway, 1974). The result is that readers can then conclude that there is no meaningful link between animal and human aggression. Animal researchers, however, have failed to communicate the critical role of domestication in modifying behaviors with a biological base. The controlled conditions of captivity can considerably obviate the usual sex role differences in some animals (Poirier, 1974). Similarly, there is good reason to believe that in humans these roles are even more susceptible to modification through education.

As long as psychologists subscribe to the exclusivity of the causative view, evolutionary arguments will not be viewed openly. A broader view of biological and functional factors would admit observation of genetic as well as experiential aspects of behavior. In this way, by considering these animal data, we might learn much about the potential for sex role and aggression in humans when education is minimized. Open consideration of domestication could narrow the assumed gulf between man and other animals. No longer, then, would it be safe to assert, for example, that man alone is capable of being bored (Fromm, 1955).

Perhaps the best way to promote some of the functionalism of ethology within American psychology is to show evidence of generalizations about animals in humans. The lead has been taken by social psychologists in a modest venture beyond the laboratory (e.g., Bickman & Henchy, 1972). Results of the new human ethology are interesting (see Ellsworth, Carlsmith, & Henson, 1972; Mehrabian, 1971) but only preliminary; thus far, these studies lack the kind of substantive significance demanded by psychologists who have been imprinted on causative values.

One of the benefits that could result from the inclusion of ethology into psychology is an emphasis on observational skills. Despite the obvious value of training good observational skills (Turner, 1973), these are rarely taught as core material in psychology. Until psychologists develop the special sensitivity that comes from watching patiently and carefully they will probably not realize the full potential of behavioral research:

> Animal behavior is in the same position as politics and medicine: almost everybody feels entitled to have an opinion about it. Worse still, there are not a few learned men who put these opinions in print, without being aware of their ignorance of simple observational data. Ignorance of another type is often found among scientists who focus attention on one special part of behavior and study this in the laboratory. While this tendency has led to splendid research and has yielded important results . . . it

cannot be denied that as a method it is insufficient for acquiring an understanding of behaviour as a whole. [Tinbergen, 1967, pp. 276–277].

Summary

It is traditional for psychologists to preface other considerations with a recapitulation consisting of primitive and nonhuman examples. In contemporary form, this recapitulation typically concerns animal research, and it inevitably includes apologetic appeals to convince the reader of its worth. The persistence of these apologies suggests a disinterested audience and ambiguous offerings by animal behaviorists.

Studies of aggression in animals have generally offered the social psychologist little more than polar extremes of simplified emphasis. European views, exemplified by Tinbergen, are naturalistic and entertaining but are vaguely defined and speculative. The favorite research subjects of ethologists (fish, birds, and insects) are ideal for showing the stereotyped, fixed action patterns emphasized by these researchers, but similar patterns in mammals, including man, are difficult to specify. Conversely, American views, typified by Ulrich, are objectivistic and thorough but seem to offer little generality. Biology and heredity are denied, behaviors are simplified and automatically recorded, and laboratory conditions and obstrusive controls may distort behaviors. While animal aggression is ordinarily a complex and social process, behaviorists often reduce it to a single response in the absence of another organism.

This state of affairs is apparently the result of Darwinian influence. The Darwinian notion of mental continuity between animals and man was a great prod to modern scientific psychology, specifically to an emphasis in America on learning in animals as evidence of subhuman consciousness. In American Darwinism, the constraints of objectivism grew to overwhelming importance.

A related emphasis is adaptiveness of behavior; learning is assumed by behaviorists to be the most adaptive and most important behavior in nature; learning is studied to the near exclusion of other, seemingly less important, behaviors such as aggression. The premium placed on control has nearly excluded naturalistic research in America in favor of laboratory research with domesticated animals, usually rats. The overall climate is one of learning and environmentalism and a general denial of instincts. This maximizes conflict with European animal behaviorists who reacted to Darwinism as a call to naturalism and the study of instincts. There are a few individuals, such as Hailman and Hess, attempting a compromise, but generally the middle ground on research in animal aggression is uninhabited.

It may be that animal psychologists need to reevaluate the traditional interpretations of Darwinism. Domesticated animals are protected and do face boredom and crowding; emphasis on learning in captivity might distort natural behaviors and create new ones. At the moment, psychologists know little about how much laboratory learning or aggression is artifact and how much is natural. Psychologists often speculate with surprising self-righteousness as to the characteristics of nature, and they are correspondingly indignant if asked to evaluate distortions of natural behaviors in the constraints of their experimental situations. It may be that evolutionary bases can be modified to the extent that an organism is domesticated and educated. Recent research suggests that, in the case of aggressive behaviors, some can be intensified, others inhibited.

Until animal psychologists know more of effects of captivity and domestication, social psychologists may be justified in treating claims of evolution and insights about aggression lightly. For the moment, animal psychology may be valuable in suggesting hypotheses for human research. More legitimately, its quandries may lead to productive criticism of unquestioned ideas and to the training of better observers of behavior.

REFERENCES

Allport, G. W. *Becoming: Basic considerations for a psychology of personality.* New Haven: Yale Univ. Press, 1955.

Azrin, N. H., Rubin, H. B., & Hutchinson, R. R. Biting attack by rats in response to aversive shock. *Journal of the Experimental Analysis of Behavior,* 1968, *11,* 633–639.

Beach, F. A. The snark was a boojum. *American Psychologist,* 1950, *5,* 115–124.

Bickman, L., & Henchy, T. (Eds.) *Beyond the laboratory: Field research in social psychology.* New York: McGraw-Hill, 1972.

Boice, R. Some behavioral tests of domestication in Norway rats. *Behaviour,* 1972, *42,* 198–231.

Boice, R. Domestication. *Psychological Bulletin,* 1973, *80,* 215–230.

Boice, R. A test for degeneracy in laboratory rats: Indoor and outdoor burrowing by wild and domestic rats. Paper presented at the Psychonomic Society, Boston, 1974.

Boice, R., Quanty, C. B., & Williams, R. C. Competition and possible dominance in turtles, in toads, and in frogs. *Journal of Comparative and Physiological Psychology,* 1974, *86,* 1116–1131.

Bruner, J. S. Nature and uses of immaturity. *American Psychologist,* 1972, *27,* 687–708.

Burnham, J. D. Thorndike's puzzle boxes. *Journal of the History of Behavioral Sciences,* 1972, *8,* 159–167.

Carter, M. H. Romanes' idea of mental development. *American Journal of Psychology,* 1899, *11,* 101–118.

Darwin, C. *The variation of animals and plants under domestication.* Vols. 1 & 2. London: John Murray, 1868.

Dethier, V. G., & Stellar, E. *Animal behavior.* Englewood Cliffs, New Jersey: Prentice-Hall, 1970.

Ekman, P. (Ed.) *Darwin and facial expression.* New York: Academic Press, 1973.

Ellenberger, H. *Discovery of the unconscious.* New York: Basic Books, 1970.

Ellsworth, P. C., Carlsmith, J. M., & Henson, A. The stare as a stimulus to flight in human subjects: A series of field experiments. *Journal of Personality and Social Psychology,* 1972, *21,* 302–311.

Fromm, E. *The Sane Society.* New York: Rinehart, 1955.

Ghiselin, M. T. Darwin and evolutionary psychology. *Science,* 1972, *179,* 964–968.

Grant, F. C., & Mackintosh, J. H. A comparison of the social postures of some common laboratory rodents. *Behaviour,* 1963, *21,* 246–259.

Hafez, E. S. E. (Ed.) *Behaviour of domestic animals* (3rd ed.). Baltimore: Williams & Wilkins, 1975.

Hailman, J. P. How an instinct is learned. *Scientific American,* 1969, *221* (6), 98–106.

Hall, E. Ethology's warning. *Psychology Today,* 1974, March, 65–80.

Harlow, H. F. The evolution of learning. In A. Roe & G. G. Simpson (Eds.), *Behavior and evolution.* New Haven: Yale Univ. Press, 1958.

Harlow, M. K., & Harlow, H. F. Affection in primates. *Discovery,* 1966, *27,* 11–17.

Hebb, D. O. What psychology is about. *American Psychologist,* 1974, *29,* 71–79.

Hebb, D. O., & Thompson, W. R. The social significance of animal studies. In G. Lindzey & E. Aronson (Eds.), *The handbook of social psychology,* (2nd ed.), Vol. 3. Reading, Massachusetts: Addison-Wesley, 1969.

Hediger, H. *Wild animals in captivity.* New York: Dover, 1964.

Herrnstein, R. J. Nature as nurture: Behaviorism and the instinct doctrine. *Behaviorism,* 1972, *1,* 23–52.

Hess, E. H. "Imprinting" in a natural laboratory. *Scientific American,* 1972, *227* (2), 24–31.

Hirsch, J. *Behavior-genetic analysis.* New York: McGraw-Hill, 1967.

Hodos, W., & Campbell, C. B. G. *Scala naturae:* Why there is no theory in comparative psychology. *Psychological Review,* 1969, *76,* 337–350.

Holloway, R. L. Introduction. In R. L. Holloway (Ed.), *Primate aggression, territoriality, and xenophobia.* New York: Academic Press, 1974.

Holmes, S. J. *Studies in animal behavior.* Boston: Richard G. Badger, 1916.

James, W. *The principles of psychology.* New York: Holt, 1890.

Jaynes, J. The historical origins of 'ethology' and 'comparative psychology.' *Animal Behaviour,* 1969, *17,* 601–606.

Johnsgard, P. A. *Animal behavior.* Dubuque: Wm. C. Brown, 1967.

Kantor, J. R. The evolution of mind. *Psychological Review,* 1935, *42,* 455–465.

Lack, D. *The natural regulation of animal numbers.* Oxford: Oxford Univ. Press, 1954.

Latané, B. Gregariousness and fear in laboratory rats. *Journal of Experimental Social Psychology,* 1969, *5,* 61–69.

Lawick-Goodall, J. van. The behaviour of free-living chimpanzees on the Gombe Stream Reserve, *Animal Behaviour Monographs,* 1968, *1,* 161–311.

Lockard, R. B. Reflections on the fall of comparative psychology: Is there a message for us all? *American Psychologist,* 1971, *26,* 168–179.

Logan, F. A., & Boice, R. Aggressive behaviors of paired rodents in an avoidance context. *Behaviour,* 1969, *34,* 161–183.

Lorenz, K. *On aggression.* New York: Harcourt, 1966.

Mehrabian, A. Nonverbal betrayal of feeling. *Journal of Experimental Research in Personality,* 1971, *5,* 64–73.

Mills, W. The nature of animal intelligence and methods of investigating it. *Psychological Review,* 1899, *6,* 262–274.

Montagu, M. F. A. (Ed.) *Man and aggression.* New York: Oxford Univ. Press, 1968.

Morgan, C. L. *Habit and instinct.* New York: Edward Arnold, 1896.

Morris, D. *The naked ape.* New York: McGraw-Hill, 1967.

Petrinovich, L. Darwin and the representative expression of reality. In P. E. Ekman (Ed.), *Darwin and facial expression: A century of research in review.* New York: Academic Press, 1973.

Poirier, F. E. Colobine aggression: A review. In R. L. Holloway (Ed.), *Primate aggression, territoriality and xenophobia.* New York: Academic Press, 1974.

Ratner, S. C., & Boice, R. Effects of domestication on behavior. In E. S. E. Hafez (Ed.), *Behaviour of domestic animals.* Baltimore: Williams & Wilkins, 1975.

Revusky, S. Alas, poor learning theory, I knew it well. *Contemporary Psychology,* 1974, *19,* 692–694.

Reynierse, J. H. Submissive postures during shock-elicited aggression. *Animal Behaviour,* 1971, *19,* 102–107.

Romanes, G. J. *Animal intelligence.* London: Kegan Paul, 1904.

Schneirla, T. C. An evolutionary and developmental theory of biphasic processes underlying approach and withdrawal. In M. R. Jones (Ed.), *Nebraska Symposium on Motivation.* Lincoln: Univ. of Nebraska Press, 1959.

Scott, J. P. The social psychology of infrahuman animals. In G. Lindzey & E. Aronson (Eds.), *The handbook of social psychology.* (2nd ed.), Vol. 4, Reading, Massachusetts: Addison-Wesley, 1969.

Scott, J. P. Agonistic behavior of primates: A comparative perspective. In R. L. Holloway (Ed.), *Primate aggression, territoriality, and xenophobia.* New York: Academic Press, 1974.

Segal, E. F. Induction and the provenance of operants. In R. M. Gilbert & J. R. Millenson (Eds.), *Reinforcement: behavioral analyses.* New York: Academic Press, 1972.

Seligman, M. E. P. On the generality of the laws of learning. *Psychological Review,* 1970, *77,* 406–418.

Skinner, B. F. The phylogeny and ontogeny of behavior. *Science,* 1966, *153,* 1205–1213.

Skinner, B. F. *Beyond freedom and dignity.* New York: Bantam, 1972.

Skinner, B. F. The steep and thorny way to a science of behavior. *American Psychologist,* 1975, *30,* 42–49.

Southwick, C. H., Siddiqi, M. F., Farooqui, M. Y., & Pal, B. C. Xenophobia among free-ranging rhesus groups in India. In R. L. Holloway (Ed.), *Primate aggression, territoriality, and xenophobia.* New York: Academic Press, 1974.

Thorpe, W. H. *Learning and instinct in animals.* London: Methuan, 1963.

Thorndike, E. L. *Animal intelligence.* New York: Macmillan, 1911.

Thorndike, E. L. Edward Lee Thorndike. In C. Murchison (Ed.), *A history of psychology in autobiography,* Vol. 3. Worchester: Clark Univ. Press, 1936.

Tinbergen, N. *The study of instinct.* New York: Oxford Univ. Press, 1951.

Tinbergen, N. *Social behaviour in animals.* London: Methuen, 1953.

Tinbergen, N. *Curious naturalists.* New York: Basic Books, 1958.

Tinbergen, N. *The Herring Gull's world.* New York: Anchor, 1967. (Originally published: 1961).

Tinbergen, N. On war and peace in animals and man. *Science,* 1968, *160,* 1411–1418.

Turner, J. L. Powers of observation. Unpublished Ph.D. dissertation, Univ. of Missouri, 1973.

Turner, J. L., Boice, R., & Powers, P. C. Behavioral components of shock-elicited aggression in ground squirrels. *Animal Learning & Behavior,* 1973, *1,* 254–262.

Ulrich, R. Pain as a cause of elicited aggression. *American Zoologist,* 1966, *6,* 643–662.

Wasmann, E. *Instinct and intelligence in the animal kingdom.* St. Louis: B. Herder, 1903.

Watson, J. B. *Behavior as an introduction to comparative psychology.* New York: Holt, 1914.

Watson, J. B., & MacDougall, W. *The Battle of Behaviorism.* New York: W. W. Norton, 1929.

Wundt, W. *Lectures on human and animal psychology.* New York: Macmillan, 1894.

Zajonc, R. B. (Ed.), *Animal social psychology.* New York: Wiley, 1969.

Zajonc, R. B. *Animal social behavior.* Morristown, New Jersey: General Learning Corporation, 1972.

Zeuner, F. E. *A history of domesticated animals.* New York: Harper, 1963.

Zimmerman, R. R., & Geist, C. R. A primer of animal behavior for the lay person. *Contemporary Psychology,* 1974, *19,* 115–116.

Moral Judgment of Aggressive Behavior[1]

BRENDAN GAIL RULE

ANDREW R. NESDALE

Introduction

Events in recent years have heightened the social scientist's interest in questions about society's attitudes toward aggression. The documentation of people's attitudes toward Viet Nam war demonstrations, police violence, and ghetto riots has revealed the apparently differing values that people place on aggressive behavior. This differentiation in the evaluation of acts of violence and aggression has been recently discussed in the literature both at the theoretical and empirical levels. For example, rioters' comments about participation in the ghetto riots reflect, in some cases, their assumption that violence serves a good end, that of calling attention to the plight of the blacks. Others, however, see the riot as an opportunity to express hostility resulting from long periods of frustration (Tomlinson, 1970). Similarly, Kahn (1972) conducted a survey that revealed that police violence was viewed as jus-

[1] The authors' research reviewed in this article was partially supported by Canada Council Research Grants to B. G. Rule. Preparation of this chapter was facilitated by a Canada Council Doctoral Fellowship to A. R. Nesdale. Thanks are extended to Michael Enzle, Geri Lynn Hewitt, Elizabeth Percival, and Warren Thorngate for comments on an earlier draft of the manuscript.

tified by some people, but as unjustified by others. The former considered the violence to be justified in terms of its value for social change or for social control.

Such varying attitudes presumably are reflected not only in current major social issues or in cases of extreme violence but also in everyday situations involving aggression. The opportunity to evaluate aggressive acts often presents itself in everyday experience, as, for example, when a person observes teenage boys engaging in a fight or a parent striking a child. The present concern is with two related questions regarding such situations. First, will the aggressive act be judged as right or wrong by an observer? Second, what considerations influence the moral judgment that is made? For example, are people's judgments influenced by the amount of harm done, the age of the participants, the observer's own attitudes about fighting, or the observer's social role?

Somewhat surprisingly, the systematic assessment of such questions has been largely ignored in psychology until quite recently when the importance of morality as a legitimate focus of inquiry has been stressed (Kelley, 1971), especially with reference to aggression (Feshbach, 1971). In fact, the scientific study of moral judgments in general seems to have become acceptable only within the past few years (e.g., Brown, 1965; Hoffman, 1969; Kohlberg, 1969). Part of the reason for the neglect of such studies appears to have been due to such considerations as concern about the mentalistic overtones of moral judgments, disdain for the fuzzier cognitive concepts invoked, and fear of scientific erosion from the consideration of such value-laden issues.

In addition to the continuing convergence of cognitive and noncognitive concepts (e.g., Baldwin, 1969; Campbell, 1963; Scheerer, 1954), however, Feshbach (1971) has argued that psychologists' methods are especially appropriate "to describe variations in the moral evaluation of violent acts, to isolate dimensions of the context and of the action which contribute to differences in evaluation, and to determine the degree to which personality and socio-cultural factors influence moral attitudes [p. 281]." Certainly an analysis of the factors determining the evaluation of aggression can be impartial in its own value perspective and need not pronounce on what is ethically right or wrong. Instead, such an analysis can provide information regarding those aggressive acts that are perceived as being ethically right or wrong. Given that moral judgments constitute phenomena which should be intrinsically interesting to psychologists, Kelley (1971) has stressed the ramifications of systematically examining the determinants of moral judgments by pointing out that "these judgments play an important mediating role between the social or moral system and the behavior of individuals [p. 208]."

The purpose of this chapter is to review the research which has focused on the factors influencing people's judgments of an aggressor. Before embarking on this task, it is necessary to consider the concepts of "aggression" and "moral judgment," especially as they will be treated within the context of the present discussion.

Definition of Aggression

The question of what constitutes an aggressive act has been the focus of considerable attention by a number of scholars. Examples of aggression which pervade both the lay and scientific literature include war, gossip, children's fights, firing employees, spanking a child, and destroying toys. Because classification of many different responses as exemplars of the same phenomenon has led to confusion, attempts have been made to limit the definition of aggression to a more scientifically viable concept.

In discussing various definitions, Feshbach (1964, 1971) has noted that although aggression can be defined as injury at the descriptive level, some typing of aggression is necessary at the construct level. Feshbach has classified aggressive acts into unintentional and intentional aggression. Although they result in injury, unintentional aggressive acts are not contingent upon their injurious consequences for their commission. Of the three intentional reasons for committing aggression which Feshbach has delineated (i.e., expressive, hostile, instrumental), the ones that have been given the most attention in current theory and research are those that serve either hostile or instrumental functions. Hostile aggressive behavior is directed primarily at injuring another person. In delineating their field of inquiry, many theorists have concentrated upon aggressive behavior serving this function (Dollard, Doob, Miller, Mowrer, & Sears, 1939; Berkowitz, 1962). Instrumental aggressive behavior is directed toward attaining a nonaggressive goal; it refers to an aggressive act that attempts to attain a reinforcer from the victim or from some source external to the victim. For example, injury may be perpetrated for money, prestige, or social approval (Bandura, 1969; Borden, Bowen, & Taylor, 1971; Buss, 1961; Milgram, 1963; Silverman, 1971): personal–instrumental goals.

Instrumental aggressive behavior may be further classified in terms of whether the aggression is used for some social purpose. This classification was noted by Sears (1961) who discusses prosocial aggression as "aggression used in a socially approved way for purposes that are acceptable to the moral standards of the group [p. 471]." Such aggression includes socially approved controls and disciplinary behaviors that have injurious outcomes as by-products of attaining another individual's or society's goals. Some authors have argued against considering injury which serves a social purpose as aggression (Buss, 1961, 1971; Feshbach, 1964). For example, Buss (1971) has asserted that punishment is usually excluded from theoretical concern if it occurs in the context of a socially approved role, such as parent, teacher, judge, or dentist. According to this view, if what is considered an appropriate level of punishment is exceeded, then the act would be labeled as aggression. Thus, dentists are probably not considered to be engaged in aggressive behavior simply because their good intention (which is to help, not to harm, the patient) is recognized. If aggression is not defined according to its hostile connotation but rather as an injurious response that serves different functions, injurious responses directed toward even a socially approved goal are appropriately labeled as aggressive.

In summary, "aggression" refers to a response, some element of which is injury, but a response that requires typing for predictive value. Rule (1974) has summarized arguments and data which bear on the differing antecedents and consequences of these varying kinds of aggression. It appears, for example, that while hostile and personal-instrumental aggression produce similar consequences (Rule & Percival, 1971), hostile and prosocial aggression have differing antecedents and consequences (Rule & Hewitt, 1971; Rule & Nesdale, 1974). Whether the antecedents and consequences differ, however, is an important issue in understanding the expression of aggression. The relevance of these distinctions for this review is that these functions of aggression are the most commonly differentiated and have received the most emphasis in the moral judgment literature.

In the present context then, aggression will be treated as an action that injures the recipient, and the review will include such behavior committed for hostile, personal-instrumental, and prosocial reasons.

Definition of Moral Judgment

"Moral judgments" are defined as attitudes about how right or wrong a person is for behaving in a certain way. Measurement of this attitude is typically accomplished by ratings on a bipolar scale of judgment whose end points are denoted "right" and "wrong." In addition to this direct measurement, researchers have often asked subjects to indicate how much punishment should be meted out to the aggressor (e.g., number of years imprisonment, fines). Given that these latter judgments have no real consequences for the aggressor, measures of punishment are regarded in this chapter as secondary ways of assessing perceived morality. Although it is recognized that there is a body of research dealing with attribution of responsibility, the view taken here is that judgment of responsibility is conceptually closer to attribution of causality (cf. Heider, 1958) than to judgment of right or wrong. Although the assignment of responsibility or causality might be involved in the process of judging morality, it is not seen as being synonymous with a moral judgment.

The moral judgments that are relevant to this review are those made by people as they ordinarily react to aggressive incidents they have observed directly, as well as to aggression that is more indirectly experienced through different media, such as television, newspapers, and books. Thus, morality judgments of aggressive acts ranging from verbal abuse to murder fall within the purview of this chapter. The experimental paradigm which has been employed in research studies usually involves the presentation of information describing aggressive incidents to research participants who then make their judgments in terms of "rightness" or "wrongness," or "punishment deserved."

Observers' Reactions to Aggression

Although research on the factors influencing observers' judgments of aggressive acts has increased in recent years following the encouragement of such inquiry by social scientists (Feshbach, 1971; Kelley, 1971) and the observations of legal scholars interested in judicial reform (Evan, 1962; Kalven & Zeisal, 1966; Toch, 1961), the area is notable for the fragmentary nature of the research undertaken thus far.

Consequently, in order both to facilitate this review of the research and to indicate the gaps in our knowledge, the extant literature is categorized according to several aspects of the total judgment situation. These include: (1) the aggressive act itself, which involves both the severity and mode of aggression; (2) the perceived characteristics of the aggressor and the victim, including such factors as their physical attractiveness, personal favorableness, and momentary and enduring dispositions; (3) the characteristics of the observer, such as sex, age, stable dispositions, and relationship with both the aggressor and the victim; and (4) the specific situation in which the judgment is made, emphasizing the conditions under which, and in the presence of whom, the observer makes his judgments.

Nature of the Act

As Feshbach (1971) has noted, aggressive acts differ in their mode and severity; they may range from verbal abuse, slander, and defamation of character to murder, rape, and assault. While the varieties of aggressive behavior have been recognized, there has been little systematic treatment of these differences in either theory or research. Some empirical data relating to the nature of the act were provided by Thurstone (1927) and Coombs (1967), both of whom asked University of Michigan students to indicate the seriousness of different crimes. The judgments made by persons surveyed in 1967, compared with those made in 1927, were less uniform and indicated that offenses such as homicide, kidnapping, and assault were considered to be more serious than were those of a sexual nature (e.g., rape). These results show that although the seriousness of these acts is institutionalized in the legal code, societal norms or attitudes toward such aggression vary over the years.

It is important to note, of course, that although some aggressive acts are defined by the severity of consequences for the victim (e.g., homicide), the psychological and physical consequences of other acts for the victim (e.g., rape and assault) may vary. Despite the potential influence of this differentiation into the nature of the act and the severity of the consequences on observers' judgments, however, no attempt has been made to survey or scale acts with differing consequences. In addition, it is not known how the nature of the act, unconfounded by severity of harm, combines with other factors, such as characteristics of the victim or aggressor, to influence morality judgments.

With regard to the nature of aggressive acts, researchers' efforts have focused on the examination of the effects on observers' judgments of variations in the consequences of a specific act. Moreover, the inquiry has been restricted to interpersonal aggression situations where one person engages in a comparatively moderate, rather than a serious, transgression against another. It has been found, for example, that varying the severity of consequences of an aggressive act (one adult striking another) produced no effect on judgments of adults' aggression (Nesdale, Rule, & McAra, in press). While this finding might seem surprising, it is nevertheless consistent with Piaget's suggestion (1965) that, whereas children make moral judgments on the basis of severity of outcome, mature persons, who are presumably at higher stages of moral development, are less responsive to outcome information. Piaget's notion has also received support from several studies that have examined age trends in the influence of consequences on childrens' moral judgments of aggression (Costanzo, Coie, Grumet, & Farnill, 1973; Gutkin, 1972; Hebble, 1971; Rule & Duker, 1973; Shantz & Voydanoff, 1973).

It should be noted that at least one other study employing adult sub-jects has reported a consequence effect on judgments of aggression (Dion, 1972). It is possible, however, that the consequence effect ob-tained in Dion's study (1972) may be attributed to the absence of other information concerning the transgression (e.g., intentions) which could be used as a basis for judgments. It is also possible, of course, that the lack of consequence effect in the Nesdale *et al.,* study (in press) may be due to the outcome severity which subjects observed; the severe condi-tions may not have been serious enough to exert a significant influence on judgments. Further studies are needed to assess these possibilities.

Characteristics of the Aggressor and the Victim

Although the level of indictment in a murder trial depends on the ag-gressor's motive, the recognition of such motives or intentions is also likely to be vital in the evaluation of aggressive acts and subsequent retaliation even when sanctions are not institutionalized in a legal code. Accordingly, both theorists and researchers have given some attention to how, and to what extent, different intentions influence judgments of aggression. Aside from reviewing the contributions of researchers interested in the influence of the aggressor's intentions on observers' judgments, we will also consider the influence on judgments of other less well recognized factors. These factors relate to both the aggressor's and the victim's physical attractiveness and personal favorableness or attractiveness.

AGGRESSOR'S INTENTIONS

Apart from discerning whether a particular act was intended or acci-dental, the nature of the aggressor's actual goal is also important. Draw-ing the distinction between aggression serving personal (hostile or per-sonal-instrumental) versus prosocial purposes, Feshbach (1971) proposed that the former is viewed more unfavorably than the latter. This suggestion was evaluated in several investigations in our laboratory (Nesdale & Rule, 1974; Nesdale *et al.,* in press; Rule, Dyck, McAra, & Nesdale, 1975). In these experiments, subjects were asked to read a transcript of an interview in which the person interviewed described an aggressive act he committed against another person over a wallet they had jointly found. The aggressor's stated intentions for the aggression were either to hurt the victim (hostile aggression), to return the wallet to its rightful owner (prosocial), or to keep the wallet for himself (personal-instrumental). The results of these studies have disclosed that an ag-gressor who hits for prosocial reasons is viewed as more right and as less deserving of punishment than the aggressor who hits for personal reasons (hostile and personal-instrumental). Although it might be expected that one of the boundary conditions for viewing prosocial aggression as less wrong would be the specification that it is the only response available, such is not the case. Rule, Dyck, McAra, and Nesdale (1975) found no difference in judgments of prosocial aggression regardless of whether subjects were or were not told that this was the only response available. It is possible, of course, that if subjects were told that specific, alternative, nonaggressive responses were available, the aggressor's chosen action would be judged as more wrong.

While it is apparent from these findings that an aggressor's intent influences another person's judgment, it is also possible that knowledge of the consequences of aggression may interact with intentions to influence judgments. Thus, one might speculate that the severity of aggression would exert a greater influence on judgments of its morality when an aggressor's intentions are bad. One might feel that a serious consequence from an act maliciously intended is much worse than a serious consequence with other intentions. Alternatively, one might also conjecture that when the consequences of an act are severe, the intentions underlying the action might be disregarded.

In an attempt to shed some light on these questions, Rule and Duker (1973) manipulated the intentions of an aggressor and the consequences of his action within the same study. They found that the moral judgments were not affected by differences in intention when the aggressive act had serious consequences, but intentions were differentially important when the aggressive act had less harmful consequences. However, the subjects in the Rule and Duker study were young Dutch boys, and, according to Piaget (1965), intentions exert a greater influence on morality judgments as individuals become more mature or reach higher stages of moral development. The overpowering effect of serious consequences might be diminished for more mature individuals. Consequently, a second study was undertaken using adult subjects as observers (Nesdale et al., in press). In this study, university students were asked to judge the mild or severe aggression of a person who hit another for either prosocial or personal-instrumental reasons. The results provided no support for the hypothesis that an adult's judgments of an action depends on the combined effect of the consequences of the act and the intentions underlying it.

In view of these findings and those on consequence effects cited earlier, it seems likely that when only one source of information is available to an adult observer (i.e., intentions or consequences), it is used as a basis for judgments, but when both sources are available, the intentions rather than the consequences are used as the basis for the judgment. A person's need to make sense out of his world (Heider, 1958; Lerner, 1970) may lead him to use whatever source of information presents itself, even if it is a less preferred one. When several sources of information are presented, it is not necessary to rely on the less preferred one.

FAVORABILITY OF THE AGGRESSOR AND THE VICTIM

Although the importance of the motive underlying an aggressive act has long been recognized, people have also suspected that, contrary to the spirit of justice and fair play for all, personal characteristics of both the aggressor and the victim are important factors affecting judgments. In fact, this suspicion has apparently been accepted by the producers of television legal dramas. In these shows, the lawyer frequently manipulates the appearance or personal impression of his client in order to influence the jury's judgment. Moreover, well-known practicing lawyers have stated unequivocally that such a manipulation is one of their main aims. For example, Clarence Darrow asserted that "jurymen seldom convict a person they like or acquit one they dislike. The main work of the trial lawyer is to make a jury like his client, or at least to feel sympathy for him; facts regarding the crime are relatively unimportant [Sutherland, 1966, p. 442]." Furthermore, in relation to the victim, Percy Foreman has noted that "the best defense in a murder case is the fact that the deceased should have been killed regardless of how it happened [Smith, 1966, p. 96]."

What factors affect the degree to which a person is favorably evaluated? So far, researchers have used a variety of ways to create favorable impressions of the transgressor and the victim. For example, researchers have examined the effects on judgments of physical attractiveness, respectability through marital status (married versus divorced), previous criminal record, and a foreigner's attitudes toward the observer's country. As will be evident from subsequent discussion, these favorability or likeability manipulations have generated uniform judgments of serious (death) and less serious (hitting) aggressive acts.

Some work has focused specifically on victim characteristics. In mock jury situations, college students advocated longer sentences for a defendant who killed a personally favorable as opposed to an unfavorable person (Landy & Aronson, 1969) or who raped a more respectable as compared to a less respectable victim (Jones & Aronson, 1973). Thus, it seems that the more positive the characteristics of the victim, the more lengthy is the sentence given to the aggressor.

Similarly, several studies have demonstrated that the personal characteristics of the aggressor determine moral judgments of his ac-

tion. The same act is judged as worse and/or deserving more punishment when the aggressor is personally unfavorable (Landy and
Aronson, 1969; Nesdale & Rule, 1974; Nesdale *et al.*, in press; Rule *et
al.*, 1975; Shepherd & Bagley, 1970) or physically unattractive (Dion,
1972). Moreover, characteristics of the victim and the aggressor produce
their effects independently of each other (Landy & Aronson, 1969).

Given this evidence of the importance of the favorability of the aggressor, the issue is how favorability combines with other factors that
are commonly associated with the evaluation of aggressive behavior to
produce effects on judgments. For example, would knowing about the
aggressor's personal characteristics affect interpretation of the apparent intentions underlying an act and interactively influence moral
judgments?

According to attribution theorists (Heider, 1958; Jones & Davis,
1965; Jones & Nisbett, 1971), observers make attributions about enduring dispositions on the basis of information that is available to them.
Moreover, information about temporary events is displaced toward the
enduring disposition, if the latter is known (Hastorf, Schneider, &
Polefka, 1970). Thus, aggression committed with a bad intention by an
otherwise favorable person might be perceived as externally caused,
whereas the good intention of an unfavorable person might be dis-
believed. In effect, the latter would render the stated differences in
intention ineffective for unfavorable persons. The resultant impression
of the aggressor based on his favorableness and intentions presumably
would determine the attribution of greater or lesser enduring aggressiveness to the actor; this would then affect the observer's moral judgments
(Dion, 1972; Nesdale & Rule, 1974). In a similar vein, Sigall and Ostrove (1975) have proposed that the judgment that a transgressor is less
likely to transgress again in the future means that one should "go easy"
on the transgressor and give him a second chance. Although this would
be especially pertinent to actual sentencing, it is possible that it would
even affect judgments which are devoid of any real consequences for the
aggressor.

Contrary to expectations, the intentions and favorability of the aggressor do not interact to affect moral judgments. In studies designed
specifically to detect these effects (Nesdale & Rule, 1974; Nesdale *et
al.*, in press; Rule *et al.*, 1975) both intentions and favorability independently affected the moral judgments.

Moreover, the empirical results have provided little support for the
view that attributional processes mediate observers' moral judgments.
In one study, the experimental manipulations (i.e., intentions and personal favorability) produced their effects on judgments, but there was
no evidence that attributions of enduring aggressiveness accounted for

the effects (Nesdale & Rule, 1974). The investigators found that only variation in the intention underlying the aggression affected estimates of whether an aggressor would engage in similar behavior in the future. Nonetheless, both a personal favorability and intention manipulation independently affected the moral judgments and sanctions applied.

Some data have also indicated that although some factors affect attributions in the expected way, they do not alter moral judgments in a like manner. For example, Nesdale *et al.* (in press) found that a personally unfavorable aggressor was perceived as more likely to engage in subsequent aggression when he aggressed with bad rather than good intentions, but that the favorable aggressor was perceived as somewhat more unlikely to engage in subsequent aggression when he aggressed with bad rather than good intentions. Paralleling this finding, Dion (1972) has reported an analogous interaction between physical attractiveness and severity of consequences on the probability of the aggressor's engaging in an aggressive act in the future. The observers' attributions, however, were not matched by similar effects on moral judgments in either experiment.

In summary, the results thus far indicate that information concerning the aggressor's favorability and the intentions underlying his action are simply combined independently to determine the favorableness of the observer's impression of the aggressor, and that the favorability of this judgment is then reflected in the observer's moral judgment. In essence, when unambiguous information is provided, the moral judgment seems to reflect a judgment on a favorability dimension. Perhaps the mediating effects of attributions occur when ambiguous information or no information is available about particular factors, and an observer must make inferences about the causes of behavior. Such a possibility, however, remains to be assessed empirically.

Finally, in considering characteristics of the aggressor and the victim, the age and sex of each would seem to be dimensions affecting moral judgments. Do observers react differently to aggression committed by adults versus children? Do observers view aggression differently when commited by men versus women? Vidmar and Ellsworth (1974) have reported opinion poll data indicating that capital punishment is endorsed more for men than women and more for adults than for children. No experimental research, however, has been addressed to these questions.

Characteristics of the Observer

The observers who have been the subject of much attention are jurors. According to Winick (1961), lawyers have long exploited characteristics of the juror for their own purposes. In fact, a number of writers have recently documented how selection of jurors according to various criteria can exert an influence on decisions (Kaplan, Klein, & Fried, 1973; Rokeach & Vidmar, 1974; Schulman, Shaver, Colman, Emrich, & Christie, 1973; Shaver, 1973). For example, Rokeach and Vidmar (1974) have indicated that current American selection procedures often favor authoritarian, dogmatic, and older persons, all of whom are biased toward more punitive sentences. Although Rokeach and Vidmar's work was directed toward a particular issue (selection of jurors for a Black Panther trial), they proposed several relevant categories of observer characteristics that are likely to influence moral judgments of aggression.

SEX OF THE OBSERVER

Many authors (Berkowitz, 1962; Buss, 1961; Feshbach, 1970) have indicated that sex differences are important considerations in understanding the expression of aggression, and, indeed, it has often been observed that males are more aggressive than females (reviewed by Feshbach, 1970). Would similar differences obtain in moral judgments of aggression? Because females are more inhibited in their expression of aggression, would they view such expression as being more wrong? Lending indirect support to this possibility, Sears (1961) found that girls reported that they were more willing to engage in prosocial aggression than hostile aggression. Thus, the young girls in his study expressed more aggression for punishment and corrective purposes. In view of these findings, it might be expected that females would view hostile aggression as more wrong than prosocial aggression. Conversely, since males are less inhibited in their expression of aggression, their moral judgments might not be differently influenced by aggression serving different purposes.

Contrary to these expectations, studies addressed to this issue have shown that the sex of observers does not have an important influence on moral judgments. For example, Rule et al. (1975) found that both male and female high-school and university students judged an aggressive act motivated by personal reasons as more wrong and more deserving of punishment than an aggressive act motivated by social reasons. Furthermore, in another study using preschool and elementary school children, no sex differences were found in judgments of the morality of the aggressive acts (Rule et al. 1974). Both boys and girls judged personally motivated aggression as "naughtier" than socially motivated aggression.

Personality Characteristics of Observers

Although research on the effects of the observer's stable personality characteristics on moral judgments of aggression is particularly sparse, it is likely that an assessment of the effects of such variables as authoritarianism, dogmatism, and cognitive complexity on moral judgments would be especially fruitful.

Some research has been undertaken that indicates that the authoritarian's tendency to be rule bound, law oriented, and hostile (as measured by the F-scale, Adorno, Frenkel–Brunswik, Levinson, & Sanford, 1950; or dogmatism scale, Rokeach, 1960) results in his being more harsh in his moral judgments of transgressors and in his recommendations of more severe punishment than a less authoritarian person (Boehm, 1968; Jurow, 1971) particularly for low-status transgressors (Berg & Vidmar, in press). The fact that authoritarians are people whose needs for certainty lead them to avoid or dislike potentially inconsistent information (Hastorf *et al.*, 1970) also has important implications for moral judgments in those situations in which an observer is confronted with inconsistent information concerning an aggressor's intentions versus his more enduring personal qualities. In these situations, knowledge of an aggressor's enduring favorable or unfavorable qualities might lead the high authoritarian, as compared to the low authoritarian, to ignore or suppress knowledge of the aggressor's inconsistent, more momentary intentions when making his judgments. That is, the high authoritarian's judgments would be more likely to reflect the favorableness of the aggressor's enduring personal qualities, regardless of his present intentions, whereas the low authoritarian's judgments would reflect both the favorable qualities and present intentions.

Because cognitive complexity is another personality variable that refers to the way in which a person perceives his world, one would also expect the moral judgments of cognitively simple persons to differ from those of more cognitively complex people. Hastorf *et al.* (1970) have noted that, although there is some disagreement among researchers as to the specific definition and measurement of cognitive complexity, most have agreed that the cognitively simple person has fewer categories and makes less distinctions in his categories than the cognitively complex person. The implication for moral judgments is that the cognitively simple person is likely to be more extreme in his judgments because he has fewer categories available to him. Furthermore, it has been suggested that, when faced with contradictory information concerning an aggressor, the judgments of a cognitively complex person would be more likely to reflect finer discriminations made on the basis of all of the information, since he has more dimensions available to handle such information (Hastorf *et al.*, 1970). Thus, one would expect the judgments of a cognitively complex person to reflect information concerning both the aggressor's favorableness and his intentions, whereas the judgments of the cognitively simple person would reflect only one of these sources of information.

Aside from the influence of the observer's personality characteristics, various relational considerations linking the observer to the aggressor and/or the victim in different ways might influence the observer's judgments. For example, different status or role relationships (e.g., teacher–pupil, father–son, employer–employee, policeman–citizen) between the observer and the aggressor and/or the victim might influence the harshness of the observer's judgment depending on the role or status that the observer is assuming at the time of judgment. Although the effects of such relationships have not been systematically assessed, one study has examined the influences of the observer's perception of his own and the aggressor's wealth on the observer's judgments (Gordon & Jacobs, 1969). It was reported, however, that subjects who indicated that their wealth was more or less than the aggressor's did not differ in the degree of guilt that they attributed to the aggressor. Whether or not this or similar variables exert a differential influence on moral judgments remains to be examined.

It is also possible that the observer's perception of similarity between himself and the aggressor or victim influences his judgments. Although this question has also not been extensively researched, Mitchell and Byrne (1973) found that authoritarians perceived that a similar defendent was more guilty than was a dissimilar one and recommended greater punishment for those who held dissimilar attitudes. In contrast, egalitarians were not so influenced in their judgments by the transgressor's similarity to themselves.

DIFFERENCES IN THE AGE OF OBSERVERS

The factors that influence moral judgments at various ages have received little theoretical and empirical attention in the field. One theorist, Piaget (1965), has commented extensively on the development of moral judgments in children. He suggests that children in the stage of moral realism (usually under the age of about 10) do not rely on inferences about intentions but rather rely on other features of the situation to form their judgments. According to his view, the formation of moral judgments progresses from an egocentric perspective, in which outcomes or consequences are used as the basis for inferences, toward a greater reliance on the intention underlying a particular act. In accordance with his view, Rule and Duker (1973) predicted that only boys older than 10 years of age would respond to differences in intentions underlying an aggressive act. Instead, they found that both 8- and 12-year-old Dutch boys evaluated an aggressor as worse when his intentions were hostile rather than prosocial. Costanzo *et al.* (1973) found that 5-year-old boys used differences in intentions to arrive at their evaluations only in dealing with incidents having positive but not negative outcomes. Shantz and Voydanoff (1973) reported that 7-year-old boys failed to distinguish intentional from accidental aggression, whereas their older counterparts did. The differences in perceived aggression were due to the greater inhibition of aggression by the older boys when the instigation was accidental. In this study, however, no provision was made for responses to differing kinds of intentional aggression.

In order to examine whether very young children use information about differing intentions as a basis for their judgments about aggression, Rule *et al.,* (1974) conducted two studies in which young boys and girls of varying ages were asked to evaluate an aggressor whose intention was either personal or prosocial. In these studies, kindergarten, second-, and fifth-grade girls, and first-, third-, and sixth-grade boys evaluated the naughtiness of children who aggressed either for personal (hostile or personal–instrumental) or prosocial reasons. It was found that, regardless of age, the children viewed the personal reasons for aggressing as more wrong than the prosocial reasons.

The results from this study clearly demonstrated that girls as young as 5 years of age and boys as young as 6 do distinguish differing intentions underlying aggression in their moral evaluations. Information about intentions exerts an influence at an earlier age than that proposed by Piaget (1965) but consistent with that suggested by Kohlberg (1969). Apparently the complex inferential processes operative at higher stages of cognitive development are not involved in making these discriminations. Instead, it seems likely that adults emphasize the difference between personally and socially motivated aggression in the training of even very young children. As Piaget suggested, however, the consequences of the act are also influential in determining moral judgments for younger children.

One additional point to note about these studies is that the children have typically been provided with unambiguous information about the intentions underlying the act. Although this is consistent with Piaget's presentation of information to his research subjects, it is not known whether children actually make inferences about intentions when the information is not explicitly given. This possibility should be assessed in future studies.

Results based on university and high school populations (Rule *et al.*, 1975) have also demonstrated that the personal (hostile and personal-instrumental) versus social motivation underlying an aggressive response is a major determinant of moral judgments and sanctions. Both university and high school students judged aggression motivated by personal goals as more wrong than aggression motivated by social goals. The university students, however, evaluated hostile and personal-instrumental aggression as equally wrong, whereas the high school students evaluated the aggressor who hit for personal-instrumental reasons as more wrong and as more deserving of punishment than the aggressor who hit for hostile reasons. It is possible that the manipulation of personal-instrumental aggression in this study (stealing someone else's wallet) provided an increment to the negative moral judgments. This may be especially salient for the lower middle-class high school students used in the study. The fact that the results from middle-class, pre- and elementary-school children directly paralleled those of university students strengthens the latter interpretation.

Considered together, the studies that have been reviewed indicate that, in accord with Feshbach's notions (1971), people varying in age from the preschool to university level view personal reasons (both hostile and personal-instrumental) as more wrong than prosocial reasons for aggressing. Although hostile and personal-instrumental aggression have been considered as functionally different bases for expressing aggression (Feshbach, 1971), the results of these studies demonstrate that they elicit similar evaluations from persons judging aggression. Furthermore, it seems that the way in which personal-instrumental goals are defined makes very little difference. In the work with university and high school students, the personal-instrumental reasons for aggression were described as an attempt by the aggressor to keep for himself a wallet which he jointly found with another person, a manipulation which involved stealing. In contrast, the manipulation of personal-instrumental aggression in the study with young children did not involve stealing. In spite of these different manipulations, however, the results obtained from preschool, elementary, high school and university students were markedly similar.

Finally, few studies have been addressed to the question of at which age children's judgments are influenced by such supposedly irrelevant factors as aggressor and victim characteristics. Dion and Berscheid (1974) found that for both younger and older nursery school children, the physically unattractive boys were perceived as more aggressive than the more physically attractive boys. Rule *et al.*, (1974) designed a study specifically to examine how the moral judgments of children varying in age were affected by physical attractiveness. They found that in spite of the fact that the children perceived differences in the physical attractiveness of an aggressor as was intended, the variation had no effect on moral judgments for kindergarten, second-, or fifth-grade girls. Perhaps physical attractiveness and personal favorability do not exert an influence on moral judgments until adolescence, when such factors assume greater importance in everyday life.

The Judging Situation

The judging situation assumes considerable importance when one realizes that various situations may serve to introduce considerations that will differentially influence observers' judgments. For example, different judgment situations may differentially affect the salience of the norm of impartiality. When compared with an anonymous judgment situation, one in which the observer is forced to explain the basis for his judgment may engage the norm of impartiality or "fairness to all." This would preclude judgments from being influenced by less relevant considerations, such as the clothes, physical appearance, or personal favorability of the aggressor or victim.

In order to test this assumption, Nesdale and Rule (1974) designed an experiment in which the aggression of a personally favorable or unfavorable person was judged by an observer who was, or was not, accountable for his judgment. They found that the usually obtained difference in judgments for a favorable versus an unfavorable aggressor was markedly diminished when observers were led to believe that they would be accountable for their judgments.

Aside from situations in which an observer is accountable for his judgments, a number of other judgment situations can be specified in which considerations peculiar to the situation might influence judgments. These include situations in which the observer expects to interact subsequently with the person judged or situations in which the observer's judgment has real consequences for the aggressor. Finally, if the observer is directly or indirectly linked to the outcome for either the aggressor or the victim, his judgments might differ from those of an uninvolved judge. None of these factors, however, has been examined in moral judgment situations focusing on the aggressor, although some have been shown to affect impressions of victims or other nonvictimized targets (Bond & Dutton, 1973; Stokols & Schopler, 1973; Lincoln & Levinger, 1972).

Summary and Conclusions

The empirical results which have been reviewed in this chapter document the variations in society's attitudes toward aggression. It is evident that the mere act of causing harm to someone is not the sole criterion for judging the morality of an aggressive act. Instead, observer's judgments are influenced by many factors. Some of these factors are usually considered to be more appropriate for judging the morality of aggression (e.g., the aggressor's intentions) than others (e.g., likeableness of the victim), depending upon the particular judgment situation.

The review also highlights the relative sparsity and fragmentary nature of the research which has been accomplished. To take but one example, little is known about the influence of the observer's personality characteristics or the effects of his relatedness to the aggressor and/or the victim on his moral judgments of the transgression. Much more systematic empirical work needs to be undertaken before a complete understanding of the determinants of moral judgments is achieved.

Although there is little research, enough has been accomplished in some areas to demonstrate the importance of certain factors in determining moral judgments. One example of this comes from studies that have varied the intentions underlying the harmful act. The research has consistently demonstrated that people view aggression committed for prosocial reasons as less wrong than aggression committed for personal reasons. These results parallel the judgments that people have made of acts of police violence (Kahn, 1972) and riots (Tomlinson, 1970). Viewed together, they suggest that tolerance for extreme violence may have its roots in tolerance for more minor aggressive incidents. This suggestion is buttressed by the data indicating that even kindergarten children differentiated, and were more approving of, aggression of a more minor nature when it was undertaken for prosocial rather than personal reasons. The important implication of these findings is that if some modification of attitudes toward aggression is desired, it would have to be attempted at a very young age. Nevertheless, given that people are more approving of prosocial aggression, it would be particularly interesting to ascertain at what point the anticipated harm done would outweigh the presumed beneficial goals of aggression, thereby inhibiting prosocial aggression and/or leading to a less favorable moral judgment of it.

Another finding that has been consistently reported is that moral judgments are significantly influenced by the characteristics of the aggressor and the victim. While the demonstration of this effect has occurred primarily in situations of private judgment, the important implication of this finding is that people who are likely to be in judgment situations should be aware of this bias. It is also recognized, of course, that the favorability effect has been obtained in situations in which the judgment carries no real consequences for the aggressor. Future research should be directed at determining whether judgments are biased by the aggressor's and/or the victim's characteristics when the person making the judgment is in a position to administer real sanctions (e.g., jurors, teachers). This also implies, of course, that far more attention must be directed toward the situation in which the judgment is made because, aside from the norm of impartiality, different judgment situations might activate other normative considerations (e.g., equity and equality) which presumably would influence judgments.

The present discussion has also indicated that the research that has been accomplished has not been guided by any systematic theoretical framework. Although attribution theory seemed promising, it did not have predictive value in the few studies in which it has been assessed. The findings obtained suggest that individuals simply combine the information presented to them in a noninteractive fashion to reach their judgments (cf. Anderson, 1971; Kaplan & Kemmerick, 1974). Perhaps predictions based on notions of attribution will be verified when intentions are less explicit. Further consideration of the role of attribution theory could be directed toward situations in which an aggressor's intentions must be inferred.

An additional implication from the accumulated body of data bears on how the interpretation of witnessed aggressive incidents affects the viewer's expression of aggression. Some studies have demonstrated that children and young adults who view justified, rather than unjustified, aggression are subsequently more aggressive (e.g., Berkowitz, Corwin, & Heironimus, 1963; Berkowitz & Geen, 1967). In these studies, justification was varied by describing the victim in unfavorable terms, which is analogous to the variation in moral judgment studies of favorability of the victim. On the other hand, a study by Bandura, Ross, and Ross (1963) has revealed that even though children disapproved of a model's aggression, they imitated his behavior. Because the model's rewards for aggressing were high in that situation, however, it seems likely that this factor overrode whatever effect moral judgments may have had on aggression.

Several studies have been addressed to whether the expression of aggression is affected by an observer's awareness of a filmed aggressor's goals. One study (Liefer & Roberts, 1971), which varied the consequences of aggression and the motivation underlying the act failed to reveal that the experimental variations affected instigation to aggression. The manipulations, however, were confounded with the story content, and the dependent measure was a paper and pencil response rather than overt behavior. In other experiments, more aggression was expressed toward a provoking partner after angered persons viewed a film in which violence had occurred for vengeful in contrast to other purposes, such as filling the professional role of a fighter (Geen & Stonner, 1973), or in self-defense (Hoyt, 1970), or for altruistic reasons (Geen & Stonner, 1974). It is evident that further studies designed to investigate the influence of characteristics of the aggressor and the victim as well as motivation and consequences of the aggression on subsequent aggression would be particularly fruitful.

One final consideration concerns the relevance of the reviewed findings to our understanding of jury functioning. Although some of the studies reviewed have been conceptualized within a mock jury paradigm (e.g., Landy & Aronson, 1969; Mitchell & Byrne, 1973), the many differences between the simulated and actual courtroom severely restrict the relevance of the obtained findings to real courtroom judgments. In terms of the operationalizations employed in these studies, the findings are more appropriate to an understanding of everyday moral judgments rather than to those made by a jury in a criminal trial. For example, compared with a real courtroom situation, the hypothetical jury situations do not typically entail real consequences for the defendant, the instructions given by a judge to the jury, defense or prosecution statements, or group discussion by the jurors. Only a more realistic and more complex simulation (e.g., Strodtbeck, James, & Hawkins, 1958), or research undertaken in an actual trial would provide data appropriate to an understanding of courtroom outcomes and their underlying processes.

REFERENCES

Adorno, T. W., Frenkel-Brunswik, E., Levinson, D. J., & Sanford, R. M. *The authoritarian personality.* New York: Harper, 1950.
Anderson, N. H. Integration theory and attitude change. *Psychological Review,* 1971, *78,* 171–206.
Baldwin, A. A cognitive theory of socialization. In D. A. Goslin (Ed.), *Handbook of socialization theory and research.* Chicago: Rand, McNally and Company, 1969. Pp. 325–345.
Bandura, A. Principles of behavior modification. New York: Holt, 1969.
Bandura, A., Ross, D., & Ross, A. Vicarious reinforcement and imitative learning. *Journal of Abnormal and Social Psychology,* 1963, *67,* 601–607.
Berg, K. S., & Vidmar, N. Authoritarianism and recall of evidence about criminal behavior. *Journal of Research in Personality,* 1975, *9,* 147–158.

Berkowitz, L. *Aggression: A social psychological analysis.* New York: McGraw Hill, 1962.

Berkowitz, L., Corwin, R., & Heironimus, M. Film violence and subsequent aggressive tendencies. *Public Opinion Quarterly,* 1963, *27,* 217–229.

Berkowitz, L., & Geen, R. G. Stimulus quality of the target of aggression: A further study. *Journal of Personality and Social Psychology,* 1967, *5,* 364–368.

Boehm, B. R. Mister prejudice, miss sympathy and the authoritarian personality: An application of psychological measuring techniques to the problem of jury bias. *Wisconsin Law Review,* 1968, 734–750.

Bond, M. H., & Dutton, D. G. The effects of interaction anticipation upon the extremity of trait ratings. *Canadian Journal of Behavioral Science,* 1973, *5,* 226–233.

Borden, R. J., Bowen, R., & Taylor, S. T. Shock setting behavior as a function of physical attack and extrinsic reward. *Perceptual and Motor Skills,* 1971, *33,* 563–568.

Brown, R. B. *Social psychology.* New York: Free Press, 1965.

Buss, A. H. *The psychology of aggression.* New York: Wiley, 1961.

Buss, A. H. Aggression pays. In J. L. Singer (Ed), *The control of aggression and violence.* New York: Academic Press, 1971. Pp. 7–18.

Campbell, D. T. Social attitudes and other acquired behavioral dispositions. In Sigmund Koch (Ed.), *Psychology a study of a science.* Vol. 6. New York: McGraw Hill, 1963. Pp. 94–172.

Costanzo, P. R., Coie, J. D., Grumet, J. F., & Farnill, D. A reexamination of the effects of intent and consequences on children's moral judgments. *Child Development,* 1973, *44,* 154–161.

Coombs, C. H. Thurstone's measurement of social values revisited forty years later. *Journal of Personality and Social Psychology,* 1967, *6,* 85–91.

Dion, K. K. Physical attractiveness and evaluation of children's transgressions. *Journal of Personality and Social Psychology,* 1972, *24,* 207–213.

Dion, K. K., & Berscheid, E. Physical attractiveness and peer perception among children. *Sociometry,* 1974, *37,* 1–12.

Dollard, J., Doob, L. W., Miller, M. E., Mowrer, O. H., & Sears, R. R. *Frustration and aggression.* New Haven: Yale Univ. Press, 1939.

Evan, W. M. *Law and sociology.* New York: Free Press, 1962.

Feshbach, S. The function of aggression and the regulation of aggressive drive. *Psychological Review,* 1964, *71,* 257–272.

Feshbach, S. Aggression. In P. H. Mussen (Ed.), *Carmichael's manual of child psychology* (rev. ed.). New York: Wiley, 1970. Pp. 159–259.

Feshbach, S. Dynamics and morality of violence and aggression: Some psychological considerations. *American Psychologist,* 1971, *26,* 281–292.

Geen, R. G. & Stonner, D. Context effects in observed violence. *Journal of Personality and Social Psychology,* 1973, *25,* 145–150.

Geen, R. G. & Stonner, D. The meaning of observed violence. Effects on arousal and aggressive behavior. *Journal of Research in Personality,* 1974, *8,* 55–63.

Gordon, R. I., & Jacobs, P. D. Forensic psychology: Perception of guilt and income. *Perceptual and Motor Skills,* 1969, *28,* 143–146.

Gutkin, D. C. The effect of systematic story changes on intentionality in children's moral judgments. *Child Development,* 1972, *43,* 187–195.

Hastorf, A. H., Schneider, D. J., & Polefka, J. Person Perception. Reading, Massachusetts: Addison-Wesley, 1970.

Hebble, P. W. The development of elementary school children's judgment of intent. *Child Development,* 1971, *42,* 1203–1215.

Heider, F. *The psychology of interpersonal relation.* New York: Wiley, 1958.

Hoffman, M. Moral development. In P. Mussen (Ed.), *Carmichael's manual of child psychology*. New York: Wiley, 1969. Pp. 261–359.

Hoyt, J. L. Effect of media "justification" on aggression. *Journal of Broadcasting*, 1970, *6*, 455–464.

Jones, C., & Aronson, E. Attribution of fault to a rape victim as a function of respectability of the victim. *Journal of Personality and Social Psychology*, 1973, *26*, 415–419.

Jones, E. E., & Davis, K. E. From acts to dispositions. In L. Berkowitz (Ed.), *Advances in experimental social psychology*, Vol. 2. New York: Academic Press, 1965. Pp. 219–266.

Jones, E. E., & Nisbett, R. E. The actor and the observer: Divergent perceptions of the causes of behavior. New York: General Learning Corporation, 1971.

Jurow, G. Y. New data on the effect of a "death qualified" jury on the guilt determination process. *Harvard Law Review*, 1971, *84*, 567–611.

Kahn, R. L. The justification of violence: Social problems and social solutions. *Journal of Social Issues*, 1972, *28*, 155–175.

Kalven, H., & Zeisal, H. *The American jury*. Boston: Little, Brown, 1966.

Kaplan, K. J., Klein, K. W., & Fried, M. General aims of prosecution versus defense in the selection and influence of jurors in a criminal trial: A brief working model. Unpublished manuscript, Wayne State Univ., 1973.

Kaplan, M. F., & Kemmerick, G. D. Juror judgment as information integration. *Journal of Personality and Social Psychology*, 1974, *30*, 493–499.

Kelley, H. H. Moral evaluation. *American Psychologist*, 1971, *23*, 293–300.

Kohlberg, L. Stage and sequence: The cognitive-developmental approach to socialization. In D. A. Goslin (Ed.), *Handbook of socialization theory and research*. Chicago: Rand, McNally & Company, 1969.

Landy, D., & Aronson, E. The influence of the character of the criminal and his victim on the decisions of simulated jurors. *Journal of Experimental Social Psychology*, 1969, *5*, 141–152.

Leifer, A. D., & Roberts, D. F. Childrens' responses to television violence. In J. P. Murray, E. A. Rubenstein, & G. A. Comstock (Eds.), *Television and social behavior: Television and social learning*. Vol. 2. Washington, D.C.: U.S. Department of Health and Education and Welfare, 1971. Pp. 43–180.

Lerner, M. J. The desire for justice and reactions to victims. In J. Macauley & L. Berkowitz (Eds.), *Altruism and helping behavior*. New York: Academic Press, 1970. Pp. 205–229.

Lincoln, A., & Levinger, G. Observers' evaluations of the victim and the attacker in an aggressive incident. *Journal of Personality and Social Psychology*, 1972, *22*, 202–210.

Milgram, S. Behavioral study of obedience. *Journal of Abnormal and Social Psychology*, 1963, *67*, 371–378.

Mitchell, A. E. & Byrne, D. The defendant's dilemma: Effects of jurors attitudes and authoritarianism on judicial decisions. *Journal of Personality and Social Psychology*, 1973, *25*, 123–130.

Nesdale, A. R., & Rule, B. G. The effects of an aggressor's characteristics and an observer's accountability on judgments of aggression. *Canadian Journal of Behavioral Science*, 1974, *6*, 342–350.

Nesdale, A. R., Rule, B. G., & McAra, M. J. Moral judgments of aggression: Personal and situational determinants. *European Journal of Social Psychology*, in press.

Piaget, J. *The moral judgment of the child*. New York: Free Press, 1965.

Rokeach, M. *The open and closed mind*. New York: Basic Books, 1960.

Rokeach, M., & Vidmar, N. Testimony concerning possible jury bias in a Black Panther murder trial. *Journal of Applied Social Psychology,* 1973, *3,* 19–29.

Rule, B. G. The hostile and instrumental functions of human aggression. In W. Hartup & J. de Wit (Eds.), *Determinants and origins of aggressive behavior.* The Hague: Mouton, 1974. Pp. 125–145.

Rule, B. G., & Hewitt, G. L. Effects of thwarting on cardiac response and physical aggression. *Journal of Personality and Social Psychology,* 1971, *19,* 181–187.

Rule, B. G., & Percival, E. The effects of frustration and attack on physical aggression. *Journal of Experimental Research in Personality,* 1971, *5,* 111–118.

Rule, B. G., & Duker, P. The effect of intentions and consequences on childrens' evaluations of aggressors. *Journal of Personality and Social Psychology,* 1973, *27,* 184–189.

Rule, B. G., Dyck, R., McAra, M., & Nesdale, A. R. Judgments of aggression serving personal versus prosocial purposes. *Social Behavior and Personality: An International Journal,* 1975, *3,* 55–63.

Rule, B. G., & Nesdale, A. R. Differing functions of aggression. *Journal of Personality,* 1974, *42,* 467–481.

Rule, B. G., Nesdale, A. R., & McAra, M. J. Children's reactions to information about the intentions underlying an aggressive act. *Child Development,* 1974, *45,* 794–798.

Scheerer, M. Cognitive theory. In G. Lindzey (Ed.), *Handbook of social psychology.* Cambridge, Massachusetts: Addison-Wesley, 1954. Pp. 91–142.

Schulman, J., Shaver, P., Colman, R., Emrich, B., & Christie, R. Recipe for a jury. *Psychology Today,* May, 1973, 37–84.

Sears, R. R. Relation of early socialization experiences to aggression in early childhood. *Journal of Abnormal and Social Psychology,* 1961, *63,* 466–492.

Shantz, D. W., & Voydanoff, D. A. Situational effects on retaliatory aggression at three age levels. *Child Development,* 1973, *44,* 149–153.

Shepherd, J. W., & Bagley, A. The effects of biographical information and order of presentation on the judgment of an aggressive action. *Journal of Social and Clinical Psychology,* 1970, *9,* 177–179.

Shaver, P. Lessons from the Harrisburg Conspiracy Trial. Presented at the 81st Annual Convention of the American Psychological Association, Montreal, 1973.

Sigall, H., & Ostrove, N. Beautiful but dangerous: Effects of offender attractiveness and nature of the crime on juridic judgments. *Journal of Personality and Social Psychology,* 1975, *31,* 410–414.

Silverman, W. H. The effects of social contact, provocation, and sex of opponent upon instrumental aggression. *Journal of Experimental Research in Personality,* 1971, *5,* 310–316.

Smith, M. Percy Foreman: Top trial lawyer. *Life,* 1966, *60,* 92–101.

Stokols, D., & Schopler, J. The actions to victims under conditions of situational detachment: The effect of responsibilities, severity, and expected future interaction. *Journal of Personality and Social Psychology,* 1973, *25,* 199–209.

Strodtbeck, F. L., James, R. M., & Hawkins, C. Social status in jury deliberations. In E. E. Maccoby, T. M. Newcomb, & E. L. Hartley (Eds.), *Readings in social psychology.* New York: Holt, 1958. Pp. 379–388.

Sutherland, E. *Principles of criminology.* Philadelphia: Lippincott, 1966.

Toch, H. (Ed.) *Legal and criminal psychology.* New York: Holt, 1961.

Tomlinson, T. M. Ideological foundations for negro action: A comparative analysis of militant and non-militant views of a Los Angeles riot. *Journal of Social Issues,* 1970, *26,* 93–120.

Thurstone, L. L. The method of paired comparisons for social values. *Journal of Abnormal and Social Psychology,* 1927, *21,* 384–400.

Vidmar, N., & Ellsworth, P. Public opinion and the death penalty. *Stanford Law Review,* 1974, *26,* 1245–1270.

Winick, C. The psychology of juries. In H. Toch (Ed.), *Legal and criminal psychology.* New York: Holt, 1961. Pp. 96–120.

Personality Variables as Mediators of Attack-instigated Aggression

H. A. DENGERINK

Introduction

Personality is a term that has been so diversely defined that several authors have declined to specify its limits and have left this task to individual theorists (Hall & Lindzey, 1970). There are, however, certain concepts that have, with some regularity, been identified with the term personality. Recently a number of persons have begun to consider mediational behaviors and processes as the specific domain of personality. Shontz (1965) states that, "put most directly, personality is identified by its concern for inferred mediational processes that account for organization in the behavior of the individual [p. 7]." That is, certain processes or behaviors of a person, such as anger, anxiety, guilt, expectations, and attributions, serve as mediators that can alter the effects of environmental stimuli on behaviors such as aggression. This chapter will follow the aforementioned definition of personality and will attempt to focus on those behaviors and processes of a potential aggressor that mediate the effect of environmental events on aggressive behavior.

Behaviors that are considered to be aggressive are nearly as diverse as the concepts of personality. Behaviors labeled as aggressive include the utterance of verbal insults (James & Mosher, 1967), interference with another person's performance on a task (Peterson, 1971), and the delivery of shock (Buss, 1961), as well as a myriad of other behaviors. For purposes of expediency, this chapter will focus on those aggressive behaviors that involve the delivery of noxious stimuli or causing injury to another person. This category of aggression has been referred to as physical aggression by Buss (1961), but even physical aggression can take on several different dimensions. Physical aggression can occur in response to or in the absence of attack (Pisano & Taylor, 1971), with intent to help, or with intent to harm (Baron & Eggelston, 1972).

Several authors have suggested that one of the most pervasive and consistent instigators of aggression is attack. Buss (1961) suggested that attack is a prepotent stimulus for aggression, and Bandura (1973) stated that "if one wished to provoke aggression, the most dependable way to do so would be simply to physically assault another person, who would then be likely to oblige with a vigorous counterattack [p. 153]." Numerous investigations have supported this notion. Patterson and Cobb (1971) recorded several different behaviors on the part of children and other members of their families. They reported that while the child hit another child only during .2% of the periods sampled, this behavior occurred during 32% of the periods following those in which the child had been hit. Thus, it appears that physical attack (receipt of noxious stimuli) is an important facilitator of aggressive behavior.

In another study, O'Leary and Dengerink (1973) reported that the intensity of shocks delivered to an opponent varied with the intensity of attack from that opponent. If the opponent delivered consistently high intensity shocks to the subject, the subject responded by choosing consistently high intensity shocks for the opponent. If the opponent chose low shocks, the subject chose low shocks. If the opponent increased the intensity of his shock choices for the subject, the subject increased his, and if the opponent decreased the intensity, so did the subject. O'Leary and Dengerink concluded that the intensity of the immediately preceding attack is a major parameter in the control of physical aggression.

These findings of Patterson and Cobb (1971) and O'Leary and Dengerink (1973) support the position of persons, such as Buss (1961) and Bandura (1973), who feel that attack may be the most important social instigator of aggression. Since attack instigated aggression appears to be the most important and most frequent form of aggression, this chapter will focus on personality variables that mediate the effects of attack on aggression. Two major classes of such personality variables will be considered: emotional variables including anger, guilt, and anxiety, and cognitive variables such as attribution and expectations.

Because this chapter will focus on attack-instigated aggression, the findings discussed here may not generalize to aggressive behaviors that occur in the absence of attack. For example, Dengerink and Bertilson (1974) recently reported that aggression occurring in response to attack was most likely to decrease if the attacker suddenly withdrew and adopted a strategy of being as nonaggressive as the situation permitted. In contrast, Pisano and Taylor (1971) selected subjects who were aggressive in the absence of attack and reported that these persons were most likely to reduce their aggression if the opponent matched the aggression level of the subject. This matching was only minimally effective for Dengerink and Bertilson, whose subjects were aggressive after being attacked. Clearly, some social conditions differentially influence attack-instigated and uninstigated aggression. Personality variables may also differentially influence attack-instigated and uninstigated aggression.

Basic Experimental Procedures

Research on attack-instigated aggression has most often relied on two basic sets of experimental procedures. Since the studies described later have relied heavily on these procedures, it may be helpful to readers if these procedures were described in some detail at this point.

One set of laboratory procedures that permits close examination of the relationship between attack and aggression is the set designed by Taylor (1965). These procedures are referred to as the competitive reaction time task. They require two persons to compete, during a series of trials, in achieving the faster reaction time. Prior to each trial, each competitor chooses an intensity of shock that he wishes the other to receive if the other has a slower reaction time during the ensuing portion of the trial. Typically the subjects have five different shock intensities from which to choose. These range from a mild level up to a level that the opponent had previously indicated was definitely unpleasant and the maximum he would take voluntarily.

After choosing shock for the other person, both competitors respond to a reaction time signal and receive feedback. Feedback is given in two forms: On some trials (usually half), the subject receives a shock which indicates that his reaction time was slower than that of the opponent. The intensity of this shock varies from high (the level that the subject had indicated was definitely unpleasant before the task) to low. In addition, on all trials a light is illuminated to indicate which of the five intensities the opponent chose for the subject. This light is illuminated regardless of whether or not the subject lost that particular trial. There is, in fact, no opponent; rather, the shock intensities for the subject and whether or not the subject receives shock on any given trial are programmed by the experimenter. The shock chosen for and delivered to the subject can be varied to manipulate the level of attack. The intensity of shock chosen for the opponent by the subject serves as the primary measure of aggression.

A second set of procedures used by several investigators are those devised by Berkowitz and his associates (Berkowitz & Geen, 1966). In these procedures, interactions between the subject and an accomplice are fabricated prior to the interaction in which the subject chooses shock for the accomplice. During this initial interaction, the subject typically is asked to write what he feels would be the best solution to some problem, such as the rising crime rate. This solution is then evaluated by the accomplice, who is permitted to communicate his evaluation by delivering a number of shocks and writing a response to the subject. In the attack conditions, the accomplice delivers shocks (often 9 of a possible 10) to the subjects and writes a very insulting response. In the control conditions, the accomplice delivers only one shock and then writes a complimentary response to the subject.

The interaction in which subjects deliver shock to the accomplice is often the more widely known procedure designed by Buss (1961). In these procedures, subjects are asked to teach a concept to the accomplice by providing shocks for errors that the accomplice makes. The intensity and duration of the shocks that the subject chooses to administer to the accomplice serve as the dependent measures of aggression.

Personality Research

As was pointed out earlier, the focus of this chapter will be some of those inferred behaviors and processes that mediate the effect of attack on aggression. Because the primary focus of this chapter is mediational processes, it is appropriate to discuss some of the limitations of such personality research.

Experimental procedures for psychological research require manipulation of an independent variable while assessing changes or differences in the dependent variable. Such manipulation is relatively simple when the variables under investigation are environmental ones, such as attack. Attack is something external to the subject and can be manipulated simply by varying the behavior of the accomplice. Personality variables, however, often consist of covert behaviors of the subject. As such, they are difficult if not impossible to manipulate directly. One cannot generate anger in the same sense that one can provide attack. To solve such a problem, researchers have adopted two different strategies, both of which have their own limitations.

The first strategy, and the one that has been employed most frequently in the history of personality, is to select persons who differ in some independent measure of the mediational process under investigation. Most frequently, personality researchers have selected groups of subjects who differ in some self-report measure, such as anxiety. These two groups of subjects are then compared on some dependent measure of aggression. Differences between the groups are attributed to the previously assessed differences and the mediational process that those differences presumably measure. These procedures have the advantage of permitting investigations of aggressive behaviors associated with mediational behaviors that occur naturally rather than with those that are generated in the laboratory. These procedures do not, however, lead to the conclusion that differences in aggressive behavior are caused by the assessed differences in mediating behaviors. It is also possible that both the differences in the assessed characteristics and the differences in aggression are the result of some third variable.

The second strategy, which has been employed with increasing frequency in recent studies, is to manipulate the inferred mediating behavior indirectly. That is, some variable, which can be manipulated directly and which is presumed to cause differences in the mediating behavior, is used. For example, insult is presumed to result in anger. If insulted subjects are later observed to be more aggressive than those who were not insulted, this difference is attributed to differences in anger. These procedures have the advantage of permitting causal inferences. Since the mediating behaviors are not manipulated directly, however, manipulation checks are required to determine whether or not the mediating behaviors have in fact occurred. Unfortunately, a large number of studies, which may have implications for the relationship between personality variables and aggression, have not employed such manipulation checks. Other investigations have employed manipulation checks after the person has had the opportunity to act aggressively. This latter strategy has a disadvantage in that persons may describe themselves as being angry, for example, because they were aggressive, not because they were angry before or while aggressing. Bem (1967) has argued cogently that persons' self-descriptions depend as much or more on their overt behavior as on other variables, such as subjectively felt emotions. Ideally, such manipulation checks would be taken before the opportunity to aggress arose.

Emotional Inhibition of Aggressive Behavior

Aggressive behaviors are commonly assumed to be influenced by emotions. The legal distinction between first degree murder and manslaughter rests, in part, on the degree to which the defendant is judged to have been angry or cooly premeditated at the time of the aggressive act. Persons who are not aggressive, even when severely provoked, are often assumed to be very anxious or stoically insensitive. These common assumptions will be the topic of these first two sections. Emotional variables, including anxiety, guilt and anger, will be reviewed for their effect on aggressive behavior.

Anxiety and Fear

Anxiety and fear are complex concepts. These terms most often refer to emotional behaviors but are often associated with the cognitive variable of expectation. A social learning approach to anxiety and fear stresses the notion that these are emotional responses to anticipation of, or uncertainty about, aversive consequences (Epstein, 1972). As such, anxiety and fear involve both emotional arousal and expectations. For purposes of this review, an arbitrary distinction will be made. Those studies with implications primarily for the effects of emotional arousal will be reviewed here. Those with major implications for expectancy mediation of aggression will be reviewed in a later section.

When two persons are engaged in an aggressive interchange, they are subject to several contingencies. If a potential aggressor chooses to be passive, he may be the subject of ridicule and disapproval by the opponent or by observers, particularly if he is male. When there are rewards for defeating an opponent, the passive person foregoes these instrumental rewards. If the aggressor chooses to return the attacks of an opponent or to escalate the aggressive exchange, he risks harm and possibly disapproval if he initiates the escalation or exceeds the bounds of culturally defined norms. These potential consequences create uncertainty regarding the potential aggressors' choice of behaviors, and, according to anxiety theory, these potential consequences also generate anxiety. Various experimental manipulations that alter the likelihood of these conflicting consequences should then result in differences in aggression if, in fact, anxiety does influence aggression. Increasing the possibility that observers would disapprove of a subject's aggressive behavior should reduce the intensity of counterattack.

Consistent with this notion, Borden (1975) has demonstrated that the perceived values of an observer will influence aggression. He employed the competitive reaction time task but modified it to provide shock intensities from 1 to 10. In this case, the number 10 corresponded to the intensity judged definitely unpleasant by the subject or the opponent. The opponent in Borden's studies chose moderately low shocks for the subject—intensities 3 and 4. During the first half of the trials, an observer was present; during the last half of the trials, the observer was absent. Borden reported the male subjects chose more intense shock for the opponent with a male observer than with a female observer. Subsequently, subjects who had been observed by a male decreased the intensity of their choices after the observer left, while removal of the female observer did not result in any change in shock choices. Borden replicated this experiment and added a manipulation of the observer's values. In one condition, the observer was an instructor in the university karate club and indicated much enthusiasm for this aggressive sport. In another condition, the observer was a member of the Society Against Nuclear Expansion and, in fact, was a cofounder of this pacifistic group. Bordon reported that there was a significant reduction in shock setting after the aggressive observer left but not after the pacifistic observer left (see Figure 1). These findings indicate that the perceived values of an observer may facilitate aggressive behavior.

In a related study, Borden and Taylor (1973) employed active ob-

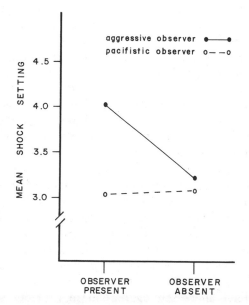

Figure 1. Mean shock settings of subjects in the presence of either an aggressive observer or a pacifistic observer, and on subsequent trials when the observer was absent (From Borden, 1975).

servers who attempted to change the aggressive behavior of the subjects. If the opponent was nonaggressive, the subjects were consequently non-aggressive, and the observers (two females and one male) attempted to cajole the male subjects into becoming more aggressive. If the opponent was very aggressive (choosing only maximum shocks for the subject), the observers attempted to persuade the subject to lower his shock choices. Borden and Taylor reported that observers were able to increase the shock choices of the subjects who were competing with the nonaggressive opponent. Furthermore, after the observer left, the sub-jects continued to set elevated shocks for the opponent. The observers were also effective in reducing the shock level chosen for the unmitigat-ing opponent, but this reduction disappeared after the observers left.

Baron (1972) similarly reported that insulted subjects were more ag-gressive after witnessing the aggressive model than before. If the model had been criticized by a peer for being too aggressive, however, the modeling effect was smaller than if the model had not been censured.

These studies suggest that social disapproval from a third party can inhibit aggression even when the subject has been insulted, after he has observed an aggressive model, and when he is under intense attack from the opponent. It is also possible that subjects may be responsive to the disapproval of the opponent or victim. Savitsky, Izard, Kotsch, and Christy (1974) have explored this possibility. They asked subjects to shock a learner in the Buss procedures while subjects were able to see the learner over a closed-circuit television monitor. When the learner received shock, he either smiled, indicated anger, was neutral or indi-cated fear. Savitsky *et al.* reported that if the victim was neutral or indi-cated fear, the intensity of shock chosen by the subjects did not change over trials. If the victim smiled after receiving shock, the subjects chose shocks which increased in duration and intensity across trials. If the victim indicated anger, then the subjects chose shocks which decreased, particularly in duration, across trials.

Unfortunately, it is not clear from the Savitsky *et al.* study whether these social consequences would have the same effect if the subjects had been attacked or angered first. Prior to the testing for aggression, half of the subjects learned that the victim disagreed with their opinions re-garding the value of closed-circuit television and punishment in teach-ing. The disagreeing victim further stated "directly that the subject's opinions were wrong and misinformed [p. 350]." This manipulation of insult did not influence the subject's aggressive behavior. Since similar manipulations have increased aggression in previous studies (Baron, 1971a), it may be appropriate to conclude that this was a weak manipu-lation of attack and that these findings may not generalize to aggressive behavior that is instigated by attack.

One other social variable that may lead subjects to anticipate social approval or disapproval for acting aggressively is the sex of the victim. Males especially are more likely to have experienced punishment and disapproval for acting aggressively toward females than toward males. Accordingly, Taylor and Epstein (1967) reported that female opponents in the competitive reaction time task elicited lower shock settings than male opponents. Furthermore, even though the opponent gradually increased the shock settings for the subject, both male and female subjects increased the intensity of their counterattack more for males than for females.

These studies indicate that the social relationship between the subject and the opponent may be important in the control of aggression. In addition, insofar as these social variables imply disapproval for aggression, it may be appropriate to conclude that mediating emotional variables, such as anxiety and fear of disapproval, are, in fact, causally related to reduced aggression. The most direct manipulation of anxiety or fear of disapproval was part of a study by Turner and Simons (1974). In this experiment, which is discussed in another context in Geen's chapter in this volume, "Observing Violence in the Mass Media: Implications of Basic Research," the investigators manipulated fear of disapproval by telling half of the subjects that their behavior in the aggression situation would indicate whether or not they were "psychologically maladjusted [p. 343]." The subjects then attempted to reach a solution to a problem, and this solution was evaluated negatively by an accomplice who delivered several shocks to the subject as part of this evaluation. The subjects were then given a chance to evaluate the confederate's solution to a problem by delivering a variable number of shocks. Those subjects who were told that their psychological adjustment was being evaluated delivered fewer shocks than those who were not told that they were being evaluated. Thus, it appears that potential social disapproval, whether manipulated via alterations in the sex or values of an observer or manipulated via evaluation apprehension, can reduce aggression.

The possibility that fear of social censure may inhibit aggression has also been studied by Taylor (1970). He selected subjects who scored on either extreme of the Crowne Marlowe Social Desirability Scale (Crowne & Marlowe, 1960) and exposed them to an opponent in the competitive reaction time task who gradually increased the intensity of attack across trials. He reported that persons with low need for approval chose high levels of shock across all trials. High need approval persons, on the other hand, began by setting low intensity shocks and gradually increased the intensity across trials approaching, but not reaching, the levels chosen by the low need approval persons.

In a subsequent study, Dengerink (1971) examined the relationship between self—reported anxiety and attack-instigated aggression. He identified high and low anxious persons by administering an early version of the Activity Preference Questionnaire (Lykken, 1957). This scale requires that persons indicate their preference for various activities by choosing between pairs of alternative activities that have been equated for unpleasantness. In each pair, one alternative is an onerous or tedious activity and the other is a dangerous or embarrassing activity (e.g., working during the summer on a garbage truck versus having a wreck with a borrowed car). Those persons who consistently prefer tedious or onerous tasks to dangerous or embarrassing ones are considered relatively anxious.

Dengerink then tested these two groups of subjects with the competitive reaction time task. The opponent gradually increased the intensity of shock for the subject from low to high across trials. Dengerink reported a significant interaction between the effects of anxiety and trial blocks. As Figure 2 indicates, the two anxiety groups did not differ significantly during the first block of testing in which the opponent chose mild shocks for the subject. As the opponent increased his attack during subsequent blocks, the low anxious group increased the intensity of their shocks for the opponent. The high anxious group, however, increased their shock choices for the opponent at an initially slower rate. During the second and third blocks, the high anxious group chose shocks that were less intense than those chosen by the low anxious

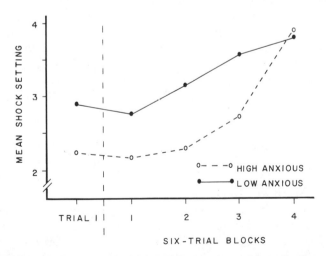

Figure 2. Mean shock setting by high and low anxious subjects during trial one and subsequent six-trial blocks (From Dengerink, 1971).

group. Between the third and fourth block, the high anxious group increased the rate of their escalation and, during the fourth block, chose shocks for the opponent that were as intense as those chosen by the low anxious group.

During the third block of testing, when the high anxious subjects were still less aggressive than the low anxious subjects, the opponent had not yet chosen the maximum intensity shock. During the third block, the opponent chose intensities Number 3 and 4 an equal number of times. During the fourth block, when the high anxious subjects chose shocks that were not different from those of the low anxious subjects, the opponent chose intensities Number 4 and 5 an equal number of times. That is, not until the beginning of the fourth block did the opponent choose the maximum shock for the subject. Dengerink reasoned that the lower shock settings of the high anxious subjects during the middle blocks may have occurred because the high anxious subjects were trying to avoid provoking the opponent into choosing the maximum shock. Once the opponent had chosen this intensity, there was no longer any hope of avoiding the maximum shock. Perhaps as a consequence, they escalated their counterattack to the level chosen by the low anxious subjects.

Dorsky and Taylor (1972) subsequently replicated this study but employed a different measure of anxiety and an additional measure of aggression. They selected as subjects college males who scored on the extremes of the Taylor Manifest Anxiety Scale (Taylor, 1953). The competitive reaction time apparatus was also modified to permit recording the duration of the subject's pressure on the shock buttons. They reported that the high and low anxious groups did not differ in their shock choices for the opponent; rather, both groups consistently increased the intensity of shock for the escalating opponent. They did observe, however, that the low anxiety subjects increased the duration of time that they pressed the shock buttons across blocks of trials, but the high anxious subjects decreased the amount of time that they pressed these buttons.

This finding is at variance with that reported by Dengerink (1971). Donnerstein, Donnerstein, Simon, and Ditrichs (1972) have suggested that the intensity of shock choices for a victim may be a direct measure of aggression and that the duration of shock choices may represent a measure of indirect aggression. Insofar as this distinction applies to the competitive reaction time task, it may be appropriate to conclude that Dorsky and Taylor (1972) demonstrated a relationship between manifest anxiety and indirect aggression while Dengerink (1971) demonstrated a relationship between anxiety, as measured by the

Activity Preference Questionnaire, and direct aggression. Dorsky and Taylor (1972) suggest that this difference in findings may be related to the difference in the measure of anxiety employed in these two studies.

Although both the Activity Preference Questionnaire and the Taylor Manifest Anxiety Scale both purport to measure anxiety, there are a number of differences between the scales. Manifest anxiety is heavily weighted in favor of pathology. That is, the anxiety is presumably suffi-ciently intense and prolonged to result in physiological manifestations of the emotional stress. On the other hand, anxiety, as measured by the Activity Preference Questionnaire, is purportedly normal anxiety that involves the anticipation of environmental consequences for engaging in certain activities. This latter scale does not correlate with measures of social desirability and correlates only minimally with the Taylor Manifest Anxiety Scale (Lykken, Tellegen, & Katzenmeyer, 1973). Dorsky and Taylor (1972) further suggested that the early version of the APQ employed by Dengerink measured primarily social anxiety. They implied that the inhibition of aggression intensity observed by Dengerink, but not observed by them, may have stemmed from antici-pation of social censure on the experimenters part or implied in the op-ponent's escalating attack, rather than from anticipation of escalated shock per se.

This possibility was explored in a subsequent study by Dorsky (1972). A revised form of the Acitivity Preference Questionnaire permit-ted Dorsky to select subjects who described themselves as being high or low anxious on both the social and physical anxiety subscales of the revised test. Dorsky reported that there was little effect of physical anxiety in the shock settings chosen by subjects for the opponent. High socially anxious subjects, however, were less aggressive than the low socially anxious subjects while the opponent chose increasing shock for the subjects. Following the increasing attack, Dorsky varied the com-petitive reaction time procedures to include an additional shock alterna-tive. This alternative was described to the subjects as being twice as intense as that judged previously as definitely unpleasant. When this al-ternative could be chosen by the opponent but not by the subject, the high socially anxious subjects decreased the intensity of shocks chosen for the opponent. Low anxious subjects evidenced a slight increase in shock settings chosen for the opponent when the opponent could deliver the massive shock to them. In a final block of trials, the subject could deliver the massive shock alternative to the opponent, but the opponent was unable to use that alternative. In this block of trials, the high socially anxious subjects chose the massive alternative for the opponent four times as often as did the low socially anxious subjects.

This finding supports Dorsky and Taylor's (1972) suggestion that social anxiety rather than physical anxiety is related to the inhibition of aggression. At least within the measures of anxiety and aggression employed, physical anxiety has not been observed to be related to aggression while social anxiety appears to be related to the inhibition of aggression. Dorsky's observations also support Dengerink's (1971) suggestion that the inhibition of aggression by high anxious persons is related to anticipation of escalated attack from the opponent. High socially anxious subjects reduced the levels of their counterattack when the opponent's aggressive capabilities were greater than their own but increased their aggressiveness when their aggressive capabilities were greater than those of the opponent.

These studies all demonstrate that aggression may be inhibited by manipulations that increase the possibility of social disapproval and that reduced aggression is associated with self-reports of anxiety and need for approval. Although this evidence is not conclusive, it implies that arousal of aversive emotional states, such as anxiety and fear, can inhibit aggression. It is not clear, however, that such emotional variables are always associated with reduced aggression. The effect of such emotional mediators should vary with environmental cues that punishment or disapproval will accrue to the person who is aggressive. For example, if the experimental situation were arranged such that subjects would experience disapproval for not acting aggressively, then anxious or approval-seeking persons should be more, not less, aggressive. Borden (1975) and Borden and Taylor (1973) have demonstrated that social pressure can facilitate aggression. If persons who were excessively in need of social approval were exposed to those procedures then they would be more aggressive than persons who are low in a measure of need for approval. Furthermore, similar findings would be anticipated for persons who are excessively anxious. To date, little research has been conducted that attempts to assess the interaction of individual difference measures and situational variables.

Guilt

Mosher (1965) suggests that, as pointed out earlier, expectations of social disapproval or punishment will inhibit aggression only in the presence of environmental cues indicating the existence of such consequences. Mosher further suggests that more stable inhibitors of aggression are expectations of self-criticism, self-blame, and self-remorse. Mosher labels generalized expectancies for such self-mediated punishment as guilt. Expectations of self-disapproval should be present

whenever a person engages in or anticipates engaging in some self-pro-
hibited behavior. As a result, guilt should inhibit aggression regardless
of situational variations.

Brock and Buss (1964) have demonstrated that being excessively aggressive can result in subjects experiencing guilt. Buss (1966a,b) and
Baron (1971a) have further provided evidence that conditions that may
increase the tendency for self-criticism will inhibit aggression. Buss
(1966a) asked subjects to teach a problem to two different learners by
delivering shocks to them for mistakes. Half of the subjects were led to
believe that they had harmed the first learner with the shocks that they
delivered. He reported that if the victim was female, female subjects
were less likely to be aggressive toward the second learner if they had
harmed the first than if they had not harmed the first learner. Buss
(1966b) also demonstrated that subjects were less aggressive if the
victim vocalized feelings of pain than if the victim did not express pain.
Similarly Baron (1971a) demonstrated that subjects delivered less
intense shock to a learner if a "Psychoautonomic Pain Meter" indicated
that the victim were experiencing intense pain than if the meter indicated that the victim were experiencing mild pain. Baron further
demonstrated that this reduction occurred whether or not the subject
had previously been attacked (received nine shocks) or not been attacked (received only one shock) by the victim.

Baron did not attempt to provide independent evidence that the information indicating that the victim was experiencing intense pain
resulted in guilt on the part of the aggressor. Buss (1966a), however, did
pursue this possibility. He asked subjects, after they had completed
testing of the second learner, whether or not he or she was concerned
about the first learner who had been harmed. He reported that the
amount of reduction in aggression from the first to the second learner
was not related to the degree of concern reported for the first learner.
Although this finding may suggest that the reduction in aggression as a
function of having harmed someone else is unrelated to guilt, these
procedures may not be an adequate test of this hypothesis. First, the
measure of concern was taken after the subject had delivered shock to a
second learner without harmful results. This intervening experience
could easily have colored the subject's concern for the first victim.
Geen, Stonner, and Kelly (1974) have demonstrated that if a victim
expresses suffering when receiving shock, subjects may, under certain
circumstances, underrate the aggressiveness of aggressive cues. Second,
Buss does not provide a comparison on the guilt measure between those
who had supposedly harmed the first learner and those who had not.
Despite a failure to discern a relationship between reduction of ag-

gression and concern within the group that had harmed the first victim, it is possible that those who had harmed the victim were more concerned than persons who had not harmed the victim.

Thus these studies of the effect of harm on subsequent aggression fail to provide any conclusive evidence that aggression is inhibited by guilt. Their relevance to the effect of guilt on aggression is further clouded by the observation of Feshbach, Stilles, and Bitter (1967) that observing a victim in pain can actually facilitate rather than inhibit aggression. They first exposed female subjects to either an insulting or a neutral confederate. The subjects were then given the opportunity to observe the confederate receiving shock or, in a control condition, a light. The subjects could control the delivery of shock or light to the confederate by choosing the correct pronoun response to a question. Those subjects who had been insulted gradually increased the choice of the responses that resulted in the confederate receiving shock. No such effect occurred when the confederate received a light instead of a shock.

The reason for the difference between these findings and those of Buss (1966a) and Baron (1971a) is not immediately clear. One possibility is that the clarity and intensity of the pain cues may not have been as great in the Feshbach et al. study as they were in the studies of Buss and Baron. Another possibility is that, in the Feshbach *et al.* study, the subjects were not directly responsible for delivering shock to the victim. Rather, they could increase or decrease the frequency of shocks delivered by a third party to the confederate. It is possible that the displaced nature of the aggressive responsibility reduced the inhibiting social sanctions against harming another. If the difference between these studies can be attributed to the lack of social sanctions, then the aggression inhibiting effect noted by Baron and Buss may be a function of anxiety or fear (anticipated social disapproval) rather than a function of guilt (anticipation or experiencing of self-disapproval).

Ulehla and Adams (1974) provide some support for the idea that anticipated self-disapproval may serve as a control of aggressive behavior. They report that persons who are identified as aggressive by teachers or peers were less able to discriminate between aggressive behaviors resulting in self-approval and those which would not. They were concerned, however, with ability to discriminate rather than the frequency or magnitude of the self-disapproval. Furthermore, while their procedures do demonstrate that aggressive behavior is related, among adolescents, to the ability to discriminate reinforcers, they are unable to conclude that differences in aggressive behavior are caused by the ability to discriminate reinforcers.

Only two studies have directly assessed the relationship between aggression and guilt. James and Mosher (1967) first asked Boy Scout troops to complete the Mosher Forced Choice Guilt Inventory (1966) and then to nominate members of their troop who fought the most and who fought the least. They reported no significant differences in the sociometric aggression ratings between those who scored above and below the median in hostility guilt. Sociometric measures of aggressiveness are, of course, subject to distortion by the rater, and these procedures may not provide the best test of the relationship between guilt and aggression.

Knott, Lasater, and Shuman (1974) measured aggression directly and attempted to relate this behavior to the Mosher measure of hostility guilt. They modified the minimal social situation used by Hokanson (Hokanson, Willers, & Koropsak, 1968) to measure aggression. Knott *et al.* modified these procedures so that the subject and the confederate could exchange rewards and a series of variable intensity shocks rather than just one shock intensity. The confederate began the interaction by choosing rewards and shocks randomly for the subject and then returned to this baseline procedure between and following the two conditioning phases. In one of the conditioning phases, the confederate responded to the subject's choosing shock by delivering rewards; in the other conditioning phase, the confederate responded to the subject's choice of shocks by delivering shock to the subject. Two weeks after the initial testing, the male subjects were telephoned and asked to participate in an ostensibly separate experiment which required them to complete the Mosher hostility guilt subscale. Knott *et al.* reported that subjects who scored relatively high on the guilt measure delivered shock less frequently than those who scored relatively low. High guilt subjects also delivered less intense shock than low guilt subjects. Furthermore, high guilt subjects were less likely to become aggressive when rewarded for doing so than were low guilt subjects.

This study would seem to indicate that guilt does inhibit aggression even when subjects are being shocked by their victim. Mosher (1965) suggests, however, that guilt develops as "a function of the person's past history of reinforcement in regard to violating standards of proper behavior [p. 162]." Anxiety appears to occur in the same fashion, that is, as a function of reinforcements and punishments for violating standards of proper behavior. As a result, it is appropriate to expect a high correlation between measures of guilt and anxiety. Consequently, the differences in aggression between high and low guilt subjects may have been dependent on anxiety rather than guilt. Particularly in the presence of cues that imply that social disapproval or punishment may accrue when the subject is aggressive, it should be difficult to distinguish between the effects of guilt and the effects of anxiety. In the absence of such cues, however, guilt should continue to inhibit aggression but anxiety should not. Clearly a welcome study at this point would be one varying the potential disapproval or punishment for aggressive behavior on the part of high and low guilt subjects. Until such a study demonstrates that high guilt subjects continue to be nonaggressive when the potential for disapproval is minimized, it may be more parsimonious to conclude that the currently demonstrated inhibition of aggression is more a function of anxiety than of guilt.

Experimental Reduction of Aggression-inhibiting Emotions

If, as the previous evidence suggests, aggression is inhibited by emotional behaviors, such as anxiety, fear, and guilt, then measures that alleviate these emotions should facilitate aggression. One means of alleviating aversive emotional states may be the consumption of alcohol. Alcohol is commonly assumed to have a tranquilizing effect (Williams, 1931; Vogel–Sprott, 1967) and to dissipate negative emotional responses (Vogel–Sprott, 1967). If alcohol does have an emotion-dissipating effect and if anxiety and fear do reduce aggression, then persons who have consumed alcohol, particularly under threatening situations, should be more aggressive than those who have not consumed alcohol.

In the first study of the effects of alcohol on attack instigated aggression, Shuntich and Taylor (1972) employed the competitive reaction time task and a confederate who increased the intensity of attack across trials. Prior to participating in the competitive reaction time task, their subjects either consumed nothing, consumed a placebo, or consumed a large dose of bourbon. They reported that the subjects who had consumed a large dose of bourbon were more aggressive than those who had consumed a placebo or those who had consumed nothing.

In a subsequent experiment, Taylor and Gammon (1975) assessed the effects of alcohol dosage and type of alcoholic beverage on aggression in the competitive reaction time task. Their subjects consumed either a moderate or a high dose of either vodka or bourbon prior to competing with an increasingly aggressive opponent in the reaction time task. They reported that on the first trial, before the subject knew what the opponent had chosen, subjects who had consumed a large dose of alcohol chose more intense shock than subjects who had consumed a moderate dose. During the trials, a similar difference was noted with somewhat greater dosage effects occurring among those who had consumed vodka (which contains relatively few impurities) than among those who had consumed bourbon (which contains relatively high levels of impurities). These studies confirm, therefore, that alcohol does have a facilitating effect on aggression and further indicate that this effect increases with large doses of alcohol.

Whether or not the effects of alcohol on aggression are mediated by changes in emotional variables, however, is not immediately clear. Williams (1966) has reported that while small doses of alcohol are related to reduced anxiety, large doses of alcohol are related to higher levels of anxeity. That is, high levels of alcohol appear to increase aggression (Taylor & Gammon, 1975) and to increase anxiety. Taylor and Gammon asked their subjects, after the task, to indicate how anxious they had been during the competition. Unfortunately, their results from this question are mixed. They reported that subjects who had consumed the small dose of bourbon indicated that they were more anxious than persons who had consumed a large dose of bourbon. Persons who had consumed the small dose of vodka, however, indicated that they were much less anxious than those who had consumed the large dose of vodka. That is, juxtaposition of the anxiety self-reports and aggressive behavior of their subjects would indicate a negative relationship among those who had consumed bourbon. Among those who had consumed vodka, however, aggression and anxiety appear to rise or fall together.

Thus, it appears that alcohol will facilitate aggression particularly in situations that involve exchanges of shock between subject and their opponents. It is not clear, however, despite our original speculation, that this reduction is related to the interference of emotions that can inhibit aggression.

Emotional Facilitation of Aggression

The consistent finding that attack instigated aggression has led several authors to suggest that anger may be an important emotional mediator of aggression. Certainly the common or lay assumption is that if a person acts aggressively his behavior implies anger on his part.

Empirical efforts to demonstrate the relationship of anger to attack instigated aggression have often relied on indirect manipulations of anger and postexperimental manipulation checks. Hartmann (1969), for example, exposed subjects to confederates who either insulted their intelligence, sophistication, and competence or acted neutrally toward the subject. Hartmann subsequently observed that those subjects who had been insulted delivered more intense and longer shocks to the confederate than did neutrally treated subjects in the Buss aggression procedures. Following the teaching procedures, subjects were asked to

indicate how much they liked the confederate. Those who had been insulted indicated that they liked the confederate less than those who had
been treated neutrally.

Baron, in a series of experiments (1971a,b,c, 1972) employed similar
measures to arouse anger. Half of his subjects encountered a confederate who evaluated their solutions to problems positively by delivering one shock and praising them. The other half of Baron's subjects
encountered a confederate who evalauted their solutions negatively by
delivering nine shocks and then proceeded to insult their intelligence.
Subsequently, those subjects who had received negative evaluations delivered longer and more intense shocks to the confederate in the Buss
procedures than those who had received the positive evaluation. In a
postexperimental questionnaire, those who had received the negative
evaluations indicated that they had been angrier at the confederate
than those who had been positively evaluated.

Insofar as attack or insult does constitute an adequate manipulation
of anger, the effects of anger appear to be pervasive. These investigations indicate that anger will facilitate aggression even after the subject
has had an opportunity for catharsis through watching an aggressive
film (Hartmann, 1969), when given feedback that the victim was
experiencing intense pain from the shock (Baron, 1971a,b, 1974a), and
in the presence of an observer (Baron, 1971c).

The second source of evidence that anger mediates aggression arises
from self-report measures of ability to control aggression. In a series of
studies, Megargee and his colleagues (Megargee, 1966; Megargee &
Mendelsohn, 1962; Megargee, Cook, & Mendelsohn, 1967) reported that
persons who describe themselves as overcontrolled are less likely to
have engaged in mildly or moderately aggressive criminal behaviors
(battery). These same persons, however, are as likely or even more
likely than undercontrolled persons to engage in extremely aggressive
criminal behavior (murder). These findings have been replicated by
Blackburn (1968). Although Megargee does not indicate precisely what
is controlled—anger, other emotions, or some nonemotional behavior—
he implies that anger may be involved in this inhibition. Overcontrolled
persons disavow such items as "At times I feel like swearing" or "Often
I can't understand why I have been so cross and grouchy" and affirm
items such as "I don't mind being made fun of." It appears that under
conditions of mild or moderate provocation, overcontrolled persons will
inhibit their anger and not act aggressively. When the provocation is
extreme or repeated, however, such persons appear unable to inhibit
their anger and become extremely aggressive.

The relationship of extreme aggression to overcontrol of anger is not amenable to laboratory verification. The first part of Megargee's position, however, has been tested in the laboratory. Taylor (1967) first asked subjects to describe their tendency to control hostility on a self-rating scale. Those persons who described themselves as overcontrolled and those who described themselves as undercontrolled were then tested in the competitive reaction time task with an opponent who steadily increased the level of attack. Taylor observed that both groups increased the intensity of shock chosen for the opponent as the attack increased. The undercontrolled group, however, chose shocks for the opponent which were consistently higher than those chosen by the overcontrolled group. Furthermore, Taylor reported a significant tendency for the overcontrolled subjects to slow the rate of increase in their shock settings as testing progressed. These findings provide support, although indirect, that anger may be an important facilitator of aggression.

If anger does facilitate aggression, then it would seem likely that emotions that are imcompatible with anger, such as sexual arousal and enjoyment, should inhibit attack instigated aggression. Although several studies have investigated the effects of humor and sexual arousal on verbal aggression, only three have attempted to examine the effect of these variables on attack instigated physical aggression. Baron and Ball (1974) first exposed subjects to either an insulting and aggressive confederate or to a complimentary and nonaggressive confederate. They then asked subjects to rate nonhostile cartoons or nonhumorous pictures for interest value and amusing properties. They reported that subjects who had previously been insulted and shocked repeatedly by the confederate and then rated the cartoons were less aggressive than those who rated the pictures. In a subsequent experiment, Baron (1974b) employed the same design but asked subjects, after interacting with the confederate, to rate pictures of *Playboy* nudes or pictures of scenery. Baron reported that sexual arousal had an inhibiting effect on aggression only among subjects who had been attacked and insulted first.

These findings may indicate that pleasant emotional arousal does not influence aggression per se. If the subjects have become angry, however, then subsequent arousal of pleasant emotions may interfere with the incompatible anger and inhibit aggression. Baron and Baron and Ball report one finding, however, that may indicate that the arousal of pleasant emotions did not interfere with anger. Following the aggression procedures, they asked subjects to indicate their degree of anger toward the confederate. In both studies, subjects who had been attacked and insulted indicated that they were more angry than subjects who had not been attacked or insulted. No differences in self-report of anger were observed between those who rated cartoons and those who rated neutral pictures (Baron & Ball) or between those who rated scenery and those who rated the nudes (Baron). It is possible that these subjects were indicating the degree of anger at any time during the experiment, rather than the degree of anger at the time of the report. Nevertheless, this finding suggests that the effect of simultaneously evoked competing emotions on aggression is not clearly understood.

Furthermore, Zillman (1971) has reported findings that are very different from those reported by Baron (1974b). All of Zillman's subjects were first attacked by a confederate who delivered nine shocks to the subject. Subsequently, subjects viewed a segment of either a neutral, aggressive, or sexually arousing film. Following the film, the subjects were given the opportunity to shock the confederate in the Buss procedures. Zillman reported that those subjects who had viewed the erotic film were much more aggressive than those who had viewed the aggressive or neutral film. With the exception of the medium and intensity (erotic film versus still photos) of emotional arousal, Zillman's and Baron's procedures appear to be identical.

One rather subtle difference, however, may account for these differing observations. Buss's procedures require subjects to deliver shocks to a confederate for errors in order to teach the learner a concept. That is, the general requirement for the subjects is that they engage in a prosocial activity. To the extent that subjects believe that delivering higher intensity shocks will facilitate learning, their behavior may be very different from delivery of shock that has no prosocial function. Baron (1974b) told his subjects immediately before the task that the intensity of the shock was unrelated to performance. If Baron's description of the shock's effect on performance did remove any prosocial motivation in the delivery of shock, then the aggressive behavior studied by Baron and Zillman may have been very different. That is, sexual arousal may facilitate aggression which is helpful to the victim and inhibit aggression which is not helpful to the victim. It is, of course, not clear whether or not such an explanation of these differential findings will withstand empirical scrutiny.

One other variable would seem important in this context as well. The effects of sexual arousal may be quite different for male and female subjects and for aggression directed at male or female opponents. The effects of sexual arousal on aggression as it interacts with the sex of the subject and the sex of the opponent have not yet been studied.

One other notion concerning the concept of anger should be explored. Emotions are often viewed as driving a person, sometimes uncontrollably, to act. The legal discrimination between first degree murder and manslaughter rests, in part, on differentiating the degree to which a person was calmly premeditated or blindly driven to the same act. Such a causal relationship between emotions like anger and behaviors like aggression, however, is poorly understood.

Berkowitz, Lepinski, and Angulo (1969) provide some evidence that anger may function in other ways than as a driving force. Berkowitz et al. first exposed their subjects to a confederate who was quite obnoxious. Although the confederate did not attack the subject directly, he derogated the experimenter, the university, and, by implication, the subject as well. Physiological recording electrodes were then attached to the subject, and he was asked to observe a meter which would presumably indicate the degree of experienced anger as he thought about various persons. When asked to think about the obnoxious confederate, the meter indicated that the subject was either mildly, moderately, or extremely angry. The subjects were then able to shock the confederate in the Buss procedures. Berkowitz et al. reported that persons who were informed that they were moderately angry chose more intense and longer shock than those who were informed that they were mildly or extremely angry. In a subsequent study, Berkowitz and Turner (1974) replicated this finding. They also demonstrated that information about one's own anger level did not influence aggression when the target of the aggression was not the person who had presumably aroused the anger.

Berkowitz et al. and Berkowitz and Turner concluded that persons will be more aggressive if they believe that they are angry at their victim than if they do not hold such a belief. They also suggest, however, that if the person believes that he is more angry than is appropriate to the situation or to his experience, he will inhibit his aggression. It is difficult to determine whether false feedback of this sort has any influence on actually felt arousal or whether such effects would occur in the absence of meter assisted feedback. Nevertheless, these results raise the real possibility that emotional responses to some situation may influence behavior just like any other stimulus. Internal and external events may combine to form a complex set of stimuli which a person processes prior to engaging in aggressive behavior.

In this vein it may be appropriate to return to the concept of overcontrolled personality types as discussed by Megargee. Megargee suggests that overcontrolled persons become extremely aggressive not in response to a single extreme provocation but to instigations of aggression that have accumulated over time. He states that "through some form of temporal summation . . . instigation to aggression builds up over time [1966, p. 3]." If, as suggested earlier, anger functions as a cue that a person processes rather than as an unavoidable impetus to act, then another interpretation of Megargee's findings may be warranted. If overcontrolled persons have a history of not even engaging in mild aggressive behaviors, as Megargee (1966) suggests, then they may lack the social experience that permits most persons to learn discriminations between appropriate and inappropriate emotional arousal. They may also lack the experience that teaches most persons to attribute their arousal to the true instigator. As a result, the overcontrolled person may underreact at some times and overreact at others because of inadequate socialization, not because of an accumulation of anger.

Cognitive Mediators

As noted earlier, a great deal of effort has been devoted to investigating the effects of certain emotions on aggressive behavior. While these emotional mediators of aggression may have been the most popular, they are not the only, nor necessarily the most important, mediators of aggression. Another set of variables that are potentially important mediators of aggressive behavior may be classified as cognitive. These are mediational behaviors that involve the thought process, labels, categorizations, and expectations in which persons engage.

Labeling and Attribution

The competitive reaction time task, as designed by Taylor, provides two forms of feedback to the subjects. On some trials, the subject receives a shock if he presumably loses the competition on that trial. In addition, whether or not the subject receives shock, a numbered light is illuminated to indicate the intensity chosen by the opponent. Aggressive behavior which occurs in natural settings also occurs in response to multiple cues. Typically, the attacker provides both verbal and physical attack, to which persons may respond aggressively. Both forms of attack, verbal and physical, appear capable of instigating aggression (O'Leary & Dengerink, 1973; Baron & Eggelston, 1972). When both forms of attack are present, it is appropriate to expect that aggression would be more likely to result than if either alone were present. If these cues are discrepant, however, it is not clear what the effect will be on aggressive behavior.

Greenwell and Dengerink (1973) explored the possible interaction of the two different forms of feedback in the competitive reaction time task. For half of their subjects, the feedback lights indicated that the opponent chose levels of shock for the subject which increased from low to high across trials. The feedback lights indicated to the other half of the subjects that the opponent constantly chose a moderate shock intensity. Within each of these two groups, half of the subjects received shock on half of the trials which increased from low to high and half received shock which was always moderate. Greenwell and Dengerink reported a highly significant effect of the feedback lights. If the lights indicated increasing attack, the subjects responded with increasingly intense shocks for the opponent. If the lights indicated constant moderate shocks, then the subjects responded with consistently moderate shocks. The effects of constant versus increasing actual shocks, however, were not significant either as a main effect or in interaction with the increasing versus constant lights.

These results clearly indicate that certain aggressive cues are more effective in controlling aggression than others. Furthermore, if one can conceive of the lights as an imposed label for the opponent's aggressive behavior, then it is appropriate to conclude that human subjects are more likely to respond to labels of another person's behavior than to the other person's behavior per se. In support of this notion, several authors have demonstrated that increases in aggressive verbalizations are followed by an increase in physical aggression. Parke, Ewall, and Slaby (1972), for example, replicated and extended a previous study by Loew (1967) which demonstrated the effects of helpful or hostile verbalizations on aggressive behavior. They first read three words to a subject on a series of trials and reinforced them for choosing either helpful, neutral, or hostile words. Parke *et al.* then tested these subjects with the Buss aggression procedures. Those subjects who had been verbally reinforced for selecting hostile words chose more intense and longer shocks for the confederate than those who had been reinforced for choosing helpful words.

While Parke *et al.* and Loew's results may simply indicate that increased aggressive behavior in one modality will generalize to aggressive behavior in another modality, other studies suggest that verbal behaviors may mediate aggression. One such verbal mediator has been studied in an experiment by Mallick and McCandless (1966). In the first phase of their experiment, a confederate child interfered with the performance of one half of the subjects who were engaged in a task for which they could receive money. The subjects were then given an opportunity to play with toys, to talk to the experimenter about irrelevant topics, or to discuss with the experimenter a reasonable explanation for the confederate's objectionable behavior. Mallick and McCandless reported that when the children were given a chance to interfere with the the performance of the confederate, those who had been frustrated were more likely to interfere than those who were not frustrated, unless they had been given a reasonable explanation for the confederate's behavior. That is, if the frustrator's behavior was labeled as appropriate and nonarbitrary, these children were less likely to become aggressive than they were without such a label.

Similarly, labeling one's own behavior or emotional arousal can also affect one's aggressive behavior. Geen, Rakosky, and Pigg (1972) asked subjects to read a sexually arousing passage while receiving shock from an accomplice. Those subjects who were led to believe that their emotional arousal was caused by the shock were subsequently more aggressive toward the accomplice than those led to believe that their arousal was caused by the reading material.

Kanouse (1971) has argued that labeling one's own or someone else's behavior or emotion often accomplishes more than simple description of that behavior or experience. Labels often carry excess meaning, and, when applied to ourselves or to others, characteristics are assigned or attributed to that person or to ourselves.

One potentially important attribution is that of intent. That is, if one decides that another person intended to attack him, then one may be very likely to respond aggressively. If one decides that an attacker's behavior was accidental, then one may not respond with counterattack. The importance of perceived or attributed intent has been explored by Epstein and Taylor (1967). They varied both the frequency of shock received by the subject and the intensity chosen by the competitor. Epstein and Taylor reported that regardless of how often the subjects received shock, they chose high intensity shocks for the opponent who chose only high intensity shock and low intensity shocks for the opponent who chose only mild shocks. These findings suggest that the perceived intent of the opponent may be a more potent portion of attack than the pain or discomfort caused by the attack. As a result, it would not be surprising to find that seemingly minor events could elicit massive retaliation, if those events elicit attributions of hostile intent.

In a subsequent study, Nickel (1974) demonstrated this same phenomenon. In that study, subjects were first given high intensity shocks by a confederate in the Buss procedures and then were given the opportunity to shock the confederate. After the attack, however, the experimenter explained to the subjects that the buttons had been reversed due to an error on his (the experimenter's) part and that while the subject had received high intensity shocks the confederate had intended to give low shocks. The subjects who were told that the opponent's intent was the opposite of what the subject had received were less aggressive than those who were not given this information. Thus, it appears that attribution of intent is a major control of aggressive behavior. If such attributions are discrepant with the discomfort or pain experienced, then subjects appear to ignore the discomfort and respond to the attribution rather than the discomfort.

Furthermore, attribution of intent appears to be a mediator that influences a number of aggression-related behaviors. The aforementioned studies demonstrate that attribution of intent is an important mediator of aggressive instigation. In Rule and Nesdale's chapter in this volume, they more extensively discuss the effects of perceived intent on judgments of aggressive behavior.

One personality variable that may be closely related to perception of intent is paranoia. Hartemink (1971) measured the aggressive behavior of paranoid schizophrenics, nonparanoid schizophrenics, and nonschizophrenics in the competitive reaction time task. His findings may be interpreted as indicating that differences in the aggressive behavior of paranoid and nonschizophrenic subjects are dependent upon differences in perceived intent. Under increasing attack from the opponent, paranoid and nonparanoid subjects increased the intensity of their shock choices for the opponent and both were less aggressive than the nonparanoid schizophrenic group. When the opponent withdrew to a very passive strategy after the escalating attack, the nonschizophrenic subjects likewise became less aggressive. As Figure 3 indicates, both the paranoid and nonparanoid schizophrenics, however, continued to choose relatively intense shock after the opponent returned to mild

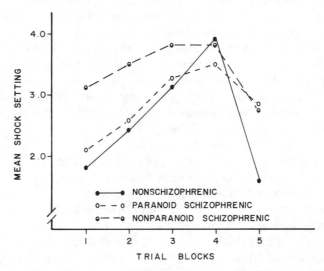

Figure 3. Mean shock settings during successive blocks by nonschizophrenic, paranoid schizophrenic, and nonparanoid schizophrenic groups (From Hartemink, 1971).

levels of attack. The failure of the paranoid group to reduce their level of aggression in response to the lowered level of attack may imply that these persons were less willing to trust the opponent than were the nonschizophrenic subjects.

While human aggression appears to vary with the perceived intent of the attacker, it may also depend on the intent of the aggressor. Rule and Nesdale (1974) pursued this suggestion which had been proposed by Baron and Eggelston (1972) and Rule and Hewitt (1971). Rule and Nesdale used the Buss procedures with two different sets of instructions. One set of instructions informed subjects that higher intensity shocks would help the learner's performance. The other instructions indicated that the higher intensity shocks would hinder performance. Within each of these conditions, half of the subjects were insulted by the confederate–learner and half were not insulted. Rule and Nesdale reported that subjects chose more intense shocks for the insulting than for the neutral confederate, but only if they had been told that the higher intensity shocks would interfere with the confederate's performance. If the subjects had been told that the higher intensity shocks facilitate learning, they delivered more intense shocks to the neutral than to the insulting confederate.

This implies that both the perceived intent of the opponent and the intent of the aggressor are very important mediators of aggression. The instigating effects of intense attack on aggression can be eliminated or even reversed by the perceived intent of the attacker and by the intent of the subject.

Expectations

Rotter (1972) has suggested that the potential for any behavior is a function of the person's expectations of rewards or punishments which may result from engaging in that behavior and the value of these consequences for the person. Expectancies are defined by Rotter as subjective probabilities that some consequence will follow a particular behavior. Thus, Rotter would predict that persons who have a high expectation that their aggressive behavior will result in retaliation would be less aggressive than persons who do not expect retaliation. Several authors have demonstrated that high probabilities of retaliation do inhibit aggression that occurs in the absence of attack (Peterson, 1971; Donnerstein et al., 1972).

Baron (1973), however, raised the possibility that expectations of retaliation may not inhibit attack instigated aggression. In that study, half of the subjects were first attacked and insulted by a confederate.

Both attacked and nonattacked subjects were then given a chance to aggress against the confederate by delivering shocks, so that the experimenter could assess the effects of these shocks on the confederate's
physiological arousal. Among both the attacked and control subjects,
one third were informed before the aggressive task that the experiment
would be completed as soon as they had shocked the confederate. This
group presumably had a low expectancy of retaliation. Another third
was told that if enough time remained the confederate would be permitted to shock the subject. The remaining third was told that the confederate would definitely change roles with them as soon as they had
finished shocking the confederate. This latter group presumably had a
high expectancy of retaliation. As Figure 4 indicates, subjects who had
not been attacked chose less intense shock when the probability was
high that they would exchange roles with the confederate than when the
probability was low or moderate. If the subjects had been attacked by
the confederate, then they were aggressive, regardless of the chances of
retaliation. Baron concluded that expectations of retaliation will not inhibit aggression that is motivated by anger.

Similarly, several authors have varied the frequency with which subjects receive shock in the competitive reaction time task. Epstein and
Taylor (1967) reported that the frequency of receiving shock had very
little effect on the subjects' choices for the opponent. Rather, their

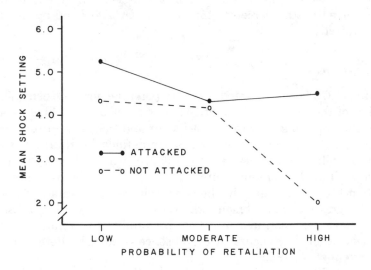

Figure 4. Mean intensity of the shocks delivered to the confederate by subjects in the
angry and nonangry conditions as a function of apparent probability of retaliation (From
Baron, 1973).

shock choices were primarily determined by the intensity of the shocks chosen by the opponent, regardless of how frequently the opponent was able to deliver these shocks to the subject. Shortell, Epstein, and Taylor (1970) also reported that the frequency of receiving shock only mildly influenced the subjects' shock choices. This same finding was also reported by Merrick and Taylor (1970). To the extent that the probability of receiving shock is an adequate manipulation of the subject's expectations of receiving shock, one would conclude that expectancies of retaliation have only minor influences on aggressive behavior that is instigated by attack.

The other variable that Rotter (1972) suggests as a major control of behavior is reward value. This concept refers to the expectation or judgment on the part of a person that the consequences of his behavior will be either rewarding, aversive, or neutral. Rotter further suggests that expectations and reward value will influence behavior independently. That is, the amount of retaliation that a person can receive from an opponent may influence aggressive behavior despite the appearance that the probability of that retaliation does not influence aggression.

Shortell et al. (1970), who reported that the probability of receiving shock did not influence aggression, also explored the effects of potential massive retaliation. Half of their subjects competed in the competitive reaction time task as it was originally designed. In the other condition, the apparatus was modified to include an additional shock button which enabled the two competitors to deliver a massive shock to their opponent. This additional shock alternative was described as twice as intense as that which the participants had previously indicated was definitely unpleasant. Shortell et al. reported that subjects who competed in the condition with the possibility for massive retaliation chose less intense shock for the opponent than those who could not receive the massive shock.

Subsequently, Dengerink, and Levendusky (1972) explored the effects of balance of power between the subject and the opponent. They employed the competitive reaction time task modified to include the massive alternative. After the task instructions, the subject and the opponent both pressed each shock button once to determine that they were working properly. After both had pressed each button, the experimenter informed both the participants that the Number 10 button (massive alternative) was apparently functioning for both, for the subject but not for the opponent, for the opponent but not for the subject, or for neither. They reported that when the opponent could deliver massive shock to the subject, the subjects chose less intense shock than when the opponent could not deliver the massive shock. This was true whether or not the subject could retaliate with the massive alternative. As noted earlier, Dorsky (1972) reported that this effect occurred only among high anxious subjects.

One should point out that this reduction in aggression occurred despite the fact that the subjects never received the massive shock. The threat of retaliation, rather than retaliation per se, inhibited aggression. In fact, it appears from the consistent evidence that attack instigates aggression, whether contingent or not, that if subjects had received the massive retaliation they would have become more aggressive. Threat of retaliation and actual retaliation appear to have opposite effects on aggression.

Up to this point, aggressive responses have been discussed as reactions to attack. This conception of aggressive behavior does not take into account the possibility that aggressive behaviors which occur in response to attack may also be instrumental attempts on the aggressor's part to reduce the level of attack. That is, aggressive responses to attack may be more than simply reflexlike reactions to attack or to the perceived intent of the attacker. Persons may respond to attack with counterattack in the hope that doing so will cause the attacker to curtail his objectionable behavior. In support of this notion, Dengerink and Bertilson (1974) have reported that subjects did respond to high intensity attack with high intensity counterattack, but, as soon as the attacker withdrew to a passive strategy, the subjects reduced the intensity of the shocks they chose for the opponent.

Rotter (1972) has suggested that expectancies may be both specific and generalized. Generalized expectancies are those that have developed with experience in a variety of situations and upon which a person relies in novel situations. Rotter has referred to one such set of generalized expectancies as expectancies of internal versus external locus of control. Persons who are characterized by an internal locus of control expect their behavior to be effective in modifying the situation in which they find themselves. Persons characterized by an external locus of control, on the other hand, expect their behavior not to be causally related to the consequences which follow their behavior. Rotter further indicates that "internal locus of control" persons are more likely to take steps to improve their situation than are "external locus of control" persons.

If, as suggested above, aggressive responses to attack are in part attempts to control the aggressive behavior of the attacker, then internal locus of control persons may be more likely than external locus of control persons to respond differentially to differing intensities of attack. Dengerink, O'Leary, and Kasner (1975) first selected subjects who scored either above the seventieth percentile or below the thirtieth percentile of a class distribution on Rotter's Internal-External Locus on Control Scale. These subjects were then exposed to opponents in the competitive reaction time task who either increased, decreased, or remained constant in their attack on the subject. Dengerink et al. reported that the internal locus of control subjects were more likely than external locus of control subjects to set high intensity shocks when the opponent chose high intensity shocks and to choose low intensity shocks when the opponent chose low intensity shocks (see Figure 5). The external subjects did respond to changes in attack with changes in aggression but not to the same extent as the internal group. In the increasing attack condition, for example, the internal group increased the intensity of shocks that they chose for the opponent by more than twice the increase observed for external subjects. Furthermore, external subjects tended not to choose shocks that were significantly different for the three different kinds of opponents. During the first block of testing, when the "decreasing" opponent set maximal shocks and the "increasing" opponent set minimal shocks, the external group did not respond with significantly different levels of counterattack. Highly significant differences were observed, however, for the internal group.

In a related, unpublished study, Dengerink and Myers attempted to manipulate the subjects' perceived ability to control the social situation. Their subjects attempted to complete a series of 15 anagrams. One

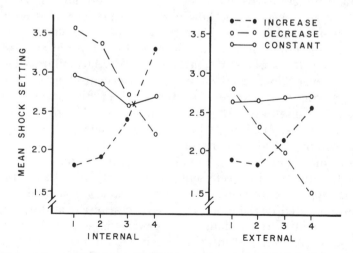

Figure 5. Mean shock settings by internal and external locus of control subjects for decreasing, increasing, and constant opponents during blocks of testing (From Dengerink, O'Leary, & Kasner, 1975).

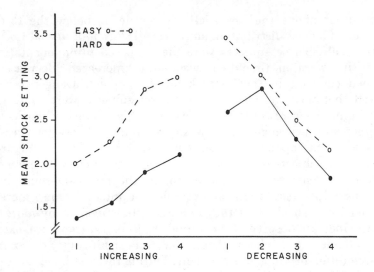

Figure 6. Mean shock settings in response to increasing or decreasing attack by subjects who had succeeded (easy) or failed (hard) to solve anagrams.

group was able to solve these anagrams easily, but the other group repeatedly failed to do so. Contrary to the predictions of the frustration–aggression theory, those persons who repeatedly failed the anagrams were less aggressive than those who were able to solve them easily. As Figure 6 indicates, however, this effect occurred only when the opponent continued to escalate the level of aggression and did not occur when the opponent steadily decreased the level of aggression. It appears that persons who have learned that this particular social situation is one over which they have very little control will be less aggressive. If the opponent reduces the level of his attack, however, perhaps in response to the subjects' shock choices, then they respond no differently than persons who had previously learned that they were successful in coping with the experiment.

These findings indicate that the effects of expectations on aggression are mixed. Differential expectations regarding the likelihood of retaliation do not appear to influence attack instigated aggression, at least as it has been measured in the laboratory. Expectations regarding the magnitude of potential retaliation, however, do appear to influence aggression. The possibility of intense massive retaliation tends to inhibit aggression. Furthermore, expectations regarding the aggressor's ability to control the behavior of the attacker also influence aggression. If one believes that one is able to influence the aggressive behavior of the attacker, then one is much more likely to respond differentially to varying levels of attack than if one lacks the expectation of being able to influence other persons' behavior.

Conclusion

It is difficult to come to clear-cut conclusions regarding the effect of personality variables on aggressive behavior. When studying the evasive effects of mediating processes on aggression, one is faced with conflicting evidence from different studies and with studies that do not provide sufficient data to state flatly that variations in aggression are caused by variations in the mediators under investigation. Furthermore, varying definitions of the mediational processes impede decisions as to which mediational variable is responsible for the observed differences in behavior. Arbitrary distinctions are often made between such related variables as anxiety and expectations. Still, when considered as a group, the studies described in this chapter indicate that it is appropriate to conclude that aggressive responses to attack are subject to the control of personality variables. In addition, there are occasions when personality variables appear to have profound effects on aggression that can even counteract the effects of potent situational variables such as attack.

Emotional variables appear to be capable of both facilitating and inhibiting aggression, but they also appear to interact with situational variables. Various manipulations of anxiety and fear of disapproval have consistently shown that these variables are related to decreased aggression. Anxiety and fear of disapproval, however, are hypothesized to vary with environmental cues which indicate that punishment or disapproval may be forthcoming. To date, no one has investigated the possibility that social anxiety and fear of disapproval will facilitate aggression in situations that provide social rewards for acting aggressively. Guilt, on the other hand, is an emotional variable which should be related to inhibited aggression regardless of situational variables. The effects of guilt on aggression have not been assessed in situations that indicate social disapproval and social approval for aggressive actions. The research which has been conducted indicates that self-reports of guilt may be related to reduced aggression even when the opponent reinforces the subjects for aggressing.

Anger may also be a consistent consequence of attack and a subsequent facilitator of aggression. There appear, however, to be three important limitations to this generalization. First, persons who have a tendency to excessive control of their emotions apparently inhibit their aggressive responses to attack. Second, if the level of anger arousal appears to the person as inappropriate to the situation, the degree of attack, and the target of the aggression, then the anger does not increase aggression. Finally, when anger is aroused simultaneously with incompatible emotions, facilitation of aggression is not always observed.

Although emotional variables have received more experimental attention, cognitive variables also appear to be important mediators of aggression. If a potential aggressor attributes aggressive intent to the attacker, he will be aggressive in return. If, on the other hand, he believes the attacker to have accidentally caused him harm, he will not counterattack. The importance of attributed intent as a control of aggression raises the possibility that other attributions may also be important controls of aggression.

Finally, some expectations appear to be viable mediators of attack instigated aggression. When a person is attacked, it appears that expectations of further retaliation from the victim for aggressive counterattack will not inhibit aggression. Expectations regarding the aversiveness of potential retaliation and one's ability to control another's behavior, however, do influence aggression. Potential massive retaliation inhibits aggression, and the belief that one can influence the attacker's behavior results in differential responses to differing levels of attack.

This chapter has not attempted to be comprehensive in its review. While some personality variables have been described here, other variables may also serve as mediators of aggressive behavior. Also, the findings described here do not necessarily apply to aggressive behaviors which occur in the absence of attack. In fact, it appears that some variables, such as expectations of retaliation, influence attack-instigated and nonattack-instigated aggression differently.

REFERENCES

Bandura, A. *Aggression: A social learning analysis.* Englewood Cliffs, New Jersey: Prentice Hall, 1973.
Baron, R. A. Magnitude of victim's pain cues and level of prior anger arousal as determinants of adult aggressive behavior. *Journal of Personality and Social Psychology,* 1971, *17*, 236–243. (a)
Baron, R. A. Aggression as a function of magnitude of victim's pain cues, level of prior anger arousal, and aggressor-victim similarity. *Journal of Personality and Social Psychology,* 1971, *18*, 48–54. (b)
Baron, R. A. Aggression as a function of audience presence and prior anger arousal. *Journal of Experimental Social Psychology,* 1971, *7*, 515–523. (c)
Baron, R. A. Reducing the influence of an aggressive model: The restraining effects of peer censure. *Journal of Experimental Social Psychology,* 1972, *8*, 266–275.

Baron, R. A. Threatened retaliation from the victim as an inhibitor of physical aggression. *Journal of Research in Personality*, 1973, *7*, 103–115.

Baron, R. A. Aggression as a function of victim's pain cues, level of prior anger arousal, and exposure to an aggressive model. *Journal of Personality and Social Psychology*, 1974, *29*, 117–124. (a)

Baron, R. A. The aggression-inhibiting influence of heightened sexual arousal. *Journal of Personality and Social Psychology*, 1974, *30*, 318–322. (b)

Baron, R. A., & Ball, R. L. The aggression-inhibiting influence of nonhostile humor. *Journal of Experimental Social Psychology*, 1974, *10*, 23–33.

Baron, R. A., & Eggelston, R. J. Performance on the "aggression machine": Motivation to help or harm? *Psychonomic Science*, 1972, *26*, 321–322.

Bem, D. Self-perception: An alternative interpretation of cognitive dissonance phenomena. *Psychological Review*, 1967, *74*, 183–200.

Berkowitz, L., & Geen, R. Film violence and the cue properties of available targets. *Journal of Personality and Social Psychology*, 1966, *3*, 525–530.

Berkowitz, L., Lepinski, J. P., & Angulo, E. J. Awareness of own anger level and subsequent aggression. *Journal of Personality and Social Psychology*, 1969, *11*, 293–300.

Berkowitz, L., & Turner, C. Perceived anger level, instigating agent, and aggression. In H. S. London & R. E. Nisbett (Eds.), *Thought and feeling: Cognitive alteration of feeling stages*. Chicago: Aldine, 1974.

Blackburn, R. Personality in relation to extreme aggression in psychiatric offenders. *British Journal of Psychiatry*, 1968, *114*, 821–828.

Borden, R. Witnessed aggression: Influence of an observer's sex and values on aggressive responding. *Journal of Personality and Social Psychology*, 1975, *31*, 567–573.

Borden, R. J., & Taylor, S. P. The social instigation and control of aggression. *Journal of Applied Social Psychology*, 1973, *3*, 354–361.

Brock, T. C., & Buss, A. H. Effects of justification for aggression and communication with the victim on post aggression dissonance. *Journal of Abnormal and Social Psychology*, 1964, *68*, 403–412.

Buss, A. H. *The psychology of aggression*. New York: Wiley, 1961.

Buss, A. H. The effect of harm on subsequent aggression. *Journal of Experimental Research in Personality*, 1966, *1*, 249–255. (a)

Buss, A. H. Instrumentality of aggression, feedback, and frustration as determinants of physical aggression. *Journal of Personality and Social Psychology*, 1966, *3*, 153–162. (b)

Crowne, D. P., & Marlowe, D. A new scale of social desirability independent of psychopathology. *Journal of Consulting Psychology*, 1960, *24*, 349–354.

Dengerink, H. A. Anxiety, aggression and physiological arousal. *Journal of Experimental Research in Personality*, 1971, *5*, 223–232.

Dengerink, H. A., & Bertilson, H. S. The reduction of attack instigated aggression. *Journal of Research in Personality*, 1974, *8*, 254–262.

Dengerink, H. A., & Levendusky, P. G. Effects of massive retaliation and balance of power on aggression. *Journal of Experimental Research in Personality*, 1972, *6*, 230–236.

Dengerink, H. A., O'Leary, M. R., & Kasner, K. H. Individual differences in aggressive responses to attack: Internal-external locus of control and field dependence-independence. *Journal of Research in Personality*, 1975, *9*, 191–199.

Donnerstein, E., Donnerstein, M., Simon, S., & Ditrichs, R. Variables in interracial aggression: Anonymity, expected retaliation, and a riot. *Journal of Personality and Social Psychology*, 1972, *22*, 236–245.

Dorsky, F. The effects of social and physical anxiety on human aggressive behavior. Unpublished doctoral dissertation, Kent State Univ., 1972.

Dorsky, F. S., & Taylor, S. P. Physical aggression as a function of manifest anxiety. *Psychonomic Science*, 1972, *27*, 103–104.

Epstein, S. The nature of anxiety with emphasis upon its relationship to expectancy. In C. D. Spielberger (Ed.), *Anxiety: Current trends in theory and research*. New York: Academic Press, 1972.

Epstein, S., & Taylor, S. P. Instigation to aggression as a function of degree of defeat and perceived aggressive intent of the opponent. *Journal of Personality*, 1967, *35*, 265–289.

Feshbach, S., Stilles, W. B., & Bitter, E. The reinforcing effect of witnessing aggression. *Journal of Experimental Research in Personality*, 1967, *2*, 133–139.

Geen, R. G., Rakosky, J. J., & Pigg, R. Awareness of arousal and its relation to aggression, *British Journal of Social and Clinical Psychology*, 1972, *11*, 115–121.

Geen, R., Stonner, D., & Kelly, D. Aggression anxiety and cognitive appraisal of aggression-threat stimuli. *Journal of Personality and Social Psychology*, 1974, *29*, 196–200.

Greenwell, J., & Dengerink, H. The role of perceived versus actual attack in human physical aggression. *Journal of Personality and Social Psychology*, 1973, *26*, 66–71.

Hall, C. S., & Lindzey, G. *Theories of personality*. (2nd ed.) New York: Wiley, 1970.

Hartemink, J. H. Physical aggression in schizophrenia. Unpublished doctoral dissertation, Kent State Univ., 1971.

Hartmann, D. P. Influence of symbolically modeled instrumental aggression and pain cues on aggressive behavior. *Journal of Personality and Social Psychology*, 1969, *11*, 280–287.

Hokanson, J. E., Willers, K. R., & Koropsak, E. The modification of autonomic responses during aggressive interchange. *Journal of Personality*, 1968, *36*, 386–404.

James, P., & Mosher, D. Thematic aggression, hostility-guilt and aggressive behavior. *Journal of Projective Techniques*, 1967, *3*, 61–67.

Kanouse, D. E. Language, labeling and attribution. In E. E. Jones, D. E. Kanouse, H. H. Kelly, R. E. Nisbett, S. Valins, & B. Weiner (Eds.), *Attribution: Perceiving the causes of behavior*. Morristown, New Jersey: General Learning Press, 1971.

Knott, P. D., Lasater, L., & Shuman, R. Aggression—guilt and conditionability for aggressiveness. *Journal of Personality*, 1974, 332–344.

Loew, C. A. Acquisition of a hostile attitude and its relationship to aggressive behavior. *Journal of Personality and Social Psychology*, 1967, *5*, 335–377.

Lykken, D. A study of anxiety in the sociopathic personality. *Journal of Abnormal and Social Psychology*, 1957, *55*, 6–10.

Lykken, D. T., Tellegen, A., & Katzenmeyer, C. *Manual for the activity preference questionnaire*. Reports from the Research Laboratories of the Department of Psychiatry, Univ. of Minnesota, 1973.

Mallick, S. K., & McCandless, B. R. A study of catharsis of aggression. *Journal of Personality and Social Psychology*, 1966, *4*, 591–596.

Megargee, E. I. Undercontrolled and overcontrolled personality types in extreme antisocial aggression. *Psychological Monographs*, 1966, *80*, No. 3.

Megargee, E. I., Cook, P. E., & Mendelsohn, G. A. Development and validation of an MMPI scale of assaultiveness in overcontrolled individuals. *Journal of Abnormal Psychology*, 1967, *72*, 519–528.

Megargee, E. I., & Mendelsohn, G. A. A cross validation of twelve MMPI indices of hostility and control. *Journal of Abnormal and Social Psychology*, 1962, *65*, 431–438.

Merrick, R., & Taylor, S. P. Aggression as a function of vulnerability to attack. *Psychonomic Science*, 1970, *20(4)*, 203–204.

Mosher, D. L. Interaction of fear and guilt in inhibiting unacceptable behavior. *Journal of Consulting Psychology*, 1965, *29*, 161–167.

Mosher, D. L. The development and multitrait-multimethod matrix analysis of three measures of three aspects of guilt. *Journal of Consulting Psychology*, 1966, *30*, 25–29.

Nickel, T. W. The attribution of intention as a critical factor in the relation between frustration and aggression. *Journal of Personality*, 1974, 482–492.

O'Leary, M. R., & Dengerink, H. A. Aggression as a function of the intensity and pattern of attack. *Journal of Research in Personality*, 1973, *7*, 61–70.

Parke, R. D., Ewall, W., & Slaby, R. G. Hostile and helpful verbalizations as regulators of nonverbal aggression. *Journal of Personality and Social Psychology*, 1972, *23*, 243–248.

Patterson, G. R., & Cobb, J. A. A dyadic analysis of "aggressive" behaviors: An additional step toward a theory of aggression. In J. P. Hill (Ed.), *Minnesota symposia on child psychology*. Minneapolis: Univ. of Minnesota Press, 1971, *5*, 72–129.

Peterson, R. A. Aggression as a function of expected retaliation and aggression level of target and aggressor. *Developmental Psychology*, 1971, *5*, 161–166.

Pisano, R., & Taylor, S. P. Reduction of physical aggression: The effects of four strategies. *Journal of Personality and Social Psychology*, 1971, *19*, 237–242.

Rotter, J. B. An introduction to social learning theory. In J. B. Rotter, J. E. Chance, & E. J. Phares (Eds.). *Applications of a social learning theory of personality*. New York: Holt, 1972.

Rule, B. G., & Hewitt, L. S. Effects of thwarting on cardiac response and physical aggression. *Journal of Personality and Social Psychology*, 1971, *19*, 181–187.

Rule, B. G., & Nesdale, A. R. Differing functions of aggression. *Journal of Personality*, 1974, *42*, 467–481.

Savitsky, J. C., Izard, C. E., Kotsch, W. E., & Christy, L. Aggressor's response to the victim's facial expression of emotion. *Journal of Research in Personality*, 1974, *7*, 346–357.

Shontz, E. C. *Research methods in personality*. New York: Appleton, 1965.

Shortell, J., Epstein, S., & Taylor, S. P. Instigation to aggression as a function of degree of defeat and the capacity for massive retaliation. *Journal of Personality*, 1970, *38*, 313–328.

Shuntich, R. J., & Taylor, S. P. The effects of alcohol on human physical aggression. *Journal of Experimental Research in Personality*, 1972, *6*, 34–38.

Taylor, J. A. A personality scale of manifest anxiety. *Journal of Abnormal and Social Psychology*, 1953, *48*, 285–290.

Taylor, S. P. The relationship of expressed and inhibited hostility to physiological activation. Doctoral dissertation, Univ. of Massachusetts, 1965.

Taylor, S. P. Aggressive behavior and physiological arousal as a function of provocation and the tendency to inhibit aggression. *Journal of Personality*, 1967, *35*, 297–310.

Taylor, S. P. Aggressive behavior as a function of approval motivation and physical attack. *Psychonomic Science*, 1970, *18(4)*, 195–196.

Taylor, S. P., & Epstein, S. Aggression as a function of the interaction of the sex on the aggressor and the sex of the victim. *Journal of Personality*, 1967, *35*, 474–486.

Taylor, S. P., & Gammon, C. B. The effects of type and dose of alcohol on human physical aggression. *Journal of Personality and Social Psychology*, 1975, *32*, 169–175.

Turner, C. W., & Simons, L. S. Effects of subject sophistication and evaluation apprehension on aggressive responses to weapons. *Journal of Personality and Social Psychology*, 1974, *30*, 341–348.

Ulehla, Z. J., & Adams, D. K. Detection theory and expectations for social reinforcement and application to aggression. *Psychological Review,* 1974, *80,* 439–445.

Vogel-Sprott, M. Alcohol effects on human behavior under reward and punishment. *Psychopharmacologia,* 1967, *11,* 337–344.

Williams, I. D. The emergency treatment of the alcoholic. *Journal of Nervous and Mental Disease,* 1931, *74,* 161–172.

Williams, A. F. Social drinking, anxiety and depression. *Journal of Personality and Social Psychology,* 1966, *3,* 689–693.

Zillman, D. Excitation transfer in communication-mediated aggressive behavior. *Journal of Experimental Social Psychology,* 1971, *7,* 419–434.

Aggression Catharsis: Experimental Investigations and Implications

MICHAEL B. QUANTY

Introduction

The concept of catharsis dates back at least to Aristotle (Poetics, 6). In explaining the popularity of Greek tragic theatre, he proposed that members of the audience, by vicariously experiencing the pity and fear portrayed on the stage, were able to purge themselves of similar feelings. Although Aristotle did not state that a similar purging of hostile and angry feelings may also occur and may not have even believed it possible (Goodman, 1964), many modern writers (e.g., Feshbach, 1961) have made such an assumption.

Sigmund Freud, who popularized the notion of aggression catharsis, accepted the idea that symbolic aggression catharsis was possible but felt that direct expression of hostile feelings produced optimal catharsis: "The reaction of an injured person to a trauma has really only . . . a 'cathartic' effect if it is expressed in an adequate reaction like revenge [Breuer & Freud, 1961, p. 5]." He believed that aggressive urges were a direct outgrowth of the death instinct and must be satisfied. If not given outward expression, the aggressive drive would lead the individual to direct his aggression inward with the subsequent development of neurotic or psychotic symptoms. If, however, "these forces are turned to

99

destruction in the external world, *the living creature will be relieved and the effect must be beneficial* [Freud, 1963, p. 143, italics added]." According to Freud, then, expression of aggressive urges is not only beneficial but is essential to the proper functioning of the individual.

A position consistent with Freud's has been accepted by many theorists who assume an instinct toward aggression in man (e.g., Ardrey, 1961, 1966; Eibl–Eibesfeldt, 1970; Lorenz, 1966; Morris, 1967), and this position is implicitly accepted in a number of clinical therapy techniques not formally associated with psychoanalysis, such as "assertiveness training" (Wolpe & Lazarus, 1966) and "primal therapy" (Janov, 1970). The acceptance of this position by large segments of the general public is obvious in the popularity of such phrases as "letting off steam" and "getting it off your chest." The frustration–aggression hypothesis (Dollard, Doob, Miller, Mowrer, & Sears, 1939) which has guided most of the research on aggression and catharsis is basically a translation of Freudian theory into learning theory terminology.

According to the frustration–aggression model, a simple, linear cause–effect relationship exists among frustration, aggression, and catharsis. Frustration leads to the arousal of aggressive drive, which motivates aggressive action. "The expression of any act of aggression *is a catharsis that reduces the instigation to all other acts of aggression* [Dollard *et al.*, 1939, p. 53, italics added]." Aggression catharsis, then, consists of two separate components—one physiological and the other behavioral. Expression of aggression should lead to *both decreased physiological arousal and decreased aggression*.

Interpretation of the research on aggression catharsis has been complicated by the fact that researchers have been content to measure only one of the two components, often assuming that the other also occurs. Thus, there are many studies that relate to what may be called "physiological catharsis" and many others that are relevant to "behavioral catharsis," but very few that have examined both within the same framework. A further complication in evaluating the viability of the catharsis hypothesis is that some authors hold to the classic "Aristotelian" view that catharsis may be experienced vicariously (e.g., Feshbach, 1961) whereas others assume the more Freudian position that direct reprisal is necessary to relieve the aggressive drive (e.g., Hokanson & Burgess, 1962b).

Some authors have suggested that this diversity in the definitions of aggressive acts and catharsis render generalizations impossible (cf. Doob & Wood, 1972). Others (e.g., Konecni, 1975) prefer to use catharsis as merely a "paradigmatic label" to denote changes that occur in either physiological arousal or aggressiveness following an aggressive (or other theoretically cathartic) act. In this review, however, I will use the term in the more traditional sense. Using this conception, catharsis can be demonstrated only when a particular activity reduces the instigation to all acts of aggression. Decreased physiological arousal is not a sufficient demonstration of catharsis nor is decreased aggressiveness when alternative explanations, such as the arousal of guilt anxiety, are possible. Although most investigations have not been designed to provide such a stringent test of the catharsis hypothesis, I will attempt to evaluate the available evidence from both physiological and behavioral studies in order to suggest some integrative constructs which will hopefully provide at least a first step toward a meaningful theoretical statement.

The Effects of Aggression on Arousal

Early Studies

One of the earliest studies purporting to show tension reduction following the expression of hostility is that of Worchel (1957). His subjects were insulted by an experimenter while performing a task in a large group. Following this anger manipulation, some subjects were allowed to express hostility directly to their antagonist. Others were allowed indirect expression for their hostility, and a third group was given no opportunity for expressions. All subjects then performed two tasks, a digit–symbol substitution task and an incidental learning task. (Worchel assumed that performance decrements would indicate greater arousal). The main finding in the study was that performance on the digit–symbol substitution task was better for subjects who were allowed to express their hostility either directly or indirectly than for those subjects allowed no expression. Although this finding has been widely interpreted as support for the catharsis hypothesis, Downey (1973) has pointed out that it may indicate the exact opposite. He maintains that if the digit–symbol substitution task may be assumed to be relatively simple, then performance on the task should be facilitated (not impaired) by moderate increases in drive (Spence, 1958). Therefore, Downey concludes that "Worchel's subjects who had aggressed may have performed differently [from nonaggressing subjects] not because they had undergone a 'tension release,' but quite possibly because they had not [p. 7]."

Data from the incidental learning task also provide equivocal evidence for arousal reduction. Here again, subjects allowed to express their aggression performed better than those who could not. Since high levels of arousal should restrict the range of cues a subject utilizes (Easterbrook, 1959) and result in poorer incidental recall, this finding does suggest that expression of hostility led to decreased arousal. Subjects, however, who expressed hostility directly (and should presumably thereby have experienced the greatest reduction in arousal), performed more poorly than those allowed indirect expression. It may be that subjects in the direct expression condition felt inhibited about aggressing against the relatively high-status experimenter (subjects in this condition actually expressed less hostility than those who gave indirect retorts) and hence remained relatively aroused. In general, although these results do seem to indicate that expressing hostility reduces arousal in angered subjects since arousal was only inferred and not measured directly, alternative explanations are possible.

The role of aggression in reducing anger-induced physiological arousal has been investigated most extensively by Hokanson and his associates. Their early studies all employed variations of the basic paradigm developed by Hokanson (1961). All subjects were assigned a relatively simple task by the experimenter. Subjects in the low frustration condition were allowed to complete the task and were then complimented by the experimenter, while those in the high frustration condition were exposed to repeated interruptions and verbal harrassment. In the second part of the experiment, subjects were allowed to aggress against the experimenter by shocking him when he made incorrect guesses about what the subject was thinking. Blood pressure readings were obtained before and after the anger manipulation and after the opportunity to aggress. Results from the studies in this series indicate that, under certain conditions, aggressive responses can lead to a cathartic-like reduction in anger-induced physiological arousal.

In the initial study, for example, Hokanson (1961) found "that the more vigorous the overt behavior [of subjects] while shocking the experimenter, the greater the reduction in systolic [blood] pressure [SBP] after the aggressive responses are completed [p. 349]." Thus, consistent with the catharsis hypothesis, the more aggressively subjects behaved, the quicker they were able to reduce their arousal. Although this study suggests physiological recovery following aggression, it does not include the essential control condition in which the subject has no opportunity to aggress.[1] It is not possible, therefore, to determine whether the drop in SBP was due to a catharsistype process following aggression or merely the passage of time.

[1] Additional problems with this study, which make it difficult to interpret in terms of catharsis, are discussed at length elsewhere (Geen & Quanty, 1975).

In a later investigation, Hokanson and Shetler (1961) added the no-aggression control group (subjects in this group informed the experimenter of his mistakes by flashing a light) and also manipulated the status of the experimenter. When the experimenter had low status (i.e., was a fellow student) the predicted autonomic recovery was found: Frustrated subjects reduced their anger arousal more quickly when allowed to aggress than when they were not given the opportunity to aggress. When the experimenter was high in status (a professor), however, responding aggressively led to slight increases in SBP while merely informing him of his mistakes led to quicker reductions in SBP. Thus, it appears that aggression against a person of higher status does not produce a reduction in physiological arousal. Merely informing a high-status frustrator of his mistakes, however, did reduce anger arousal.

A subsequent investigation by Hokanson and Burgess (1962b) in which subjects aggressed verbally (by rating the experimenter on a questionnaire) again showed arousal reduction when subjects were allowed to express hostility toward a low-status experimenter. Subjects given an opportunity to retaliate against the high-status frustrator, however, maintained SBP elevations comparable to those not allowed to aggress and higher than those allowed to aggress against the low-status frustrator. In addition, nonfrustrated subjects who were given an opportunity to evaluate the high-status experimenter exhibited higher arousal levels than nonfrustrated subjects who were not allowed to evaluate him, "as if merely having the opportunity to aggress against a high status object is 'tension' producing [p. 243]." It may be that subjects have learned to expect high levels of reprisal when they are hostile toward persons high in status, and that this fear of reprisal may contribute to their elevated arousal when given such an opportunity.[2]

Hokanson and Burgess (1962a) have also investigated the effectiveness of various types of aggressive responses in reducing physiological arousal following frustration by a "low-status" frustrator. After delivering the standard frustration manipulation, the experimenter allowed some subjects to aggress in one of three modalities—physical, verbal, or fantasy (by creating stories in response to a TAT card)—whereas subjects in a fourth condition were given no opportunity to aggress. Only direct aggression (either physical or verbal) against the frustrator reduced anger-induced physiological arousal in frustrated subjects.

[2] A study by Burgess, Reivich, and Silverman (1968), which failed to demonstrate catharsis in clinical depressive patients when they shocked a frustrating experimenter, may also be interpreted in this way. If we assume that the experimenter (a professional psychologist) had high status in the eyes of these patients, then their failure to experience arousal reduction is comparable to the college students' reactions.

Frustrated subjects in the fantasy and no-aggression conditions maintained elevated levels of SBP and heart rate. Hokanson, Burgess, and Cohen (1963) obtained similar results when they studied the effects of displaced aggression on SBP.

It appears, then, from these early studies that *direct aggression* (either verbal or physical) *against a frustrator low in status can produce a catharsislike reduction in physiological arousal.*

The Social Learning Model

Hokanson himself (Hokanson & Edelman, 1966) has noted that "there are several procedural flaws in the earlier studies which tend to limit the generality of the findings and make them difficult to replicate [p. 442]." Since the frustration manipulation involved face-to-face insult and harassment by the experimenter, it was difficult to standardize and, therefore, susceptible to the influence of individual differences among experimenters. Instructions for the aggression task were lengthy and complicated and could have been frustrating by themselves. Finally, the roles of experimenter and frustrator were confounded. Thus, the physical presence of the provocateur (experimenter) at the time blood pressure ratings were taken could have influenced these ratings.

To overcome these methodological difficulties Hokanson, and Edelman completely abandoned the previous design and carried out an experiment disguised as one on interpersonal behavior. Each subject interacted with an experimental confederate of the same sex; the subject and confederate were seated in individual booths several feet apart. A panel in the subject's booth contained three response keys labeled "shock," "reward," and "no response." Subjects in the aggression condition were told that on a given signal following the action of the other subject (confederate) they could respond by depressing any one of the three keys. By depressing the shock key they would presumably deliver a painful electric shock to the other subject. Activation of the "reward" key gave the confederate a point, and nothing happened if the "no response" key was depressed. Experimental conditions were arranged so that the confederate shocked the subject on every exchange. The subject's blood pressure was measured immediately before the confederate shocked him and immediately before and after he responded. Additional measures were taken at 20-sec intervals following the subject's response until his blood pressure reached its initial resting level. The experimental session involved five such trials. Control subjects were exposed to five similar trials but given no opportunity to respond.

Results of the investigation indicated that after being shocked subjects showed a sharp rise in SBP. When male subjects responded to this shock aggressively by "shocking" the confederate, their blood pressure returned to normal more quickly than when they made a friendly or ignoring (i.e., no) response. This pattern, however, was not found among female subjects. Female recovery rates following all three responses were essentially the same as those for males allowed no response, while the recovery rate for females allowed no response was extremely slow. Thus, it appears that allowing females to make *any* response, even a prosocial one, to another's aggression produces some physiological tension reduction.[3]

These data prompted Hokanson, Willers, and Koropsak (1968) to reformulate their hypothesis of arousal reduction in terms of social learning theory. They proposed that the efficacy of a response in promoting cardiovascular recovery depends on a person's social-learning history and that in our culture males and females learn different strategies for dealing with frustration. They postulated that, in our culture, males undergo a set of learning experiences in which responding aggressively to another's aggression is rewarded, whereas females are rewarded for adopting more passive responses to provocation.

In order to test the viability of this theory, Hokanson *et al.* modified the basic procedure used by Hokanson and Edelman. Subjects were allowed only two responses, shock or reward. The experimental session was divided into three phases. The first phase, or baseline, consisted of 32 interchanges between the subject and the confederate during which the confederate randomly shocked or rewarded the subject's responses an equal number of times. As predicted, during this phase, females exhibited more rapid vascular recovery when they responded to the confederate's aggression by rewarding her than when they counterattacked. Males, however, reduced their arousal more quickly with aggressive counterresponses than with friendly ones.

The second phase of the experiment was composed of 60-conditioning trials. Female subjects were rewarded for *aggressive* counterresponses, and males were rewarded for friendly counterresponses. By the end of this conditioning phase, the previous pattern of results had been reversed: Female subjects exhibited quicker vascular recovery following aggression, and male subjects began to recover more quickly following friendly counterresponses. During the final extinction phase, the con-

---

[3] This finding raises a serious question concerning the interpretation of data from Hokanson's earlier studies. These studies typically found evidence for aggression catharsis even though they used mostly female subjects. Since the procedure forced subjects to make either an aggressive response or no response, it is possible that the same results would have been obtained if subjects were allowed to make *any* response. A second possibility is that the male subjects, even though a minority, may have accounted for most of the catharsis effects.

federate again responded randomly, and subjects reverted to their earlier patterns of vascular recovery. Consistent with the social learning paradigm, then, these investigators were able to modify subjects' autonomic recovery patterns by teaching them new ways of effectively countering an attack.

Sosa (1968) reported further data suggesting the importance of one's social learning history for physiological recovery. Using male members of a prison population, he found that those who customarily replied to threats of violence with submissive or passive responses displayed a catharticlike vascular response only when they were allowed a passive response to aggression. Extremely slow vascular recovery resulted when they responded aggressively.

An even more impressive demonstration of how social learning can influence catharticlike responses was provided by Stone and Hokanson (1969). They employed a procedure similar to that of Hokanson *et al.* (1968) except that subjects were given a choice of three responses. They could shock the confederate, reward him, or deliver a mild shock to themselves. During the training phase, contingencies were arranged such that subjects were rewarded for responding to the confederate's aggression by shocking themselves. By the end of this training period, these self-punitive responses actually came to produce a catharticlike reduction in vascular arousal. Thus, even a "masochistic" response, which is learned to be effective in reducing another's hostility, can promote reduction of anger-induced physiological arousal.

Several other studies also suggest that whether a response enhances arousal reduction depends more on its effectiveness in avoiding further frustration than on the aggressive content of that response. Holmes (1966) and Vantress and Williams (1972), for example, using female subjects, found no arousal reduction following aggressive reactions toward a frustrator (Holmes actually found blood pressure increased when subjects shocked their frustrator). They did, however, effect reduced arousal by removing the provocateur from the subject's presence, even though the subject was allowed no retaliation. Baker and Schaie (1969) found that angered subjects can experience as much cardiovascular recovery when they merely observe another aggress against their antagonist as when they actually retaliate, again demonstrating that direct aggression is not *necessary* to produce physiological recovery.[4]

[4] This finding, however, has proven difficult to replicate. For example, Geen *et al.* (1975) found no evidence of arousal reduction when angered subjects observed the experimenter shock their antagonist, although direct aggression did reduce arousal.

The Effects of Personality Factors on Autonomic Recovery

Three personality variables (hostility guilt, need for approval, and repression-sensitization) have been shown to affect the amount of tension reduction a person experiences following an aggressive counter-response toward a frustrator. In general, it has been found that persons with personality types that would dispose them to feel uncomfortable or guilty about aggressing do not experience arousal reduction following an aggressive retaliation. To the extent that these personality dimensions can be assumed to reflect differential social learning histories, their effects on reduction of physiological tension seem to fit the social learning model well.

Guilt Anxiety

Meyer (1967), in a study of prison inmates convicted of violent crimes, found that those who continued to act aggressively while in prison had lower diastolic blood pressure (DBP) than those who were less aggressive. Among those who continued to act aggressively, however, the *lowest* blood pressures were found in inmates who were classified as low in guilt on the Mosher Incomplete Sentences Test.

An experiment by Schill (1972), using female college students, corroborates Meyer's findings. Subjects scoring high and low on the hostility guilt subscale of the Mosher Forced-Choice Guilt Inventory (Mosher, 1968) were frustrated by an experimenter who withheld a promised reward. Subjects were then allowed to retaliate by evaluating the experimenter on a questionnaire. Low guilt subjects expressed more hostility and showed greater reduction in diastolic blood pressure following retaliation than their high guilt counterparts. In a further analysis of the data, Schill identified highly aggressive subjects (those expressing greater hostility than the mean for the sample) and divided them into those who scored high and low in guilt. There were eight low-guilt subjects in this highly hostile group, and seven of them showed a decrease in DBP following their evaluation of the experimenter; of the six high-guilt subjects, only one experienced a decrease in DBP. For highly guilty subjects, then, attacking a frustrator tended to promote anxiety rather than tension reduction.

An experiment by Gambaro and Rabin (1969) failed to show any differences between subjects high and low in guilt following aggression toward a frustrator. High guilt subjects experienced as great a decrease in DBP as low guilt subjects after shocking their frustrator. When subjects were given a chance to displace their aggression by attacking the innocent experimenter, guilt anxiety did make a difference. Under

these conditions, low guilt subjects still experienced a catharticlike reduction in DBP, but high guilt subjects did not. Several procedural differences between this study and that of Schill may have contributed to
the discrepant findings. First, Gambaro and Rabin used male subjects,
who might be expected to show greater arousal reduction following aggression than Schill's female subjects (cf. Hokanson *et al.,* 1968).
Second, the frustrator in the Gambaro and Rabin study was a fellow
student whereas in Schill's experiment the experimenter served as frustrator and victim. Subjects may have felt less inhibited attacking a
fellow student. Finally, the nature of the frustration differed dramatically in the two studies. Schill used a relatively mild withholding of
reward while Gambaro and Rabin used a confederate who was
thoroughly rude and disgusting both to the subject and the experimenter and interrupted the subject repeatedly as he attempted to complete a task. In short, he may have been so obnoxious that even anxious
subjects felt little compunction when given a chance to attack him.

NEED FOR APPROVAL

Fishman (1965) found that subjects who scored high in need for approval on the Marlowe–Crowne Social Desirability Scale maintained
elevated SBP after attacking a frustrator while those low in need for approval reduced their SBP. It appears, then, that subjects who value
social approval may have learned to become anxious when they attack
another person, even one who has frustrated them.

REPRESSION-SENSITIZATION

A recent experiment by Scarpetti (1974) examined differences
between repressors and sensitizers in aggressiveness and autonomic
recovery through a social learning approach. Repressors tend to react to
stressful situations by denial of the threatening situation while
sensitizers tend to meet them "head on" (Byrne, 1964). Therefore, Scarpetti argued that sensitizers would have learned to react aggressively to
provocations while repressors would adopt more passive strategies. He
further proposed that, following an attack, arousal reduction would occur only when a subject responded in his preferred mode and that these
behavioral and autonomic patterns could be modified through a social
learning paradigm.

In order to test these hypotheses, Scarpetti subjected male repressors
and sensitizers to a procedure similar to that employed by Hokanson *et
al.* (1968). Subjects interacted with a confederate and were allowed to
respond to him on any trial by delivering either reward or electric
shock. The experiment was divided into three parts. During the

baseline portion, the subjects' aggressive counterresponses were either rewarded or punished an equal number of times. As predicted, during this phase of the experiment, sensitizers tended to respond to the confederate's aggression with more aggression and to show greater autonomic recovery when they responded aggressively. Repressors exhibited the opposite pattern, preferring reward counterresponses and recovering more quickly following such responses. During the conditioning phase of the experiment, subjects' nonpreferred responses were rewarded, that is, repressors were rewarded when they responded aggressively to the confederate's shocks, and sensitizers were rewarded for friendly counterresponses. By the end of this conditioning phase, the previous pattern of results had been reversed. Repressors showed a preference for aggressive counterresponses and recovered more quickly following them while sensitizers preferred friendly responses and showed quicker recovery following them. When the original random reinforcement contingencies of the baseline period were re-established during the extinction period, subjects reverted to their previous response patterns. Thus, using a social learning model, Scarpetti was able to predict differential recovery rates for his subjects and to modify them by means of social reinforcements.

A Final Caution

Although the results cited above seem to provide strong support for the social learning model of autonomic recovery, a qualification should be added. Several studies not directly related to the catharsis hypothesis have concluded that diastolic blood pressure is the most reliable indicator of anger arousal (cf. Ax, 1953; Funkenstein, King, & Drolette, 1957; Schachter, 1957). While some investigators have found this to be the case in catharsis research (e.g., Gambaro & Rabin, 1969; Geen, Stonner, & Shope, 1975), Hokanson and his associates (Hokanson & Edelman, 1966) typically find SBP to be the best discriminator. Holmes (1966), on the other hand, found that both DBP and SBP were correlated with aggressive arousal. Perhaps the difference between SBP and DBP is relatively unimportant, and both may serve as reliable measures of tension (McGinn, Harburg, Julius, & McLeod, 1964; Forsyth, 1974).

Further complicating the catharsis literature is the fact that cardiovascular measures of arousal may not correlate well with other measures of physiological arousal (Lacey, 1967). In studies which have included other physiological measures, the results are equivocal. Scarpetti (1974) reported that both DBP and GSR were reduced following aggression. Kahn (1966), on the other hand, found that insulted subjects who were allowed to retaliate showed quicker recoveries to baseline levels on both DBP and SBP than nonaggressing control subjects. On other arousal measures (finger temperature, specific GSRs, average skin conductance, and muscle tension), however, subjects who retaliated showed *slower* returns to baseline, but, in an interesting analysis of his data, Kahn did find somewhat different evidence for tension reduction with these measures. Comparing each subject's *recovery patterns* (Lacey, Bateman, & Van Lehn, 1953) following the insult and retaliation manipulations with his recovery patterns following a cold pressor test, Kahn found that subjects who were allowed to aggress showed patterns more similar to their normal recovery patterns than subjects who did not retaliate. Thus, Kahn concluded, "The function of catharsis might be to permit the autonomic nervous system to adopt a recovery pattern [p. 286]" rather than to cause an absolute drop in any particular arousal measure. Nevertheless, until future research clarifies this point, one must conclude that physiological catharsis, when it does occur, seems generally to be limited to cardiovascular arousal.

Conclusion

In general, the results of studies on physiological recovery seem to fit the social-learning model well. The model predicts the observed differences between males and females, guilty and nonguilty subjects, repressors and sensitizers. Furthermore, it has been demonstrated that these differences can be modified through a social-learning paradigm and that even self-punitive responses can have catharsislike effects if they are reinforced. Now we must see if this model can explain behavior following aggression.

Behavioral Investigations of Aggression Catharsis

According to the traditional formulation of the catharsis hypothesis, the reduction in physiological arousal following a retaliatory act lessens the likelihood of further aggression. If we adopt a social learning approach, however, this is not necessarily the case. The reduced arousal may actually reinforce the aggression that preceded it and thus *increase* the likelihood of further aggression. Decreased hostility following aggression, should it occur, is taken as evidence of an active inhibition of aggressiveness rather than a passive draining of the aggressive urge. A crucial point in applying the social learning model to aggression catharsis is that even when a person is taught to respond aggressively to provocation, he is probably also taught that "enough is enough." In other words, social inhibitions are learned which keep the person from becoming too aggressive, so that although he may feel like aggressing further, he actively restrains himself from doing so.

A second point inherent in a social learning analysis of aggression and catharsis is that a person may have learned to respond to frustration with responses other than aggressive ones. For example, an angry child might be told to go to his room and play with his toys. Such substitute activities may lessen aggressiveness by distracting the person or by introducing responses that are incompatible with aggression, or they may, as many authors contend, produce a catharsis in the classic sense by allowing the person to engage in vicarious aggression. Therefore, we will look at how both vicarious and direct aggression affect subsequent behavior and see how well the data support the traditional frustration-aggression hypothesis and the social-learning theory approach.

Effects of Vicarious Aggression

FANTASY AGGRESSION

The ostensibly cathartic effect of fantasy behavior was first reported by Feshbach (1955). In his study, groups of subjects were assigned to one of three experimental conditions. Subjects in two of the conditions were exposed to an insulting experimenter who derogated their ability, motivation, and maturity. Some of these subjects were then shown a series of four TAT cards and asked to make up stories about them (insult-fantasy condition), while others spent a similar amount of time engaged in various nonfantasy activities (insult-control condition). In the third condition (non-insult fantasy) the experimenter behaved politely before administering the TAT task. Upon completion of the TAT or control task, all subjects were given a sentence completion test and an experimental evaluation form designed to measure residual hostility. The results of the study were interpreted by the author as support for the catharsis hypothesis. Insult-fantasy subjects expressed more aggression in their TAT stories than did non-insult-fantasy subjects and showed less residual hostility toward the insulting experimenter than did insult-control subjects. For insult-fantasy subjects, the amount of residual hostility was negatively correlated with the amount expressed in TAT stories, offering further evidence for the cathartic value of aggressive fantasy.

Pytkowicz, Wagner, and Sarason (1967) expanded Feshbach's design into a 2 × 2 × 2 × 3 factorial, with factors of sex (male versus female), daydreaming frequency (high versus low), insult condition (insult versus noninsult), and fantasy activity (daydreaming versus TAT versus control). The effects of these manipulations were measured on two dependent variables: ratings of hostility toward the insulting experimenter and self-ratings of hostility. The major finding was that for male subjects who reported a high instance of daydreaming, the opportunity to engage in fantasy behavior (via either daydreaming or TAT) after being insulted reduced the amount of hostility expressed toward the insulting experimenter more than the opportunity to engage in the control activity did. A similar, though nonsignificant, pattern was found for low daydreaming males. It is interesting that the opposite effect occurred in the data on self-ratings of hostility. High daydreamers who engaged in fantasy activities after being insulted rated themselves as more hostile than control subjects. Perhaps subjects in the "cathartic" conditions, having observed themselves engaging in hostile fantasy, subsequently labeled themselves as more hostile than subjects who engaged in non-hostile activity. It is further possible that the realization that they were being hostile engendered guilt in these subjects and that this guilt led to the decreased hostility toward the experimenter. (The same criticism can be leveled at the Feshbach study.) Yet another possibility is that subjects who daydream often have learned to avoid stressful situations by ignoring them in this fashion.

For female subjects, the ratings of the experimenter were no more hostile when subjects were insulted than when they were not. The authors, therefore, considered the anger manipulation unsuccessful with females and did not report significance tests between groups. Nevertheless, the results show an interesting pattern. The two groups exhibiting the greatest amount of hostility are those who were insulted and then engaged in the daydreaming activity, the highest level of hostility being expressed by low daydreaming insulted subjects. Thus, it is possible that for female subjects the TAT and control activities, which required activity, may have distracted them and dissipated their anger while the more passive daydream activity may have led them to brood and maintain a rather high level of anger (such a possibility was mentioned by Hokanson and Edelman, 1966). In this regard, one should note that, on the questionnaire used to measure daydreaming frequency, females reported less of a tendency than males to engage in daydreaming. This suggests that it may have been more difficult for them to use this activity as a mode of either catharsis or distraction. The attempt to engage in such an activity may even have proved frustrating for them (among noninsulted females, low daydream subjects in the daydream condition were most hostile toward the experimenter). While we can only speculate upon the role played by distraction in the current study, both Downey (1973) and Konecni (1974, 1975) have reported that angered subjects who engaged in a distracting task were subsequently less aggressive toward their antagonist than subjects given nothing to do for the same length of time.

Spiegel and Zelin (1973) studied the effects of fantasy aggression on systolic blood pressure and ratings of the experiment. Male subjects were either insulted or not insulted by a female experimenter and then allowed to write stories for 5 min about one of three TAT-type pictures varying in aggressive pull. Following this fantasy task, subjects were asked to write a short evaluation of the experiment and to rate how angry they had felt toward the experimenter and themselves at various points during the experiment. Results indicated that the anger manipulation was effective in raising SBP of insulted subjects and that this elevated blood pressure was reduced by all three fantasy conditions. Unfortunately, this effect could be due merely to passage of time because the authors did not include a no-fantasy control condition. [In a study reported earlier, Hokanson and Burgess (1962b) found fantasy aggression to be an ineffective mode of arousal reduction.] Data from the ratings are also difficult to interpret. After the fantasy activity, insulted subjects did show a greater drop in reported anger toward the experimenter than noninsulted subjects, but this is to be expected since they started at a higher level of anger after being insulted. Again, a no-fantasy control could have clarified this point.

To summarize, it does appear that allowing angered subjects to engage in fantasy behavior can reduce their aggressiveness, but that it is most effective for males who customarily engage in a large amount of fantasy behavior. It is also not clear whether the fantasy content needs to be aggressive to reduce hostility.

Aggressive Humor

According to Freud (1960), enjoyment of hostile humor is a symbolic expression of aggression and should produce cathartic effects. Thus, subjects who are angered and then exposed to hostile humor should experience a reduction in aggressive drive and be less hostile than those who are provided no aggressive outlet for their anger. Dworkin and Efran (1967) attempted to test this notion in a laboratory setting. Three groups of subjects were angered by an insulting experimenter and then administered a modified version of the Nowlis–Green Mood Adjective Check List (Nowlis, 1965) designed to measure hostile and anxious feelings. They then listened to one of three 20-min tape recordings: a hostile humor tape, a nonhostile humor tape (matched for funniness with the hostile tape), or a control documentary and musical tape. Following this manipulation, they were again administered the "mood adjective check list." Additional control subjects listened to either the hostile or non-hostile humor selections without being angered. Both types of humor reduced feelings of anger and anxiety aroused by the insulting experimenter, while the documentary control tape had a negligible effect. Hostile humor seemed somewhat more effective than nonhostile humor in reducing reported levels of anxiety and arousal, but the difference was not significant. Minimal support for the catharsis hypothesis was found in the humor ratings. Angered subjects appreciated aggressive humor more than nonangered subjects (ratings for nonhostile humor were in the opposite direction, but the difference between the groups was not significant). Nevertheless, contrary to the catharsis hypothesis, enjoyment of the hostile humor was unrelated to subsequent reduction in hostile feelings.

A study by Singer (1968) provides somewhat stronger evidence for a cathartic effect of aggressive humor on self-ratings of hostility. The experiment was conducted by black civil rights leaders using blacks as subjects. Half the subjects were angered by listening to a tape that described incidences of degradation and torture perpetrated against black leaders and included excerpts from an arch-segregationist's speech. The remaining subjects listened to a control tape featuring a reasoned, noninflammatory discussion of race relations written by a prominent black author. Following this manipulation, subjects were exposed to one of three communications: hostile humor, neutral humor, or control. In the hostile humor condition, subjects listened to a tape of a well-known black humorist which was bitterly scornful of segregationists and policies of white leaders. The neutral humor tape consisted of excerpts from the same humorist dealing with topics other than race relations in a manner that was "wryly sympathetic." The control tape consisted of a recording by an eminent black author describing problems he encountered becoming a playwright from which humorous remarks had been deleted. Each of these tapes lasted 6 min. The principal dependent variables were ratings of the humor and self-ratings on the Nowlis–Green Mood Adjective Check List.

Interpretation of the data obtained in this study was somewhat complicated by the unexpected finding that, in the late summer, subjects, regardless of experimental condition, described themselves as feeling much more anxiety, aggressiveness, and depression than early summer subjects. These late summer subjects, then, should, in the words of the author, be "most ripe for cathartic aggression reduction [p. 6]." This, in fact, proved to be the case. For the less aroused (early summer) subjects, results paralleled those obtained by Dworkin and Efran (1967). Both hostile and nonhostile humor reduced aggressive and anxious feelings, and these reductions were unrelated to humor appreciation. For the highly aroused (late summer) subjects, however, hostile humor was considerably more effective than the other two conditions in reducing feelings of aggressiveness and anxiety. Furthermore, there was a striking negative correlation between appreciation for the hostile humor and residual hostility ($r = -.987$, $p < .001$). When subjects were moderately aroused, both hostile and nonhostile humor reduced feelings of aggressiveness and tension, but when they were highly aroused, only hostile humor produced a cathartic effect.

Landy and Mettee (1969) extended the aforementioned findings by showing that subjects who were insulted by an experimenter and then exposed to hostile and nonhostile cartoon humor were less hostile in rating their insulter than subjects who engaged in a control task or who rated the insulter immediately. Unfortunately, all subjects in the humor condition were exposed to both hostile and nonhostile cartoons, so there is no way to assess differences between the two types of humor. A more recent experiment (Leak, 1974) did find that angered subjects who were exposed to aggressive humor were less hostile toward an insulting experimenter than those exposed to nonhostile humor. Angered subjects, however, were no more appreciative of hostile humor than nonangered subjects. Berkowitz (1970), by contrast, reports results directly opposed to Leak's findings. In his study, female subjects listened to an interview with a supposed job applicant who was either insulting or neutral toward university coeds. They then rated the applicant after hearing either a recording of neutral humor by George Carlin or one of hostile "humor" by Don Rickles. Although angered subjects did appreciate Rickles more than nonangered subjects, exposure to his humor increased aggressiveness toward the applicant regardless of how she had behaved during the interview. This effect is difficult to interpret, however, since humor ratings obtained from the subjects showed that Don Rickles was not only rated as more aggressive than George Carlin but also less funny. Thus, the differences obtained could be due either to Don Rickles' relative aggressiveness or his relative lack of humor. In order to control for the latter, Berkowitz chose only those subjects from each group who rated the humor as decidedly funny (4 or 5 on the 5-point scale). An additional criterion was that subjects in the Rickles condition rated him above the median in aggressiveness and those in the Carlin condition below the median.

Using only these subjects, Berkowitz found essentially the same results as he had obtained with the entire sample: Subjects exposed to the hostile humor were less friendly toward the applicant than those exposed to the neutral humor. This selection of subjects, however, may have biased the results in this direction. Byrne (1956) has reported that "Those [subjects] who frequently express hostility, either overtly or covertly, find hostile cartoons significantly more amusing than do those [subjects] who fail to express hostility [p. 88]." In other words, it is possible that those who were most appreciative of Don Rickles may have been more aggressive even without the humor manipulation.

Taken together, these studies indicate that, under conditions of moderate aggressive arousal, exposure to both hostile and nonhostile humor appear to be effective in reducing aggressive feelings (Dworkin & Efran, 1967; Singer, 1968) and the expression of aggression (Landy & Mettee, 1969). Under conditions of high aggressive arousal, only hostile humor proved to have a cathartic effect (Singer, 1968). The latter finding could be explained without recourse to humor. Since the humorist's anecdotes represented a direct attack on the source of the subjects' ire, the ostensibly cathartic effect could be due to other factors, such as vicarious attack (Doob & Wood, 1972), equity restoration (Berscheid, Boye, & Walster, 1968), or status restoration (Worchel, 1961) not all of which involve catharsis in the traditional sense. Finally, the fact that subjects report feeling better after listening to aggressive humor does not necessarily imply that they will behave less aggressively. The evidence for behavioral catharsis following exposure to aggressive humor is mixed. Leak demonstrated that it can occur, but Berkowitz showed that the opposite result is also possible. Thus, the effects of aggressive humor on the overt expression of aggression remain uncertain.

Exposure to Media Violence

An extensive review of the literature on media violence and aggressive behavior by Goranson (1970) uncovered only a single study (Feshbach, 1961) showing a cathartic effect in subjects who view media violence. As Goranson points out:

> Evaluation of the implications of this one experiment provides a good example of the dangers inherent in generalizing too freely from the results of a single piece of research. Additional experiments have indicated that the results of this study were very likely due to the arousal of aggression anxiety and the subsequent inhibition of overt hostility, rather than the result of symbolic catharsis. More recent experiments that have minimized the factor of aggression anxiety have almost uniformly found that observed violence results in the stimulation of aggression. These results, along with the . . . findings of modeling experiments with children, all argue against the idea that observed violence results in a cathartic discharge of aggressive energies [p. 22–23].

For a more detailed discussion of the role of observed violence on aggression, the reader is referred to Chapter 8.

Sports and Vigorous Physical Activity

The notion that participation in and observation of athletic events can drain off aggressive impulses has received enthusiastic support from a number of popular theorists (e.g., Ardrey, 1966; Lorenz, 1966; Menninger, 1948; Stokes, 1958; Storr, 1968). Menninger, for example, has suggested that "competitive games provide an unusually satisfactory social outlet for the instinctive aggressive drive [p. 343]" and Storr, in a statement echoing Lorenz[5] and Ardrey, has maintained that "it is obvious that the encouragement of competition in all possible fields is likely to diminish the kind of hostility which leads to war rather than to increase it . . . rivalry between nations in sports can do nothing but good [p. 117]."

Such glowing statements, however, hardly seem warranted in view of the experimental evidence available. Husman (1955) did report data showing that boxers made less aggressive responses to projective tests than wrestlers, cross-country runners, or control subjects. While this finding seems to suggest that boxing produces a cathartic reduction in aggressive feelings, the effect may have been due to some selection factor since it was found even before the start of the season. The data also showed that boxers expressed more guilt feelings following a contest than control subjects. A similar effect has been reported by Atkins, Hilton, Neigher, and Bahr (1972) who found that angered police officers who chose to box exhibited both less aggression and more guilt in response to TAT pictures than those who chose other activities. Thus, the lower aggressiveness scores of boxers may have been due to guilt rather than catharsis. Also, contrary to the catharsis hypothesis, in the Husman study, aggression scores on the TAT *increased* rather than decreased for athletes after a season of participation. A recent field experiment by Patterson (1974) using high-school football players and physical education students likewise produced results directly opposed to the catharsis theory. Hostility scales were administered to students 1 week before the football season and 1 week after its completion. While physical education students showed a slight nonsignificant decrease in hostility at the second testing, football players showed a significant increase.

---

[5] In fairness to Lorenz, it should be noted that he has recently recanted on this point and several others that he made in *On Aggression*: "Nowadays, I have strong doubts whether watching aggressive behavior even in the guise of sport has any cathartic effect at all [in Evans, 1974, p. 93]."

A laboratory study by Ryan (1970) also found no evidence of the cathartic value of vigorous physical exercise. He angered some subjects by exposing them to an insulting accomplice while others received neutral treatment. All subjects then engaged in one of four activities before being given an opportunity to shock their antagonist under the guise of a learning experiment. One group of subjects was given 10 swings with a rubber mallet at a "cathartic pounding apparatus." Two other groups performed this task in competition with an accomplice, one group "winning" all 10 trials and the other "losing" all 10. A control group simply sat and waited before being given the opportunity to aggress. No differences were found in amount of shock delivered by subjects who had been allowed to pound (either alone or in competition) and those who merely sat. Thus, the opportunity to engage in aggressive physical activity produced no more "catharsis" than merely sitting. In another investigation Hornberger (1959) found that angered subjects who pounded nails for 10 min were later *more* verbally aggressive than subjects in a control condition.

Zillman (1971) has developed a theory of excitation transfer, which would argue strongly against physical exercise producing a cathartic effect in angered subjects. According to his viewpoint (adapted from Schachter, 1964), the amount of aggression expressed by a subject is a function of both his physiological arousal and his interpretation of that arousal. Subjects who are angered and engage in strenuous physical activity are likely to attribute their arousal level to anger. They should, therefore, feel more aroused and angry and, hence, be more aggressive than subjects who have been angered but not engaged in strenuous physical activity. An experiment by Zillman, Katcher, and Milavsky (1972) confirmed these predictions. Subjects interacted with an experimental accomplice who gave them either three (low anger) or nine (high anger) shocks. Half the subjects then engaged in the strenuous physical activity of pedaling a bicycle while the other half performed a more sedentary activity. All subjects were then allowed to aggress against the instigator by shocking him to inform him of his errors. As predicted, angered subjects who engaged in strenuous physical activity were more aggressive than angered subjects who did not. The effect of exercise was minimal when subjects were not angered. In this case, then, strenuous physical activity led to an *increase* rather than a decrease in aggression. Similar effects have been obtained when the anger manipulation is delivered shortly after the bike riding activity while subjects are still highly aroused (Zillman & Bryant, 1974).

Finally, Mallick and McCandless (1966), using grade-school children as subjects, found no more aggression in children who engaged in target shooting than in those who merely talked with the experimenter. Both groups, however, were more punitive toward their frustrator than were subjects who had the frustrator's behavior explained to them. The further observation that subjects who expressed hostility toward the frustrator immediately later expressed more dislike of him than others who did not express hostility also argues against the traditional catharsis hypothesis.

It appears, therefore, that participation in aggressive sports does not produce the cathartic drain of aggressive urges in the athletes which has been so often suggested. Perhaps, though, as the ancient Roman emperors proposed, observation of these "gladiators" allows the fan to drain off his aggressive urges. The observation of vigorous contact sports, however, probably elicits aggressive reactions similar to those produced by observation of other sorts of aggressive activity, especially if the sporting event is described in violent terms (Berkowitz & Alioto, 1973). Newspaper accounts provide additional dramatic evidence of this phenomenon. In 1964 during a soccer match in Lima, Peru, a riot erupted in which 293 fans were killed and 500 were injured. El Salvador and Honduras broke off diplomatic relations with each other over a soccer match (Lever, 1969). Here in the United States, fans at a baseball game (hardly the most aggressive of sporting events) recently attacked players on the field, and the situation seems to be worsening (Fimrite, 1974). Thus, although aggressive sports may serve a useful function in modern society, they certainly do not seem to purge the aggressive feelings of either participants or fans. Encouraging athletic competition among nations as a panacea for world conflict would seem at best ill advised.

SUMMARY OF FINDINGS ON VICARIOUS AGGRESSION AND CATHARSIS

The available literature provides some evidence suggesting that engaging in fantasy behavior or listening to humor can cause subjects to become less aggressive. It is not clear, however, whether the fantasy or humor content must be aggressive to produce reductions in hostility. The effects of engaging in aggressive sports or observing aggressive sports or media violence are more clear. Such activities typically lead to *increased* rather than decreased aggression. When decreased aggression is found, it may well be attributable to the arousal of feelings of guilt or aggression anxiety rather than catharsis.

These findings appear to be broadly consistent with the social learning model proposed earlier to account for the data obtained in investigations of autonomic recovery following aggression. The social learning model proposes that, through a series of social learning experiences, an individual is taught what constitutes an appropriate response to frustration (Bandura, 1973). Given the child rearing practices common to our culture, it seems much more likely that an angry child would be encouraged to think about something else or to "laugh it off" than he would be to play football, shoot a gun, or watch some violent TV. Through a gradual learning process, the former type of activities may come to serve as a distracting influence in mitigating the effects of anger arousal, especially when the provocateur is high in status (e.g., a parent or teacher) and direct reprisal might be deemed inappropriate. In this regard, one should note that, in every study reviewed in the sections on fantasy aggression and humor, the antagonist occupied higher status than the subject. Different results might have been obtained if the provocateurs had been lower in status. Hokanson and Burgess (1962b), for example, found no evidence of arousal reduction when subjects engaged in fantasy behavior after being angered by an experimenter low in status.

From a social learning standpoint, it is also not surprising that participation in aggressive sports tends to increase a person's hostility since the participants are constantly rewarded for aggression. Coaches and fans cheer them for aggressive play and encourage them to become even more aggressive (recall the common football cheer: "Hit 'em again, harder, harder!"). Eventually such constant reinforcements of aggression may lower inhibitions against aggression *off* the field as well as on.

Direct Expression of Aggression and Behavioral Catharsis

When we turn to a consideration of the effects of direct expressions of aggression upon subsequent behavior, we are dealing with the situation described by both Freud and the authors of the frustration–aggression hypothesis in their definitions of catharsis. Studies of the effects of direct aggression on subsequent aggressive tendencies can be divided into two categories: those which allowed subjects to express their aggression verbally and those in which aggression was physical. Since these two modes of expression may not be comparable, they will be considered separately.

VERBAL AGGRESSION AND BEHAVIORAL CATHARSIS

Most studies investigating the effects of verbal aggression on subsequent aggression have employed a design similar to that of Thibaut and Coules (1952). Subjects were verbally insulted by a confederate and were then either given a chance to reply to his insult or interrupted before they could do so. Following this manipulation, a measure of residual hostility was obtained by having all subjects write brief personality sketches of the insulter, which were scored for hostile, neutral, and friendly content. It was found that those who were allowed to reply to the confederate subsequently used a larger percentage of friendly adjectives in describing the insulter. No significant difference was found between the groups in number of hostile comments. While this finding might be accepted as marginal evidence for catharsis, results from their second study weaken that interpretation of the data. In this study, the authors found that subjects who were interrupted for 3 min before replying to an insult were reliably more hostile than those allowed an immediate reply. Apparently, interrupting subjects who are about to reply to an insult introduces an additional frustration over and above that of the insult. Differences between subjects allowed to reply and those not allowed to reply in the first experiment, then, may have been due to an increase in hostility on the part of those interrupted rather than to catharsis for those allowed to reply. Similar effects reported by Pepitone and Reichling (1955) are subject to the same criticism.

Rosenbaum and de Charms (1960) extended the design employed by Thibaut and Coules (1952) to include a vicarious communication condition in which subjects were not allowed to reply directly to their insulter but heard a confederate attack him. They also divided subjects into high and low self-esteem groups. For low self-esteem subjects, those who could reply to their insulter or who heard him being attacked were less hostile toward him in their personality sketches. For high self-esteem subjects, there were no differences in residual hostility among the various experimental treatment conditions. Although the chance to reply to an insulter seemed to be cathartic for low self-esteem subjects, the authors urge caution in accepting a catharsis explanation noting that "there is scant evidence that aggressive verbalizations during the rebuttal are the cause of the reduced hostility [p. 110]." Perhaps subjects in this condition attempted to restore their status rather than derogate their insulter. The attack upon the insulter by the confederate may have also served to restore lost status to low self-esteem subjects. Worchel (1961) has demonstrated that such a restoration of status can be an effective (though "uncathartic") means of reducing hostility in insulted subjects.

De Charms and Wilkins (1963) lowered the restraints against attacking the insulter in order to encourage more open expression of hostility toward him during the "rebuttal" period. Although rebuttal should have allowed for maximum catharsis, subjects in this condition showed *more* residual hostility than those who were restrained from expressing themselves earlier. Also, contrary to the catharsis hypothesis, subjects who were most aggressive toward the insulter also tended to be highest in residual hostility toward him.

While subsequent studies of verbal aggression have uncovered little evidence in support of the classic catharsis hypothesis,[6] their results are relevant to the social learning model. In general, these studies have shown that when subjects' responses prove instrumental in changing a frustrator's behavior, residual hostility is reduced (cf. Goldman, Keck, & O'Leary, 1969; Goldman, Kretschmann, & Westergard, 1972; Rothaus & Worchel, 1964). On the other hand, when situational restraints against aggression are lowered by various experimental procedures, such as exposing subjects to critical or aggressive models (e.g., Goldman *et al.,* 1969; Rothaus & Worchel, 1964; Wheeler & Caggiula, 1966; Wheeler & Smith, 1967) or reinforcing aggressive responses (Nelsen, 1969), expression of aggression leads to *increased* rather than decreased hostility on postaggression measures. When restraints are added (e.g., by showing the insulter suffering, Bramel, Taub, & Blum, 1968) aggression is reduced.

PHYSICAL AGGRESSION AND BEHAVIORAL CATHARSIS

Evidence to support the notion that engaging in physical aggression produces a catharsis, which lowers subsequent aggressive tendencies, is equivocal at best. Berkowitz (1966) has shown that subjects who were angered and given two opportunities to aggress against their attacker were more aggressive on the second opportunity than similarly angered subjects who were not given the initial opportunity to aggress. Similarly, subjects who were most aggressive in their attacks subsequently showed more hostility toward their victim on a rating scale. These results are exactly opposite to those predicted by the catharsis hypothesis. Other experiments (e.g., Buss, 1966a; Geen, 1968) have found that, when angered subjects were allowed to aggress over a long series of trials, they tended to become *more* aggressive over the series and that subjects who were allowed to aggress physically against an antagonist were subsequently less friendly in their ratings of him than subjects who had not retaliated (e.g., Berkowitz & Geen, 1966, 1967; Berkowitz, Green, & McCauley, 1962; Geen, 1968).

Doob and his associates, however, have reported results that are consistent with the catharsis hypothesis. Doob and Wood (1972), for

[6] Nisenson (1972) did report that subjects who were permitted to write retaliatory statements to an insulter were subsequently less hostile toward him than subjects not allowed to do so. He proposed, however, several alternatives to the catharsis explanation of these findings and also noted that retaliation was no more effective in reducing hostility than was writing on a neutral topic.

example, exposed subjects to an insulting or neutral confederate. Some of these subjects were then allowed to shock the confederate when she made mistakes on a learning task. Others watched the experimenter shock her, and a third group merely waited. All subjects were then allowed to evaluate the confederate's performance on a "creative association" task by shocking her when she made responses that the subject judged to be uncreative. Results showed that annoyed subjects who had previously shocked the confederate delivered fewer shocks than those who had not been given an earlier opportunity to aggress. Insulted subjects who observed the confederate being punished also tended to be less aggressive. A similar finding was reported by Doob (1970) for subjects who saw their insulter lose money. Konecni and Doob (1972), using a similar design, found that subjects who were allowed to "displace" their aggression by punishing an innocent confederate were also less aggressive toward their insulter.

Several methodological differences between the Doob studies and the Berkowitz study may account for the discrepant findings and also cast doubt on the traditional catharsis interpretation. Berkowitz used all male subjects and a male confederate, whereas the later Doob studies involved the use of both male and female subjects and usually a female confederate (although Doob [1970] has used only a male confederate). Previous research has shown that females tend to be less aggressive than males (Hokanson et al., 1968) and that both males and females tend to inhibit attacks against a female victim when they suspect that they have hurt her (Buss, 1966a, b).

If subjects in the Doob studies felt that the confederate had been hurt by the first attack, they may have felt guilty and restrained themselves when given a second opportunity to hurt her (or him). The anger manipulations employed in the Doob studies may have also increased subjects' restraints against aggressing. Since subjects were angered by verbal insult and responded with electric shock, it is not difficult to assume that they felt the confederate had been more than repayed the first time she was shocked and, thus, held back when given a second opportunity to inflict pain. Subjects in the Berkowitz experiment, having been aroused by electric shock, may have felt less guilty responding in the same mode.

The findings from studies on physical aggression, then, seem quite similar to those cited on verbal aggression. Direct aggression can lead to reduced hostility, but, when it does, the effect may be interpreted in terms of increased restraints against aggression rather than true catharsis. When these restraints are minimized, expression of aggression seems to lead to *increased* rather than decreased hostility. Considering these results in conjunction with those showing reduction of physiological arousal in angered subjects who are allowed to aggress without guilt, it seems that expressing hostility may "make one feel better," but it is also likely to lead to even more hostility. Two studies that have measured both physiological responses and subsequent aggressive tendencies following retaliatory aggression in situations where restraints against aggressing were low strongly suggest that this may be the case.

Studies Measuring both Physiological and Behavioral Catharsis

Kahn (1966) angered male subjects by exposing them to a vulgar and insulting experimental assistant. Half the subjects were then encouraged by the experimenter to express their feelings toward the experimental assistant, while the other half were "asked to just sit a while longer." Results showed that subjects who were allowed to express their hostile feelings showed shorter vascular recovery times than subjects who sat and waited. On a subsequent rating form, though, subjects who had expressed their feelings were more hostile toward the insulter than those who had not been allowed to do so.

Similar findings were reported by Geen, Stonner, and Shope (1975), when subjects aggressed physically. In a 2 × 3 design, half the subjects were angered by a confederate who gave them excessive electric shock, while the other half were treated more mildly. Subjects were then assigned to one of three catharsis conditions. In one condition, subjects ostensibly delivered a fixed amount of shock to the confederate every time he made a mistake on a learning task. In the second condition, the experimenter "shocked" the confederate, and, in the third condition, shock was not mentioned. Following this manipulation, all subjects were allowed to "shock" the confederate when he made errors on a second learning task. On this task, they were free to determine the intensity and duration of each shock. Upon completion of the second learning task, subjects were administered a questionnaire which assessed their feelings toward the confederate and how restrained they had felt (i.e., how much they "held back") in attacking the confederate on the second learning task.

Blood pressure readings were obtained at four points during the experiment: immediately before and after the anger manipulation and immediately following the two learning tasks. Data obtained from these readings supported the catharsis hypothesis. Angered subjects showed significant increases in DBP as compared to controls. Those who shocked the confederate on the first learning task showed a significant drop in DBP as compared to the other two groups. Also consistent with the catharsis hypothesis, angered subjects in the other two conditions showed the greatest drops in DBP on the second learning task, when they were finally able to aggress (although the difference was significant only for the group that had observed the experimenter shock the confederate).

The behavioral data, on the other hand, argue just as strongly against the catharsis hypothesis. Angered subjects who were allowed to aggress twice were more aggressive on the second opportunity than subjects in the other five conditions and were more hostile toward the confederate on the final rating scale. They also reported feeling less restrained in administering shocks on the second learning task. Thus, one act of aggression, rather than purging aggressiveness, facilitated more aggression.[7]

Concluding Remarks

Summary

Results from the studies reviewed cast serious doubt on the traditional aggression catharsis hypothesis but lend support to a reformulation of that hypothesis in terms of social-learning theory. The social learning theory of catharsis differs from the traditional concept in two important respects. First, any response that has proven effective in dealing with aggression or frustration in the past can have a "cathartic" effect on physiological arousal. (This was demonstrated most dramatically by Stone and Hokanson who "trained" subjects to experience "catharsis" when they engaged in self-punitive behavior.) Aggressive responses can serve an arousal reducing function, but only if they have been reinforced in the past. A second crucial point in the social learning approach is that aggressiveness, once learned, must be actively inhibited. It cannot be passively drained off by the commission of an aggressive response. Just as one learns to be aggressive in certain situations, one must also learn to refrain from aggressing in other circumstances. The latter lesson may be more difficult to master. Observations of nursery school children have shown that, unlike college students,

---

[7] At this point, one should also note that ethological studies of lower animals, which in the past have generally been interpreted as evidence for the traditional concept of aggression catharsis, have recently produced evidence that suggests that aggression is not cathartic. Heiligenberg and Kramer (1972), for example, found that male cichlid fish, when allowed to aggress against an aggression-eliciting dummy, were subsequently more aggressive toward innocent youngsters than when they were given no opportunity to aggress against "appropriate" targets.

they continued to aggress even when their victim was hurt (Patterson, Littman, & Bricker, 1967).

Apparently, aggression is learned far more easily than it is socialized. The socialized inhibitions against aggression also seem rather easy to overcome (e.g., the Lima soccer match incident). In this regard, laboratory studies that deliberately lower restraints against aggression (e.g., Geen *et al.*, 1975) may be seen as representing a reversal of the normal socialization process. After a subject has been angered, he is allowed (actually told) to attack his adversary. The victim emits no pain cues (he is not even visible), and the subject not only feels better but also learns that, in this laboratory situation, aggression is permissible and socially approved (i.e., condoned by the experimenter). When given a second opportunity to aggress, this subject is more aggressive than one who has not yet "unlearned" his social restraints. While such laboratory demonstrations may seem rather contrived, it is reasonable to assume that any time restraints against aggression are lowered in the "real world" similar phenomena may occur. A pertinent example is suggested by this quote attributed to a man accused of murdering four people. "He said . . . he had a funny feeling in his stomach but after the first [killing] . . . it was easy [*Kansas City Times,* 19 September 1973, p. 4]."

Implications

The implications of the social learning model of aggression catharsis for educators and clinical practitioners should be obvious. Aggressive acts are not the only ones that can reduce the tension caused by frustration; prosocial responses can prove just as effective. Moreover, for some personality types (e.g., repressors) more passive responses to frustration may be preferred. As Holt (1970) has noted, "There can be both constructive and destructive ways of expressing anger [p. 11]," and therapists should seek to discover nonviolent responses to anger that can serve both tension reduction and the maintenance of healthy interpersonal relationships.

Advocates of such therapy techniques as "assertiveness training" should consider the data and should bear in mind that aggression, when condoned, often breeds further aggression. Man may, as some authors (Ardrey, 1961; Eibl-Eibesfeldt, 1970; Lorenz, 1966) suggest, be an inherently aggressive animal, but, as Lorenz (Evans, 1974) warns, the importance of learning should not be ignored. "Teaching a child to discharge aggression more successfully could certainly enhance aggression, and it may also lessen the inhibitions against aggression. The process is more complicated than it appears [Evans, 1974, p. 93]."

Future Research Directions

Future research in aggression catharsis should examine individual differences more closely. A recent investigation by Goldman and Rhoads (1973) identified at least four broad categories representing preferred modes of responding to frustration and showed that a person's preferred mode predicted how much hostility he actually expressed. Research by Foa and his associates (Foa, Turner, & Foa, 1972; Donnenwerth & Foa, 1974) suggests that certain types of aggressive responses tend to elicit particular counterresponses more readily than others. It is possible, then, that some of the discrepancies found in the catharsis literature are the result of forcing subjects to make nonpreferred counterresponses to a particular type of frustration. A factorial study, which varies the type of instigation (e.g., verbal insult versus electric shock) and type of aggressive responses (e.g., verbal versus physical) permitted subjects and measures their effects on both physiological and behavioral "catharsis," could prove particularly informative. As Feshbach (1970) maintains, more attention should also be directed toward developmental studies tracing the acquisition of aggressive responses and inhibitions. In short, much remains to be done before any definitive statement can be made concerning aggression and catharsis. All we know for sure is that the traditional linear cause-and-effect model is woefully inadequate.

REFERENCES

Ardrey, R. *African genesis.* New York: Atheneum, 1961.

Ardrey, R. *The territorial imperative.* New York: Atheneum, 1966.

Atkins, A., Hilton, I., Neigher, W., & Bahr, A. Anger, fight, fantasy, and catharsis. Paper read at the 80th Annual Convention of the American Psychological Association, 1972.

Ax, A. F. The physiological differentiation between fear and anger in humans. *Psychosomatic Medicine,* 1953, *15,* 443–442.

Baker, J. W., & Schaie, K. W. Effects of aggressing "alone" or "with another" on physiological and psychological arousal. *Journal of Personality and Social Psychology,* 1969, *12,* 80–86.

Bandura, A. *Aggression: A social learning analysis.* Englewood Cliffs, New Jersey: Prentice-Hall, 1973.

Berkowitz, L. On not being able to aggress. *British Journal of Social and Clinical Psychology,* 1966, *5,* 130–139.

Berkowitz, L. Aggressive humor as a stimulus to aggressive responses. *Journal of Personality and Social Psychology,* 1970, *16,* 710–717.

Berkowitz, L., & Alioto, J. T. The meaning of an observed event as a determinant of its aggressive consequences. *Journal of Personality and Social Psychology,* 1973, *28,* 206–217.

Berkowitz, L., & Geen, R. G. Film violence and the cue properties of available targets. *Journal of Personality and Social Psychology,* 1966, *3,* 525–530.

Berkowitz, L., & Geen, R. G. Stimulus qualities of the target of aggression: A further study. *Journal of Personality and Social Psychology,* 1967, *5,* 364–368.

Berkowitz, L., Green, J. A., & Macaulay, J. R. Hostility catharsis as the reduction of emotional tension. *Psychiatry,* 1962, *25,* 23–31.

Berscheid, E., Boye, D., & Walster, E. Retaliation as a means of restoring equity. *Journal of Personality and Social Psychology,* 1968, *10,* 370–376.

Bramel, D., Taub, B., & Blum, B. An observer's reaction to the suffering of his enemy. *Journal of Personality and Social Psychology,* 1968, *8,* (4, Pt. 1), 384–392.

Breuer, J., & Freud, S. *Studies in hysteria.* Boston: Beacon Press, 1961.

Burgess, M. M., Reivich, R. S., & Silverman, J. J. Effects of frustration and aggression on physiological arousal level in depressed subjects. *Perceptual and Motor Skills,* 1968, *27,* 743–749.

Buss, A. H. Instrumentality of aggression, feedback, and frustration as determinants of physical aggression. *Journal of Personality and Social Psychology,* 1966, *3,* 153–162. (a).

Buss, A. H. The effect of harm on subsequent aggression. *Journal of Experimental Research in Personality,* 1966, *1,* 249–255. (b).

Byrne, D. The relationship between humor and the expression of hostility. *Journal of Abnormal and Social Psychology,* 1956, *53,* 84–89.

Byrne, D. Repression-sensitization. In B. Marher (Ed.), *Progress in experimental personality research,* Vol. 1. New York: Academic Press, 1964.

de Charms, R., & Wilkins, E. J. Some effects of verbal expression of hostility. *Journal of Abnormal and Social Psychology,* 1963, *66,* 462–470.

Dollard, J., Doob, L., Miller, N. E., Mowrer, O. H., & Sears, R. R. *Frustration and aggression.* New Haven: Yale Univ. Press, 1939.

Donnenwerth, G. V., & Foa, U. G. Effect of resource class on retaliation to injustice in interpersonal exchange. *Journal of Personality and Social Psychology,* 1974, *29,* 785–793.

Doob, A. N. Catharsis and aggression: The effect of hurting one's enemy. *Journal of Experimental Research in Personality,* 1970, *4,* 291–296.

Doob, A. N., & Wood, L. E. Catharsis and aggression: Effects of annoyance and retaliation on aggressive behavior. *Journal of Personality and Social Psychology,* 1972, *22,* 156–162.

Downey, J. An interference theory of the catharsis of aggression. Unpublished Ph.D. dissertation, Univ. of Missouri, 1973.

Dworkin, E. S., & Efran, J. S. The angered: Their susceptibility to varieties of humor. *Journal of Personality and Social Psychology,* 1967, *5,* 368–371.

Easterbrook, J. A. The effect of emotion on cue utilization and the organization of behavior. *Psychological Review,* 1959, *66,* 183–201.

Eibl-Eibesfeldt, I. *Ethology.* New York: Holt, 1970.

Evans, R. I. A conversation with Konrad Lorenz about aggression, homosexuality, pornography, and the need for a new ethic. *Psychology Today,* 1974, *8* (6), 82–92.

Feshbach, S. The drive-reducing function of fantasy behavior. *Journal of Abnormal and Social Psychology,* 1955, *50,* 3–11.

Feshbach, S. The stimulating versus cathartic effects of vicarious aggressive activity. *Journal of Abnormal and Social Psychology,* 1961, *63,* 381–385.

Feshbach, S. Aggression. In P. H. Mussen (Ed.), *Carmichael's manual of child psychology,* Vol. 2. New York: Wiley, 1970.

Fimrite, R. Take me out to the brawl game. *Sports Illustrated,* 1974, *40* (24), 10–13.

Fishman, C. G. Need for approval and the expression of aggression under varying conditions of frustration. *Journal of Personality and Social Psychology,* 1965, *2,* 809–816.

Foa, E. B. Turner, J. L., & Foa, U. G. Response generalization in aggression. *Human Relations,* 1972, *25,* 337–350.

Forsyth, R. P. Mechanisms of the cardiovascular responses to environmental stressors. In P. A. Obrist, A. H. Black, J. Breuer & L. V. DiCara (Eds.), *Cardiovascular psychophysiology.* Chicago: Aldine, 1974. Pp. 5–32.

Freud, S. *Jokes and their relation to the unconscious.* (Ed. and trans. by J. Strachey) New York: Norton, 1960.

Freud, S. Why war? In P. Reiff (Ed.), *Freud: Character and culture.* New York: Collier Books, 1963.

Funkenstein, D. H., King, S. H., & Drolette, M. E. *Mastery of stress.* Cambridge, Massachusetts: Harvard Univ. Press, 1957.

Gambaro, S., & Rabin, A. Diastolic blood pressure responses following direct and displaced aggression after anger arousal in high- and low-guilt subjects. *Journal of Personality and Social Psychology,* 1969, *12,* 87–94.

Geen, R. G. Effects of frustration, attack, and prior training in aggressiveness upon aggressive behavior. *Journal of Personality and Social Psychology,* 1968, *9,* 316–321.

Geen, R. G., & Quanty, M. B. The catharsis of aggression: An evaluation of a hypothesis. In L. Berkowitz (Ed.), *Advances in experimental social psychology,* 1975, New York: Academic Press, in press.

Geen, R. G., Stonner, D., & Shope, G. L. The facilitation of aggression by aggression: A study in response inhibition and disinhibition. *Journal of Personality and Social Psychology,* 1975, *31,* 721–726.

Goldman, M., Keck, J. W., & O'Leary, C. J. Hostility reduction and performance. *Psychological Reports,* 1969, *25,* 503–512.

Goldman, M., Kretschman, J. G., & Westergard, N. Feelings toward a frustrating agent as affected by replies to correction. *Journal of Social Psychology,* 1972, *88,* 301–302.

Goldman, M., & Rhoads, C. S. Frustration response categories and levels of hostile expression. *Journal of Psychology,* 1973, *85,* 329–338.

Goodman, P. Letter to the editor. *Scientific American,* 1964, *210* (6), 8.

Goranson, R. E. Media violence and aggressive behavior: A review of experimental research. In L. Berkowitz (Ed.), *Advances in experimental social psychology,* Vol. 5. New York: Academic Press, 1970.

Heiligenberg, W., & Kramer, U. Aggressiveness as a function of external stimulation. *Journal of Comparative Physiology,* 1972, *77,* 332–340.

Hokanson, J. E. The effects of frustration and anxiety on overt aggression. *Journal of Abnormal and Social Psychology,* 1961, *62,* 346–351.

Hokanson, J. E., & Burgess, M. The effects of three types of aggression on vascular processes. *Journal of Abnormal and Social Psychology,* 1962, *64,* 446–449. (a).

Hokanson, J. E., & Burgess, M. M. The effects of status, type of frustration and aggression on vascular processes. *Journal of Abnormal and Social Psychology,* 1962, *65,* 232–237. (b)

Hokanson, J. E., Burgess, M. M., & Cohen, M. The effects of displaced aggression on systolic blood pressure. *Journal of Abnormal and Social Psychology,* 1963, *67,* 214–218.

Hokanson, J. E., & Edelman, R. Effects of three social responses on vascular processes. *Journal of Personality and Social Psychology,* 1966, *3,* 442–447.

Hokanson, J. E., & Shetler, S. The effect of overt aggression on physiological arousal. *Journal of Abnormal and Social Psychology,* 1961, *63,* 446–448.

Hokanson, J. E., Willers, K. R., & Koropsak, E. The modification of autonomic responses during aggressive interchanges. *Journal of Personality,* 1968, *36,* 386–404.

Holmes, D. Effects of overt aggression on level of physiological arousal. *Journal of Personality and Social Psychology,* 1966, *4,* 189–194.

Holt, R. R. On the interpersonal and intrapersonal consequences of expressing or not expressing anger. *Journal of Consulting and Clinical Psychology,* 1970, *35,* 8–12.

Hornberger, R. H. The differential reduction of aggressive responses as a function of interpolated activities. *American Psychologist,* 1959, *14,* 354.

Husman, B. F. Aggression in boxers and wrestlers as measured by projective techniques. *Research Quarterly,* 1955, *26,* 421–425.

Janov, A. *The primal scream.* New York: Dell Books, 1970.

Kahn, M. The physiology of catharsis. *Journal of Personality and Social Psychology,* 1966, *3,* 278–286.

Konecni, V. J. Self-arousal, dissipation of anger, and aggression. Paper read at annual convention of American Psychological Association, 1974.

Konecni, V. J. Annoyance, type, and duration of postannoyance activity, and aggression: The "cathartic effect." *Journal of Experimental Psychology: General,* 1975, *104,* 76–102.

Konecni, V. J., & Doob, A. N. Catharsis through displacement of aggression. *Journal of Personality and Social Psychology,* 1972, *23,* 378–387.

Lacey, J. I. Somatic response patterning and stress: Some revisions of activation theory. In M. H. Appley & R. Turnbull (Eds.), *Psychological stress: Issues in research.* Appleton, 1967. Pp. 14–37.

Lacey, J. I., Bateman, D. E., & Van Lehn, R. Autonomic response specificity: An experimental study. *Psychosomatic Medicine,* 1953, *15,* 8–21.

Landy, D., & Mettee, D. Evaluation of an aggressor as a function of exposure to cartoon humor. *Journal of Personality and Social Psychology,* 1969, *12,* 66–71.

Leak, G. K. Effects of hostility arousal and aggressive humor on catharsis and humor preference. *Journal of Personality and Social Psychology,* 1974, *30,* 736–740.

Lever, J. Soccer: Opium of the Brazilian people. *Trans-Action,* 1969, *7,* (2), 36–43.

Lorenz, K. *On aggression.* New York: Harcourt, 1966.

Mallick, S. K., & McCandless, B. R. A study of catharsis of aggression. *Journal of Personality and Social Psychology,* 1966, *4,* 591–596.

McGinn, N. F., Harburg, F., Julius, S., & McLeod, J. M. Psychological correlates of blood pressure. *Psychological Bulletin,* 1964, *61,* 209–219.

Menninger, W. C. Recreation and mental health. *Recreation,* 1948, *42,* 340–346.

Meyer, R. G. The relationship of blood pressure levels to the chronic inhibition of aggression. Unpublished Ph.D. dissertation, Michigan State Univ., 1967.

Morris, D. *The naked ape.* New York: McGraw Hill, 1967.

Mosher, D. Measurement of guilt in females by self-report inventories. *Journal of Consulting and Clinical Psychology,* 1968, *32,* 690–695.

Nelsen, E. A. Social reinforcement for expression vs. suppression of aggression. *Merill-Palmer Quarterly,* 1969, *15,* 259–278.

Nisenson, R. A. Aggressive reaction to frustration in relation to the individual level of extrapunitiveness. *Journal of Personality Assessment,* 1972, *36,* 50–54.

Nowlis, V. Research with the Mood Adjective Check List. In S. S. Tompkins & C. Izard (Eds.), *Affect, cognition, and personality.* New York: Springer, 1965. Pp. 352–389.

Patterson, A. H. Hostility catharsis: A naturalistic quasi-experiment. Paper read at annual convention of American Psychological Association, 1974.

Patterson, G. R., Littman, R. A., & Bricker, W. Assertive behavior in children: A step toward a theory of aggression. *Monographs of the Society for Research in Child Development,* 1967, *32,* (5, Serial No. 113).

Pepitone, A., & Reichling, G. Group cohesiveness and the expression of hostility. *Human Relations,* 1955, *8,* 327–337.

Pytkowicz, A. R., Wagner, N., & Sarason, I. G. An experimental study of the reduction of hostility through fantasy. *Journal of Personality and Social Psychology,* 1967, *5,* 295–303.

Rosenbaum, M. E., & de Charms, R. Direct and vicarious reduction of hostility. *Journal of Abnormal and Social Psychology,* 1960, *60,* 105–111.

Rothaus, P., & Worchel, P. Ego-support communication, catharsis, and hostility. *Journal of Personality,* 1964, *32,* 296–312.

Ryan, E. D. The cathartic effect of vigorous motor activity on aggressive behavior. *Research Quarterly,* 1970, *41,* 542–551.

Scarpetti, W. L. Autonomic concomitants of aggressive behavior in repressors and sensitizers: A social learning approach. *Journal of Personality and Social Psychology,* 1974, *30,* 772–781.

Schachter, J. Pain, fear, and anger in hypertensives and normotensives: A psychophysiologic study. *Psychosomatic Medicine,* 1957, *19,* 17–29.

Schachter, S. The interaction of cognitive and physiological determinants of emotional state. In P. H. Leiderman & D. Shapiro (Eds.), *Psychobiological approaches to social behavior.* Stanford, California: Stanford Univ. Press, 1964.

Schill, T. R. Aggression and blood pressure responses of high- and low-guilt subjects following frustration. *Journal of Consulting and Clinical Psychology,* 1972, *38,* 461.

Singer, D. Aggression arousal, hostile humor, catharsis. *Journal of Personality and Social Psychology Monograph Supplement,* 1968, *8,* (1, Pt. 2).

Sosa, J. N. Vascular effects of aggression and passivity in a prison population. Unpublished Master's thesis, Florida State Univ., 1968.

Spence, K. W. A theory of emotionally based drive (D) and its relation to performance in simple learning situations. *American Psychologist,* 1958, *13,* 131–141.

Spiegel, S. B., & Zelin, M. Fantasy aggression and the catharsis phenomenon. *Journal of Social Psychology,* 1973, *91,* 97–107.

Stokes, A. Psycho-analytical reflections on development of ballgames. In A. Nathan (Ed.), *Sport and society.* London: Bowes and Bowes, 1958.

Stone, L. J., & Hokanson, J. E. Arousal reduction via self-punitive behavior. *Journal of Personality and Social Psychology,* 1969, *12,* 72–79.

Storr, A. *Human aggression.* New York: Atheneum, 1968.

Thibaut, J. W., & Coules, J. The role of communication in the reduction of interpersonal hostility. *Journal of Abnormal and Social Psychology,* 1952, *47,* 770–777.

Vantress, F. E., & Williams, C. B. The effect of the presence of the provocator and the opportunity to counteraggress on systolic blood pressure. *Journal of General Psychology,* 1972, *86,* 63–68.

Wheeler, L., & Caggiula, A. R. The contagion of aggression. *Journal of Experimental Social Psychology,* 1966, *2,* 1–10.

Wheeler, L., & Smith, S. Censure of the model in the contagion of aggression. *Journal of Personality and Social Psychology,* 1967, *6,* 93–98.

Wolpe, J., & Lazarus, A. *Behavior therapy techniques.* Oxford: Pergamon Press, 1966.

Worchel, P. Catharsis and the relief of hostility. *Journal of Abnormal and Social Psychology,* 1957, *55,* 238–243.

Worchel, P. Status restoration and the reduction of hostility. *Journal of Abnormal and Social Psychology,* 1961, *63,* 443–445.

Zillman, D. Excitation transfer in communication-mediated aggressive behavior. *Journal of Experimental Social Psychology,* 1971, *7,* 419–434.

Zillman, D., & Bryant, J. Effect of residual excitation on the emotional response to provocation and delayed aggressive behavior. *Journal of Personality and Social Psychology,* 1974, *30,* 782–791.

Zillman, D., Katcher, A. H., & Milavsky, B. Excitation transfer from physical exercise to subsequent aggressive behavior. *Journal of Experimental Social Psychology,* 1972, *8,* 247–259.

Research in the Control of Interracial Aggression[1]

EDWARD DONNERSTEIN

MARCIA DONNERSTEIN

Introduction

While large scale urban riots have become relatively infrequent in the last several years, the occurrence of more localized and direct racial confrontations has steadily increased. This is especially obvious in the public schools and in the military services. Incidents ranging in intensity from minor brawls to full-scale shipboard riots have occurred with such high frequency and have been so disruptive that racial problems have become a major concern of many educational and military professionals. Clearly, strategies are needed to control racial confrontations and aggressive interracial interactions. This chapter focuses upon a recent program of laboratory research devoted to this problem.

Although it has been noted (Katz, 1970) that there is a paucity of experimental behavioral work on interracial relations, results of an

[1] Preparation of this chapter was facilitated by Grant # DAHC19-75-G-0002 from the U.S. Army Research Institute for the Behavioral and Social Sciences, and Grant # 02-15-83 from the Office of Research and Projects at Southern Illinois University, to the authors. The comments of William Haythorn, Russ Clark, John Brigham, Steve McNeel, Arnie Kahn, Mike Latta, and Dave Wilson on various aspects of this research and chapter are appreciated.

133

increasing number of studies indicate that, in a variety of situations in which a white subject possesses no more information about another individual than his race, more negative responses will be directed toward black individuals than toward other white individuals. This pattern of results has been obtained in mixed-motive games (Wrightsman, O'Conner, & Baker, 1972), as well as in situations calling for altruistic, rewarding, and aggressive responses (e.g., Bryan & Test, 1967; Piliavin, Rodin, & Piliavin, 1969; Youssef, 1968). We have been particularly interested in the latter two forms of responding. For the past several years, a program of research has been underway in our laboratory to explore means of modifying interracial negative responses (i.e., minimally rewarding or highly aggressive responses). In a series of studies, the impact of variables, such as threat of retaliation (Donnerstein, Donnerstein, Simon, & Ditrichs, 1972; Donnerstein & Donnerstein, 1971; 1972), potential social censure (E. Donnerstein & M. Donnerstein, 1973), black–white attitude similarity (Donnerstein & Donnerstein, 1975), vicarious censure of interracial aggression (M. Donnerstein & E. Donnerstein, 1973), and exposure to minimal interracial aggression (Donnerstein & Donnerstein, 1976), have been explored. The present chapter summarizes the foregoing research in detail and examines its significance for strategies to control behavior in interracial interactions.

Here, we should note that although this chapter deals almost exclusively with interracial aggression, it is not divorced from other research that has studied aggression between members of the same race. It seems reasonable to suggest that aggression directed against blacks differs from that directed against whites only in the sense that instigations to aggressive actions are heightened in the former case. Thus, pairing an individual with a black target may be thought of as raising that individual's aggressive instigations much the same way that frustration or insult raises instigation. Therefore, the research to be summarized may be considered as relevant to more established work on aggression.

In addition to the implications which the present research may have for interracial aggression, it also bears very directly on more broadly based concerns involving the control of aggression. During the past few years, under impetus provided by such factors as the continuing war in Indochina, the rising crime rate, and the frequency of urban riots, the major emphasis of research in aggression has changed from a primary focus on instigating conditions (Buss, 1963) to one involving aggression control (Berkowitz, 1970). In the latter context, the effectiveness of a number of approaches involving heightening aggressive inhibitions, such as punishment (Parke & Walters, 1967), catharsis (Hokanson, 1970), retaliation (Baron, 1971a), and censure (Baron, 1972), have been explored. Generally, the results of this work have been interpreted as suggesting that aggression-inhibiting techniques may represent effective strategies for controlling aggressive behavior. Our research, however, clearly indicates that such a broad conclusion is probably not warranted. The effectiveness of inhibition-inducing strategies appears to be limited to situations in which threats of retaliation, censure, or punishment are present and viable. Any reduction in aggression obtained in these situations is not likely to generalize to similar situations in which such threats are not operative. Moreover, while some forms of more direct aggression may be reduced by increasing inhibitions, it has been found that other less direct types of such behavior actually are facilitated under these conditions. Given these considerations, it appears that permanent and general reductions in aggression may not be affected by increasing aggressive inhibitions and that other techniques must be explored. In the context of interracial aggression, the present chapter examines more general strategies for the control of aggression.

Inhibition-based Influences

There is wide agreement among many researchers that one may conceptualize aggression as a function of two kinds of variables: instigations and inhibitions. These variables are assumed to combine additively; aggression occurs only when the total of all instigations outweighs the total of all inhibitory influences. Given this model, two strategies for the reduction of aggression seem apparent. One involves increasing inhibitions against aggression to a point where they outweigh instigations toward such action; the other involves reducing instigations and holding inhibitions constant. Initial research in our research program was directed along the former lines, with the assumption that inhibitions are related to variables such as potential retaliation and potential censure.

The research program began with an attempt to affect inhibitions, since it was believed that naturally occurring events might have been acting to reduce aggressive responses toward blacks through this particular parameter.

The Expectation of Black Retaliation

It was believed, through anecdotal evidence, that there existed a fear of black retaliation among white individuals. That is, they expected that not only would blacks retaliate for an aggressive response but would, in fact, retaliate to a much greater degree than would a white target who had been aggressed against. If this were true, what effect would this expectation have on aggressive behavior? As noted by Dollard, Doob, Miller, Mower, and Sears (1939), "The strength of inhibition of any act of aggression varies positively with the amount of punishment anticipated to be a consequence of that act [p. 33]." We would, therefore, anticipate a reduction in aggressive behavior under conditions with the opportunity for retaliation.

Here. the question of concern is the *anticipated* effect of punishment on aggressive behavior. The interested reader is referred to Parke and Walters (1967) and Berkowitz (1970) for research pertinent to the effect of actual punishment on subsequent aggression. With respect to the present program of research, studies in which subjects have been informed that the target would have an opportunity to retaliate (Gillespie, 1961; Honhart, 1970; Shortell, Epstein, & Taylor, 1970; Baron, 1971a) have supported the notion that anticipated retaliation is an effective inhibitor of aggression.

In a study designed to examine the effects of potential retaliation on interracial aggression, Donnerstein *et al.,* (1972) allowed subjects to administer differential levels of shock to either a black or white target for errors ostensibly made on a learning task. For half the subjects, a camera was present in the experimental room, and subjects were introduced to the target via what was supposed to be closed-circuit TV. In actuality, it was a prepared video tape which allowed the experimenter to carry on a conversation with the target. For these non-anonymous subjects, the target had full knowledge of who was to administer the shock in the experiment. For the other half of the subjects, no camera was present, and the subject was assured of complete anonymity from the target. Various reasons concerned with proper experimental controls were given for the assumed anonymity. In addition, half of the subjects in each of these two conditions were informed that following the learning task performed by the target, the subject and target would switch roles, and shocks would be administered to the subject. The remaining subjects in each group were not given any information concerning role switching until after they had administered punishment to the target. Thus, we have allowed the opportunity for retaliation to operate under two conditions. First, the anonymity variable under non-anonymity allowed for potential retaliation outside the experimental situation. Results obtained in an earlier study (Donnerstein *et al.,* unpublished data) had indicated that under anonymous conditions white subjects were more aggressive toward a black target than when the target–subject relation was non-anonymous. However, certain confoundings (e.g., physical proximity) precluded any definite conclusions. A recent series of studies by Zimbardo (1970) has also indicated the facilitative effects of anonymity with regard to aggression. It could be suggested, however, that anonymity is not related to targer retaliation but to other processes (e.g., social censure). Thus, to get a more direct assessment of potential retaliation effects, the manipulation of role switching was also employed. As noted earlier, this operationally allows for target retaliation. While it was assumed that there existed a predisposition to be aggressive toward blacks, an independent measure of the type of aggressive intent that subjects attributed to the target was also needed. Consequently, following the administration of shock and after all subjects had been informed that they would be switching roles with the target, a procedure was introduced to gather data concerning subjects' anticipation of aggression from the target. The subject was informed that each time a signal light appeared on his panel he was to imagine he had made an incorrect response on a learning task. He was then to indicate the level of shock he expected to receive from the target. The subject was given a reasonable rationale for this procedure that was based on reasons related to proper experimental controls. It was possible, therefore, to examine two sets of data from our subjects: actual aggression delivered and anticipated aggression.

We should note, at this point, that throughout this research program two forms of aggression are examined. The first is a direct form of aggression that is related to the intensity of shocks administered. The second is a less direct or covert form of aggression based primarily on shock duration. This conceptualization of shock duration as an alternative form of aggression is supported by other researchers in the aggression field (e.g., Ring & Farina, 1969; Baron & Ball, 1974).

The first question might be what type of aggression did white subjects expect from the black target. An analysis of each form of aggression revealed that, independent of delivered aggression, subjects anticipated more direct aggression from a black than from a white target. An examination of the data indicated that subjects not only expected more aggressive behavior from a black target, but they expected the level of aggression to be greater than the level they themselves administered. This seems to indicate that not only do whites attribute aggressive intent to black targets, but that an expectation of heightened retaliation is anticipated. What occurs, then, when this expectation of retaliation is allowed to operate?

Results on the delivered aggression data indicated that opportunity for black retaliation was an effective inhibitor of direct aggressive responses. Under both non-anonymity and role switch conditions, subjects administered less aggression toward the black target than under conditions of anonymity and non-role switching (Figures 1 and 2). Interestingly enough, while there was less aggression toward black than white targets under the former conditions the reverse was obtained under the latter. Thus, given no opportunity for retaliation from the target, white subjects tended to behave more negatively toward a black target than white target.

The results of this initial study seem fairly convincing. It is of interest to note that in a pilot study (Donnerstein *et al.,* unpublished data), subjects were divided into high and low prejudice by their scores on the California F and E scales. There were no interactions between race of target and level of subjects' prejudice, with high F and E subjects being generally more aggressive. In addition, in the aforementioned retaliation study, there was minimal variability within any particular black target cell. These results seem consistent with those of Heller (1966)

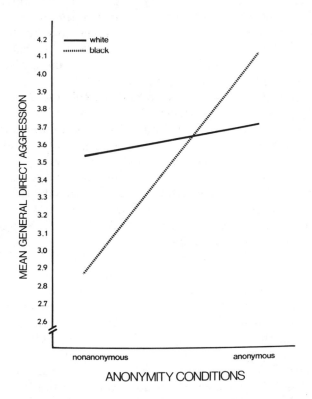

Figure 1. Mean direct aggression as a function of anonymity and race (From Donnerstein *et al.,* 1972).

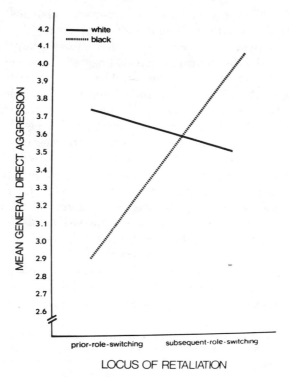

Figure 2.   Mean direct aggression as a function of role switching and race (From Donnerstein *et al.*, 1972).

and Baxter (1972) on mixed-motive games in which level of prejudice did not influence actual behavior toward a black target. More recently, Genthner and Taylor (1973), while examining interracial aggression, also obtained an insignificant effect for racial prejudice in relation to race of target.

The Effects of Vicarious Violence

Shortly after this study, a violent racial disturbance occurred at the university at which the first studies were conducted. Since this particular situation was analogous to those conditions that initially produced expectation of heightened retaliation from blacks, one might assume that such expectations would increase. If this were true, a reduction in aggressive responses would be expected in those conditions in which there was potential for black retaliation (e.g., non-anonymity). Another, and more plausible interpretation is based on the aggressive eliciting effects of observed violence (Berkowitz, 1962, 1964, 1965a,

1970, 1971). The general area of observed violence is reviewed elsewhere (cf. Singer, 1971; Weiss, 1969; Goranson, 1970, Geen, 1975) and is not of particular importance in the present context. Our main concern is with the theoretical notion that aggressive responses are more readily elicited when there are stimuli present that have been associated with the observed violence. This is the position essentially taken by Berkowitz, in that aggressive responses to aggressive stimuli are generally weak unless there are appropriate targets who are available and are in some way associated with the aggressive stimuli. It seems reasonable to assume, then, that the observation of the racial conflict elicited aggressive responses that a white subject would exhibit when confronted with a black target, who by his racial characteristics would become associated with the aggressive event. If this were true, we would expect an increase in aggressive responses to black targets, even under conditions of potential retaliation. A series of studies by Berkowitz and his colleagues (Berkowitz, 1965b; Berkowitz & Geen, 1966, 1967; Geen & Berkowitz, 1967) seem to substantiate the notion that targets who are associated with observed violence are likely to elicit aggressive responses. As recently noted by Goranson (1970):

> One possible, though speculative, implication that might be drawn from this area of research is that when members of minority groups having distinctive cue characteristics are repeatedly portrayed in the media as targets for aggression, there may be an increased likelihood that some member may, because of this association, become the victim of violence [p. 25–26].

In Experiment II by Donnerstein *et al.* (1972), white subjects were given an opportunity to administer shock to a black or white target under anonymous conditions. No information regarding role switching was given prior to aggressing. It was interesting to examine the effects of the racial disturbance by comparing subjects in analogous conditions prior to the disturbance. Results for anticipated aggression revealed that subjects still anticipated a higher level of aggression from a black than from a white target, but this showed no increase after the racial disturbance. For a direct measure of aggression, however, there was more aggression directed at the black target subsequent to the riot than before, regardless of target potential for retaliation (Figure 3). Thus, under both anonymous and non-anonymous conditions, subjects were more aggressive toward the black target. These results seem to indicate that the racial disturbance had resulted in an increase in aggressive instigation which was subsequently directed at those targets most similar to the instigating agent. With regard to the interaction of the inhibitions

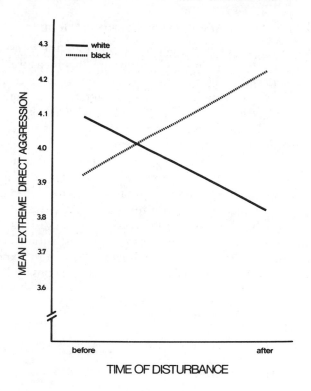

Figure 3. Mean direct aggression as a function of time of disturbance and race (Adapted from Donnerstein *et al.*, 1972).

and instigations toward aggressive responding, there are a few suggestive comments to be made. First, the level of inhibition had remained constant; there was still an expectation of retaliation. Second, the aggressive arousal on the part of the subject had increased. This increased instigation had now reached the point where it outweighed the level of inhibition. Finally, it suggests that threats of black retaliation might be an effective strategy in reducing direct forms of aggressive behavior. When threats become actual violence, however, the potential for retaliatory effectiveness may be lessened. It is interesting to note that, in a recent study by Genthner and Taylor (1973) in which subjects were both anonymous and under retaliation conditions, increased direct attack from either a black or white target facilitated the overall level of aggression. This occurred for both high- and low-prejudice subjects. Such findings tend to support the vicarious interpretation of the present results.

The Utilization of an Alternative Response Mode

There was an additional measure obtained in the present studies which was based primarily on shock duration. This measure, labeled *indirect aggression,* was suggested as a reflection of a more subtle and perhaps less cognitively mediated type of aggressive response. As was noted by Dollard *et al.* (1939) and Berkowitz (1962), the inhibition of direct aggression behavior can lead to the displacement of the aggression to another target, to another form, or both. In Experiment I, noted earlier, we found that less direct aggression was administered toward black targets under non-anonymous conditions, due presumably to the inhibitory effects of potential retaliation. In addition, however, subjects displayed a higher level of a form of hypothetically indirect aggression toward a black target under retaliation conditions (Figure 4). This finding is suggestive of the response substitution formulation alluded to earlier. The reduction in indirect aggression in Experiment II following the racial disturbance further supports this possibility.

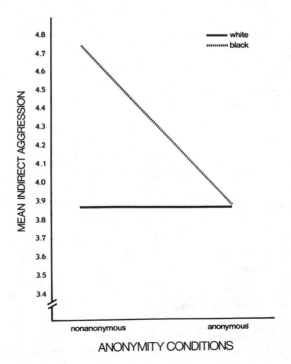

Figure 4. Mean indirect aggression as a function of anonymity and race (From Donnerstein *et al.*, 1972).

THE EFFECT OF RETALIATION ON NONAGGRESSIVE RESPONSES

At the beginning of this chapter, we noted research indicating the existence of a predisposition to behave negatively (not only aggressively) toward black targets. It would be interesting to investigate the effect potential retaliation might have on reducing these other negative responses. Research in mixed-motive games (Cederblom & Diers, 1970) and helping behavior (Bryan & Test, 1967; Wispe & Freshley, 1971; Gaertner & Bickman, 1971) has lent some tangential support to the effects of retaliation. In a more direct test, Donnerstein and Donnerstein (1972) paired subjects with either a black or white target in the same fashion as earlier studies. Rather than deliver differential shock for errors obstensibly made on a learning task, subjects were able to administer different amounts of reward to the target for correct responses. Reward consisted of points that could supposedly later be exchanged for financial payment. For every incorrect response presumably made by the target, subjects were to administer a fixed intensity shock, the duration of which was representative of an indirect form of aggression. All subjects were anonymous to the target; however, half the subjects were told that, subsequent to the first learning task, the subject and target would switch roles. The subject was told that he would be given a set amount of points, and, for every incorrect response, the target would deduct points that would later be exchangeable for money. For the remainder of the subjects, no mention was made of role switching.

Given all the information to this point, one might suggest that the delivery of a low-level reward could be considered as a negative-type response given the differential amounts that were available. Under this assumption, there would be a predisposition on the part of white subjects to deliver a lower reward level to a black target than to a white target. When there is opportunity for target retaliation, the reverse would be predicted. Results revealed that under conditions of anonymity and no opportunity for target retaliation, subjects administered a lower level of reward to a black than to a white target. When there existed opportunity for black reprisal, however, the reverse situation resulted (Figure 5). Thus, opportunity for black retaliation was effective in reducing other forms of negative behavior.

It is of more interest, however, to note the effects for indirect aggression. As seen in Figure 6, under conditions of role switching in which subjects administered a high-level reward to black targets, there were also concomitant increases for indirect aggression. Under conditions of non-role switching, subjects did not resort to an indirect form of aggression. This seems to suggest an extension of the original response

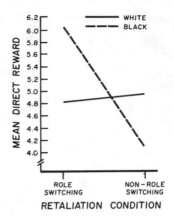

Figure 5. Mean level of reward as a function of role switching and race (From Donnerstein & Donnerstein, 1972).

substitution formulation of Dollard *et al.* (1939). It is apparent that the interaction of direct and indirect responses need not be of the same response class. When an individual is prevented from behaving in accordance with his predispositions and made to utilize a more positive type of behavior, concomitant increases in an indirect form of aggression are likely to arise.

Before proceeding, it is interesting to note that the target retaliation effect has not been found for black male subjects (Donnerstein & Donnerstein, 1971), while for black females the effect is dependent upon the level of anger arousal and race of target (Wilson & Rogers, 1975).

The Effects of Social Censure

Given the assumed limitations (indirect aggression) of potential retaliation as a means of influencing negative white behavior, it was important to examine alternative processes. One such process, which may be particularly important in view of increasing white gestures to promote racial equality, is that of potential in-group censure. It is generally recognized (Harding, Proshansky, Kutner, & Chein, 1969) that individuals are expected to behave in accordance with in-group attitudes and norms, and that failure to conform frequently results in the imposition of sanctions, such as loss of status, verbal condemnation, or group rejection. To the extent that advocacy of egalitarian racial relations by certain white groups contributes to the perception of in-group norms and attitudes as favoring nondiscriminatory behavior, whites in these groups may anticipate censure for negative actions towards blacks. Thus, the mere opportunity for in-group censure should act to reduce

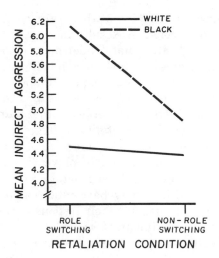

Figure 6. Mean indirect aggression as a function of role switching and race (From Donnerstein & Donnerstein, 1972).

negative behavior directed at black targets. More specifically, given liberal racial norms, the level of negative responses directed toward blacks should be lower under conditions favoring opportunity for in-group censure than under conditions reducing such opportunity. Research on the direct manipulation of social censure (Leftcourt, Barnes, Parke, & Schwartz, 1966; Wheeler & Smith, 1967; Baron, 1972; Dion, 1970) as well as indirectly through the labeling of aggression as unjustified (Albert, 1957; Berkowitz & Rawlings, 1963; Berkowitz, Corwin, & Heironimus, 1963; Berkowitz, 1965a; Berkowitz & Geen, 1967) have lent support to the notion that potential censure is effective in reducing aggressive responses.

E. Donnerstein and M. Donnerstein (1973) sought to examine the effects of potential censure in reducing negative responses toward a black target. White subjects were given an opportunity, in Experiment I, to administer differential shock levels to a black or white target, under conditions of anonymity to target and non-role switching. As noted earlier, studies in this series have found that such conditions are conducive to maximizing aggressive responses toward black targets. Half the subjects, however, were informed that their responses were being recorded via video for later use by the experimenter. For this group, then, another white individual possessed access to unambiguous information concerning how the subject had behaved. Therefore, this condition allowed for the opportunity of potential censure for negative responses toward black targets. The remaining subjects were given no information concerning the taping of their responses, thus, allowing no opportunity for in-group censure. Results on a direct form of aggression, as seen in Figure 7, indicated that, under noncensure conditions, subjects directed more aggression toward a black target than toward a white target. This, of course, was expected and replicates previous studies. Under potential censure, however, subjects reduced their aggression toward black targets to a level below that administered to white targets, thus allowing for the possibility of in-group censure to inhibit aggressive responses toward blacks. There were no race effects found for indirect aggression as was previously displayed in prior research. This could be accounted for, however, by a general procedural problem: Subjects under taping conditions may have intentionally depressed shock buttons longer in order to be sure their responses were being recorded. It was expected that Experiment II would alleviate this problem and that it would be possible to examine the effects of censure on an indirect form of aggression.

The second experiment allowed subjects to administer differential amounts of reward (money) to black or white targets under potential censure and noncensure conditions. In addition, a single fixed-intensity shock was delivered for incorrect responses ostensibly made by the target on the learning task. It was felt that distinctly separating the

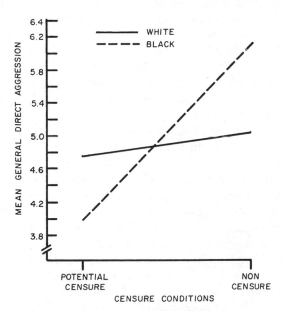

Figure 7. Mean direct aggression as a function of potential censure and race (From Donnerstein & Donnerstein, 1973).

shock button from the reward switches would alleviate the problem of subjects intentionally depressing buttons for longer durations. Results for a measure of direct reward were analogous to those found for aggression, as can be seen in Figure 8. When subjects were under conditions of noncensure, a lower level of reward was delivered to black than to white targets. These results tend to be similar to those obtained under conditions of potential retaliation (Donnerstein & Donnerstein, 1972).

The findings for indirect aggression suggested that potential censure affects inhibitions somewhat like retaliation. When subjects were presumably inhibited from administering a negative response (low reward) and were prevented from acting in accordance with their predispositions, they tended to resort to a more indirect form of aggression. Specifically, under conditions of potential censure, subjects administered a higher level of indirect aggression to black targets than under noncensure conditions (Figure 9). This finding seems to be consistent with

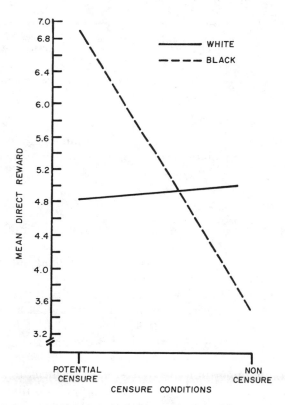

Figure 8.   Mean reward level as a function of potential censure and race (From Donnerstein & Donnerstein, 1973).

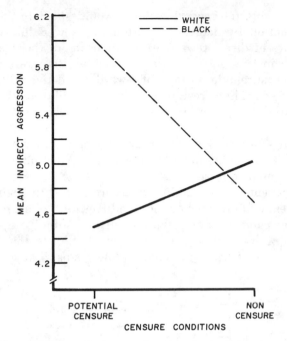

Figure 9. Mean indirect aggression as a function of potential censure and race (From Donnerstein & Donnerstein, 1973).

other research using rewarding responses (Donnerstein & Donnerstein, 1972) and research involving aggressive types of behavior (Donnerstein *et al.*, 1972).

Vicarious Censure

One further study in this series on inhibitions was intended to investigate the effects of vicarious-based censure or threat (M. Donnerstein & E. Donnerstein, 1973). A comparison was made of two kinds of threats: those which exert their influence directly on an aggressor (direct-based threats) and those which exert their influence through the observation of the experience of another individual (vicarious-based threats).

Subjects (white college students) were placed in a situation in which aggression is usually at a relatively high level. Specifically, they were provided with an opportunity to deliver electric shock to a black target under conditions in which the target was unaware of their identity and would not have an opportunity to retaliate. Prior to permitting subjects to deliver shock, operations associated with vicarious-based and direct-based threats were introduced. To manipulate vicarious-based threat, subjects were exposed to a white peer model delivering high intensity electric shocks to a black target. In one condition (vicarious censure), the behavior of the model was severely censured by the experimenter, while in a second condition (no vicarious censure), his behavior was allowed to pass without comment. To have a basis for assessing whether mere observation of aggression influenced aggressive behavior, a third condition (control) was also included. In this condition, subjects observed a model delivering shocks to a target, but the camera was positioned such that the specific buttons he depressed were not visible. As in the vicarious censure condition, the experimenter made no evaluative comments concerning the model's behavior. Following observation of the model, the direct threat manipulation was introduced. In this phase of the experiment, the probability that the subject himself would be censured for his aggressive actions was varied. Half of the subjects under each vicarious threat condition were told that their responses would be recorded on a video tape which subsequently might be viewed by an experimenter. Thus, half of the subjects were led to believe that another white individual possessed access to unambiguous information concerning how they had behaved. The other half of the subjects were given no information concerning taping of their responses and were generally led to believe that their actions were completely private.

Results indicated that direct aggression was reduced by both direct-based and vicarious-based threats (Figure 10). Lower direct aggression was delivered to black targets when response records were available to an experimenter (potential direct censure) than when such records were apparently not available (no potential direct censure). Similarly, lower direct aggression was delivered when a censured aggressive model (vicarious censure) was observed than when a noncensured aggressive model (no vicarious censure) or a model showing nonspecific behavior (vicarious control) was observed. In contrast, indirect aggression was generally facilitated by both direct and vicarious threats, with only their joint operation producing a suppressive effect. Under conditions in which only vicarious censure (vicarious censure, no potential direct censure) or only direct censure (vicarious control, potential direct censure) was operating, indirect aggression was higher than that displayed under conditions involving no censure (vicarious control, no potential direct censure). Where both vicarious censure and direct censure were operating (vicarious censure, potential direct censure), however, indirect aggression was markedly lower than that displayed under conditions involving no censure.

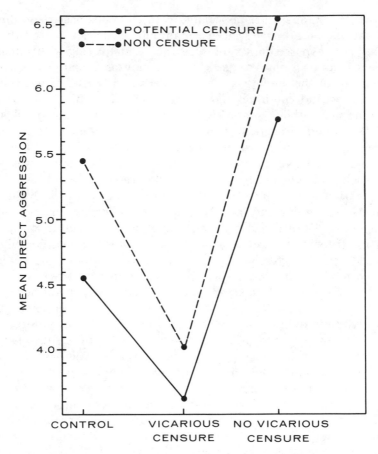

Figure 10. Mean direct aggression as a function of vicarious and potential censure (From Donnerstein & Donnerstein, 1974).

The Problem of Indirect Aggression

In all, the results of this first series of studies indicate that there exists a certain predisposition among whites to behave negatively toward black targets. Procedures that have manipulated potential retaliation and censure (both direct and vicarious) have been effective in reducing direct negative responses. The magnitude of this effect is exemplified by the finding of less negative responding toward a black target than toward a white target under these conditions. As Dollard *et al.* (1939) postulated, however, the inhibition of a direct aggressive response results in the displacement of the response to another target, another form, or both. The preceeding research program has shown that not only aggression but the blocking of other negative predispositions leads to the utilization of an indirect form of aggression. There are two questions which seem important at this point. First, suppose no mode of indirect aggression existed for the subject. Would this result in the subject not inhibiting his aggression? In other words, is the type of responding displayed by white subjects in these experiments merely a function of the inhibitory powers of retaliation and censure, or does the availability of an alternative response mode contribute to its effect. If it were true that an alternative response mode was not needed for inhibition to be effective, then one potential strategy would be to identify the particular alternative response and either rechannel it or eliminate it altogether. Given that such responses are rather subtle and most times in somewhat disguised form, however, the plausibility of this approach seems rather tenuous at best.

The other, and perhaps more realistic alternative, is to assume that such responses do occur and to consider their aversiveness. It is difficult to assess the extent to which increases in these indirect behaviors might counteract gains achieved through inhibition of more direct negative responses. In the foregoing series of studies, indirect aggression is related to duration of shock delivered. An examination of these data indicates that the mean difference in duration over censure and retaliation conditions was approximately .2 sec. In view of the fact that differences in shock intensity and monetary reward over conditions were extremely large, it appears that, in this particular case, the net effect of the operation of retaliation and censure is to produce a situation more advantageous to the black. It is possible, however, that alternative indirect responses may effectively negate any benefit derived from lowered direct behavior. Specifically, indirect responses may vary along a continuum of aversiveness, with those at the higher end detracting from the net gain obtained by the reduction of direct negative responses. A correlated possibility is that more aversive indirect responses are elicited when the net response strength of indirect aggressive behavior is high. Assuming that this strength is a function of the level of inhibition against direct aggression, various inhibitory influences may induce differentially aversive indirect aggressive responses. For example, inhibitions arising directly from the target may be relatively strong while those from sources more removed may be weaker. Thus, the use of target-based strategies, such as retaliation, may give rise to more aversive forms of indirect responding than in-group-based strategies involving potential censure. Of course, this is merely speculative, and it would be of interest for future research to explore these possibilities.

There is, however, still one additional problem. Whatever the degree of aversiveness of the indirect response, a direct mode of responding has been inhibited. This particular problem is considered by Megargee (1969) who notes that:

> By definition, response substitution and displacement take place only when inhibitions have blocked the expression of some aggressive response. As such, some additional instigation is likely to have resulted from the frustration induced by the original blocking. Moreover, by implication the substitute responses or targets are less satisfactory than the original. Therefore, we can infer that these mechanisms are generally less effective in reducing instigation to aggression, and that the individual who resorts to them probably has some residual instigation. If it does not decay with time or get reduced by some other means, this residual instigation might summate with other instigations to make the individual somewhat readier to respond aggressively than he would have otherwise [p. 1077].

Undoubtedly the problems associated with indirect aggression, particularly the form used in the present research program, are rather complex. Nevertheless, the data do seem to support this particular conceptual process of response substitution as formulated by Dollard *et al.* (1939). While these data and perhaps those of other researchers might only indicate that the process does in fact take place, its exact effect on interactions between individuals is still unclear and might remain so for some time. In light of this possibly ambiguous state of affairs, it seems more beneficial to explore methods that do not involve the inhibition of negative behaviors, but rather change the initial predisposition or instigation to behave negatively toward blacks. It was of interest in additional research in this series to investigate these possible alternatives.

Instigation-based Influences

Given the problems associated with indirect aggression, the most logical step, of course, is to reduce those particular aggressive responses through the reduction of aggressive instigation. A number of suggestions for this approach have been offered (e.g., Feshbach, 1964; Megargee, 1969; Kaufmann, 1965). Basically, the suggestions can best be narrowed down to two broad strategies. The first of these is through actual aggression against the target or through some form of displaced or vicarious aggression. There is no more controversial area in aggression theory, perhaps, than this particular reference to a cathartic process. This problem has been reviewed elsewhere (see Singer, 1971; Goranson, 1971; Berkowitz, 1965a; Weiss, 1969; Geen, 1975) and is not of immediate concern here. The notion of actual direct aggression against the anger instigator, however, has received some substantial support as a mechanism to reduce presumed aggressive arousal, at least under certain situations (Hokanson, 1970; Megargee, 1969). As Berkowitz (1964) noted, there is more involved than just an assumed reduction in aggressive drive:

> By encouraging the angry person to attack his frustrator we may actually provide him with these aggression-evoking cues (as well as lower his inhibitions by justifying such hostile acts). However, if he is thinking about aggressing against his tormentor and wants to do so . . . an inability to attack him is a frustration and may heighten his already aroused aggressive predispositions. Should he then be able to aggress against his anger instigator he may feel better . . . "Feeling better," however, does not in itself mean there is a lessened likelihood of attacking the anger instigator on some future occasion [p. 121].

There are obviously a number of problems associated with this particular approach. More important, however, is that fact that the aggressive response has actually occurred. The strategies that were mentioned with regard to inhibitions were at least able to eliminate the more overt and perhaps more aversive aspects of the aggressive response. Given this and the Berkowitz (1964) reasoning, it seems that a particular means of reducing negative behaviors toward blacks by in fact producing such behavior is not a very advantageous solution to the problem presented at the beginning of this chapter.

Another alternative is related to modifying the initial stimuli (cf. Feshbach, 1964; Megargee, 1969). The potential for this approach is best stated by Feshbach:

> The modification of the initial stimuli eliciting hostility is probably the most effective means of reducing aggressive drive . . . Those operating within the framework of a psychoanalytic drive model might argue that the hostility has been inhibitied or repressed and that it must be expressed in order for the drive tension to be reduced. The stimulus-mediating response model which has been presented here takes a simpler view of the matter. The stimulus situation has fundamentally changed and this new meaning evokes a new response. There is no need to satisfy aggressive drive because the stimulus conditions which provoked hostility are no longer present [p. 268].

This particular strategy attempts not only to reduce aggressive drive but also to reduce the probability of concomitant increases in indirect forms of aggression. Although how do you change the specific instigating stimulus? One way, for example, is to classify an instigating situation as unintentional, as when someone accidentally knocks against you. This situation might be taken as a physical attack, thus resulting in an increased instigation toward aggressive behavior. Interpreting the situation as an accident, however, arrests the development of an aggressive response and reduces the existing instigation at the time. The particular problem in the current research program, however, is not that easy. There is no situational instigation involved. The black targets do not anger subjects within the experimental session. The problem is essentially that the aggressive stimulus is not a particular act, such as attack, frustration, or insult, but it is an individual. The instigations are predispositions brought into the experimental situation, and the sight of the particular black target elicits the aggressive response. What must be changed is the whole aura surrounding the black target and the appropriate way for one to interact in a biracial situation. The stimulus is the target, and one must change certain characteristics about the stimulus and/or change the way in which subjects respond to the cues evoked by the stimulus. It was of interest, in subsequent research in this series, to investigate various techniques (e.g., attitudinal similarity and modeling) that might act to facilitate a reduction in aggressive instigation.

Attitudinal Similarity

In discussing problems associated with uncooperative behavior with black players in mixed-motive games, Wrightsman *et al.* (1972) have made the following statement:

> Another direction in which this research might go is to manipulate the information the subject receives in regard to the attitudes and personality of the other player of another race. For example, if the subject could be educated to see the Negro other player as being like himself, would he exploit less than when he sees him only in terms of his race? Rokeach's (1961) research on belief dissimilarity vs. racial dissimilarity would predict a lessened exploitation in such a case [p. 245].

These authors are suggesting essentially the same strategy alluded to earlier. While the possibility raised by Wrightsman *et al.* (1972) is merely speculative, one might, in fact, inquire as to the applicability of this method. The notion of presenting subjects with information indicating a similarity between the subject and a stranger is a well documented area of attraction research (Byrne, 1971).

Based on experiments (e.g., Rokeach, 1961; Byrne & Wong, 1962; Mezei, 1971; Hendrick, Bixenstine, & Hawkins, 1971) indicating that attitudinal similarity may influence attraction between racial groups, Byrne has proposed a relatively general theory of behavior in which attitude expressions are assumed to be an important determinant of a variety of overt evaluative responses, only one of which is attraction.

Specifically, Byrne suggests that similar attitudes act as positive reinforcers and elicit implicit positive affect. This positive affect then serves as a basis for the expression of a positive evaluative response. An analogous process is assumed to take place with respect to dissimilar attitudes. Dissimilar attitudes act as negative reinforcers, eliciting implicit negative affect and an overt negative evaluative response. If aggressive and rewarding behaviors are considered to be a type of evaluative response, this line of reasoning suggests that an important determinant of such behaviors may be the perceived attitudinal similarity between an individual and his victim.

Several recent studies bearing on this relationship have yielded inconsistent results. While Farina, Chapnick, Chapnick, and Misiti (1972) found lower aggression toward targets having similar political attitudes than toward those having dissimilar political attitudes, two other studies (Hendrick & Taylor, 1971; Baron, 1971b), which manipulated similarity in a more conventional way, failed to discern a relationship between attitudinal similarity and aggression. Clearly, the latter studies may be interpreted to cast doubt on the applicability of Byrne's conceptualization to aggressive behavior. An alternative possibility, however, is that their failure to find the hypothesized relationship was due to certain special aspects of the experimental situations that they employed. In both of these studies, two independent variables were manipulated: aggressiveness of the target and attitudinal similarity. Following introduction of the similarity manipulation, subjects were administered high-level or low-level electric shocks presumably by the target of aggression. Thus, subjects were susceptible to influence by the target's actions (aggression) as well as by his verbal statements (attitudinal similarity). Based on evidence indicating that an individual's behavior is influenced to a greater degree by another's actions than by another's verbal statements (Bryan & Walbek, 1970a,b), it seems reasonable to suggest that, in this situation, subjects' behavior may have been determined to a greater extent by the target's behaviorally expressed aggression than by his verbally expressed attitude statements. To the extent that presence of a more powerful variable may mask the influence of a weaker variable, studies treating target aggressiveness as a variable may have underestimated the effect of attitudinal similarity on aggression.

If this reasoning is correct, then attitudinal similarity should not be dismissed as a potentially important determinant of aggressive behavior. In fact, an approach based on similarity seems especially worthy of exploration since it may be more useful in controlling aggression than one based on threats involving retaliation or censure. As

noted earlier, Dollard *et al.*, (1939) suggest that, while inhibitory variables such as threats may be effective in reducing direct aggression, they
may actually operate to increase less direct aggressive responses. Presumably, the imposition of inhibitions increases frustration, and this
increased frustration acts to predispose an individual to heightened aggressive activity. Since direct aggressive behaviors are subject to greater
inhibitions, this heightened disposition is reflected in increased indirectly aggressive behaviors. In contrast, facilitation of indirect aggression should not occur where an approach based on attitudinal similarity is involved. If attitude statements are assumed to influence the
affect associated with an individual, such statements should operate to
modify aggressive instigations as opposed to aggressive inhibitions.
Dollard *et al.* suggest that, since such a modification does not influence
frustration, changes in instigations will have little effect on indirectly
aggressive behaviors.

Donnerstein and Donnerstein (1975) explored the relative effectiveness in controlling aggressive and rewarding behaviors of a strategy
based on heightening potential for retaliation and one based on increasing attitudinal similarity. It was of particular interest to determine
whether these two strategies operate in an analogous way to modify
direct aggression and direct reward while facilitating indirect aggression
to differential extents.

White college students were provided with an opportunity to deliver
aggression (electric shock) and reward (money) to a black or white
target for responses made on a learning task. Prior to administering
reinforcements, one half of the subjects in each target condition were
led to believe that they agreed with the target on a series of 14 attitude
items (attitude similar condition), while the other half were led to
believe that they agreed on only one of the 14 items (attitude dissimilar
condition). Moreover, in order to obtain some indication of the effectiveness of a strategy based on threat of retaliation, the probability of
retaliation against the subject was manipulated. Half of the subjects
under each similarity condition were told that they would subsequently
be switching roles with the target, while the other half were given no information concerning switching.

As can be seen in Figure 11, both retaliation and similarity were effective in controlling direct forms of aggression. Figure 12 also indicates
the same effect for rewarding responses. Thus, under conditions of attitudinal similarity, both black and white targets are treated equally. Of
more importance, however, is the results for an indirect form of aggression. As indicated by Figure 13, indirect aggression was only employed under conditions of potential retaliation from the black

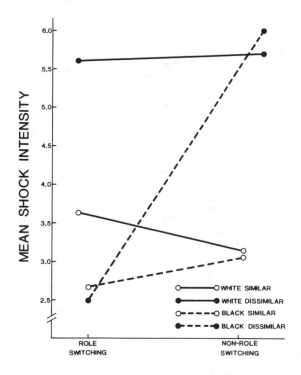

Figure 11.   Mean direct aggression as a function of retaliation, similarity, and race (From Donnerstein & Donnerstein, 1975).

dissimilar target. Therefore, while both retaliation and similarity were capable of controlling aggressive and rewarding responses, it is evident from the foregoing results that the methods employed differ.

In terms of controlling interracial aggression, the present data suggest that use of attitudinal similarity is generally more effective than use of retaliation. Introduction of attitudinal similarity was found to modify direct negative responses and did not give rise to concomitant increases in indirect aggression. Only under conditions involving an attitudinally similar target, however, did potential retaliation have an analogous salutary influence. Under conditions involving an attitudinally dissimilar target, reductions in direct reward and aggression were accompanied by increases in indirect aggression. Given that threats of retaliation influence inhibitions against aggression while modifications of affect toward an individual influence instigations toward such action, it appears that instigation-based, as opposed to inhibition-based, in-

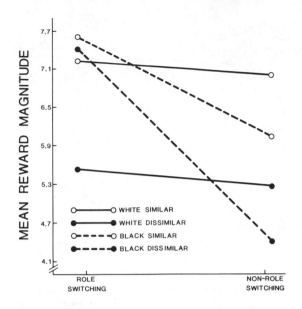

RETALIATION CONDITIONS

Figure 12. Mean reward level as a function of retaliation, similarity, and race (From Donnerstein & Donnerstein, 1975).

fluences may represent a more useful approach to the control of aggression. Strategies based on inhibitions may operate to control all types of aggression only under conditions such as target similarity, where the inhibitory influence is relatively small.

Observational Experience

There has been a large amount of research that indicates that exposure to aggressive models can facilitate aggressive behavior (e.g., Bandura, 1965; Aronfreed, 1969). As noted more recently by Krebs (1970), models make behavioral alternatives more salient in one of three ways. First, models give attention to a particular course of action and "increase the salience of social norms" (p. 268). Second, models set an example and create a type of normative standard, thus supplying some information as to appropriate behavior. Finally, models may indicate, in some instances, the consequences of a particular behavior alternative. Krebs (1970) has reviewed, in some detail, the research relevant to the effects of models on altruistic responses, and the reader is referred there for more information. One study of particular interest, however, is

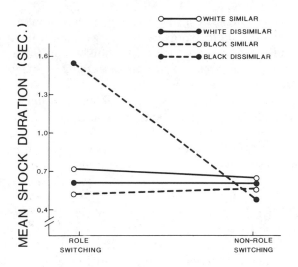

Figure 13. Mean indirect aggression as a function of retaliation, similarity, and race (From Donnerstein & Donnerstein, 1975).

that of Bryan and Test (1967) in which fewer contributions were given to a black Salvation Army solicitor than to white solicitor. In a separate experiment in which a white model made a donation, there was an increase in the amount of donations, and there was no difference in the number of donations received by the black or white solicitor. This study indicates that white models are effective in influencing at least altruistic types of behavior under conditions in which such behavior toward a black is normally minimal. With regard to aggression, a number of studies (Milgram, 1965; Wheeler & Smith, 1967; Gilmore, 1971; Walters & Willows, 1968; Baron & Kepner, 1970; Waldman & Baron, 1971; Baron, 1971c) seem to indicate that the observation of nonaggressive models is an effective means of reducing subsequent aggression, even in conditions where an aggressive response is most likely to occur (with the exception of Waldman & Baron, 1971). The effects of nonaggressive models in interracial interactions seem to be nonexistent. Epstein (1966) has shown, however, that an aggressive model raises the level of aggression (shock) to a black target as compared to a no-model control. It was interesting, in an additional study in our research program, to examine the effects of nonaggressive peer models in situations in which an aggressive response was directed toward black targets.

Donnerstein and Donnerstein (1976) gave white subjects an opportunity to aggress against a black target under anonymous, non-role switching conditions. Thus, subjects were in a condition that previous studies had indicated was conducive to a heightened form of direct aggression against black targets. Prior to aggressing, subjects observed a video tape depicting the assumed behavior of a previous subject (white model) interacting with the black target. The white model was shown administering high aggression (shocks), low aggression, or no aggression level was observable. Orthogonal to the model's behavior, subjects observed the black target administer high, low, or no indication of aggression. The aggressive behavior of the black was provided as one means of providing the subject with some information regarding the black target.

The results of this study supported the notion that observation of a nonaggressive white model is an effective means of controlling aggression toward black targets. More specifically, it was found that the highest level of aggression was administered by subjects who observed the high aggressive white model or unobservable white model. The finding of high aggression with a high white model was not surprising in view of the vast amount of research on the effects of aggressive models (e.g., Bandura, 1965). More important, however, was the finding that regardless of the level of black counter-aggression, subjects who observed a low-aggressive white model administered the least amount of aggression toward the black target.

The results of this study suggest that white models who display nonaggressive behavior toward a black target are effective in reducing aggressive behavior by other white subjects in a situation that is conducive for aggressive responses. Even more important was the finding that the reduction in aggression was not followed by concomitant increases in an indirect form of aggression. Thus, it was possible to change the predisposition to behave negatively toward the black target without in fact inhibiting the response and consequently redirecting the negative inclination. Future work may attempt to delineate other situations in which nonaggressive white models, and also counteraggression by blacks, play in determining subsequent interracial aggression.

Model Generality

Given the above data, it is interesting to speculate whether observation-based strategies may be used to control interracial behaviors in practical field situations. Considerable data suggests that white people display a large number of different negative behaviors toward blacks. Whites have been found to direct minimally altruistic and rewarding responses as well as highly competitive and aggressive responses. Clearly to deal with such a pervasive problem, any potentially useful strategy must influence a whole pattern of behavior, not merely a few selected responses. Whether a strategy based on observational experience can exert such a general effect is not clear. In the majority of experiments dealing with observational experience, the emphasis has been on controlling a single behavior by observation of an individual using that behavior in a specific way. Attempts have been made to reduce aggression by allowing subjects to view minimally aggressive behavior and to increase reward by allowing subjects to view altruistic or rewarding behaviors. These studies suggest that observational experience may exert a strong influence on behavior, but they give no information about the generality of such experience.

An additional pilot experiment was designed to explore further the influence of observational experience on both direct and indirect types of aggressive behavior (Donnerstein, Donnerstein, & Lipton, 1975). The particular focus was to determine whether observation of events other than those explicitly associated with aggressive interactions may produce changes in aggressive behavior. Clearly, it is possible that changes in aggression may be produced only through viewing a narrow range of closely related aggressive behaviors. For example, changes in aggression may be affected by observing nonaggressive or minimally aggressive behavior but may not occur as a function of observing other nonnegative events. An alternative possibility is that aggression may be influenced by observation of a relatively broad range of nonnegative response patterns. The likelihood of some kind of response generality is suggested by Bandura (1969). Bandura (1969) notes that observation of an event exerts an effect on the behavior of an observer by providing information concerning characteristics of appropriate responses. An observer presumably views a particular sequence, abstracts specific attributes of observed behaviors, and forms rules for generating similar behaviors. Under certain conditions, he then incorporates these rules into generalized behavioral orientations that operate to influence a broad class of responses. This line of reasoning suggests that considerable generality should be associated with observational experience, behavior in a particular situation being modified by observation of events containing responses that are highly similar to exhibited responses as well as by observation of events containing less similar responses.

In this initial study on generality (Donnerstein *et al.*, 1975), white college students were provided with an opportunity to administer electric shocks to a black target after being exposed to a white peer-model administering low shocks, high reward, or unspecified behavior.

Moreover, in order to obtain some indication of the relative effectiveness of a strategy based on observation and one based on increased inhibitions (retaliation), the probability of retaliation against the subject was manipulated. One half of the subjects under each observation condition was told that they would subsequently be switching roles with the target, while the other half was given no information concerning switching.

As can be seen in Figure 14, both retaliation and modeling were effective in reducing aggressive responses. It was only under retaliation conditions, however, that a type of indirect aggression was exhibited. Moreover, observation of a highly rewarding model was effective in reducing aggression. While the reduction in aggression was not as great as with the low aggressive model, the results support the generality effect of modeling.

An additional study on generality by Lipton (1973) has further demonstrated the general effects of modeling experience. In this study, it was found that helping behavior (assisting the black or white target with his experiment) could be facilitated by observation of a highly re-

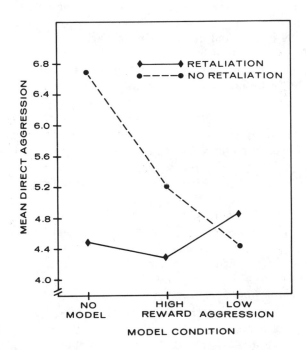

Figure 14. Mean direct aggression as a function of model condition and retaliation (From Donnerstein *et al.,* 1974).

warding model in a laboratory situation. Given these results and the aforementioned data, there is good evidence for a generality effect of modeling. It would be of interest for future research to further examine this line of research by investigating generality in terms not only of responses but across situations and targets.

Conclusion

In their discussion on reducing prejudice, Yinger and Simpson (1973) note:

> One of the most effective ways of learning about the nature of intergroup hostility is to study the techniques that are effective, and those that are ineffective, in reducing it; for such a study, to be valid, must be concerned with the causes and functions of that hostility [p. 96].

The intent of this chapter was to examine in some detail a current and ongoing program of research designed to answer the question of effective and ineffective "techniques" in the area of interracial aggression.

Initial work focused on the impact of relatively mild inhibitory influences involving threats of retaliation and potential social censure. In general, results indicated that, while such influences operate to reduce direct types of aggression, they tend to result in less directly aggressive responses. In view of this finding, more recent research has investigated the use of inhibitory influences of varying strengths. In line with previous studies, results suggested that strategies for the reduction of aggression that use mild inhibitions may be limited in their effectiveness. While reducing direct types of aggression, they may increase less direct forms of aggression. Strategies using stronger inhibitory influences or a combination of inhibitory influences, however, may be more effective in controlling aggressive behavior; these inhibitions operate to reduce both direct and indirect forms of aggression. Another line of research has focused primarily on the reduction of aggressive instigations using attitudinal similarity and observation of nonaggressive interracial interactions. These strategies were also found to be relatively effective, producing reductions in direct aggression while not increasing indirectly aggressive responses.

These studies do not answer all the questions which arise. They do suggest, however, a number of potential strategies for the control of interracial aggression. Simpson and Yinger (1973) have observed that the vast majority of research in interracial relations has been concerned with the "causes" of negative relations rather than with its reduction. Hopefully, this chapter has provided an impetus for further research on the reduction of interracial aggression and, in addition, has increased our understanding of aggression in general.

REFERENCES

Albert, R. The role of mass media and the effects of aggressive film content upon children's aggressive responses and identification choices. *General Psychological Monographs,* 1957, *55,* 221–285.

Aronfreed, J. The problem of imitation. In L. P. Lipsitt & H. W. Reese (Eds.), *Advances in child development and behavior.* Vol. 4. New York: Academic Press, 1969. Pp. 210–319.

Bandura, A. Vicarious processes: A case of no-trial learning. In L. Berkowitz (Ed.), *Advances in experimental social psychology.* Vol. 2. New York: Academic Press, 1965. Pp. 3057.

Bandura, A. *Principles of behavior modification.* New York: Holt, 1969.

Baron, R. A. Exposure to an aggressive model and apparent probability or retaliation from the victim as determinants of adult aggressive behavior. *Journal of Experimental Social Psychology,* 1971, *7,* 343–355. (a)

Baron, R. A. Aggression as a function of magnitude of victim's pain cues, level of prior anger arousal, and aggressor-victim similarity. *Journal of Personality and Social Psychology,* 1971, *18,* 48–54. (b)

Baron, R. A. Reducing the influence of an aggressive model: The restraining effects of discrepant modeling cues. *Journal of Personality and Social Psychology,* 1971, *20,* 240–245. (c)

Baron, R. A. Reducing the influence of an aggressive model: The restraining effects of peer censure. *Journal of Experimental Social Psychology,* 1972, *8,* 266–275.

Baron, R. A., & Ball, R. L. The aggression-inhibiting influence of nonhostile humor. *Journal of Experimental Social Psychology,* 1974, *10,* 23–33.

Baron, R. A., & Kepner, R. C. Model's behavior and attraction toward the model as determinants of adult aggressive behavior. *Journal of Personality and Social Psychology,* 1970, *14,* 335–344.

Baxter, G. W. Race of other player, information about other player, and cooperation in a two-person game. In Wrightsman, O'Conner, & Baker (Eds.), *Cooperation and competition: Readings on mixed-motive games.* Belmont: Brooks/Cole, 1972.

Berkowitz, L. *Aggression: A social psychological analysis.* New York: McGraw-Hill, 1962.

Berkowitz, L. Aggressive cues in aggressive behavior and hostility catharsis. *Psychological Review,* 1964, *71,* 104–122.

Berkowitz, L. Some aspects of observed violence. *Journal of Personality and Social Psychology,* 1965, *2,* 359–369. (a)

Berkowitz, L. The concept of aggressive drive: Some additional considerations. in L. Berkowitz (Ed.), *Advances in experimental social psychology.* Vol. 2. New York: Academic Press, 1965. Pp. 301–338. (b)

Berkowitz, L. The control of aggression. In B. Caldwell & H. Ricciuti (Eds.), *Review of child development research.* Vol. 3. New York: Russell Sage Foundation, 1970.

Berkowitz, L. The contagion of violence: An S-R mediational analysis of some effects of observed aggression. In W. J. Arnold, & M. M. Page (Eds.), *Nebraska symposium on motivation,* 1970. Vol. XVIII. Lincoln: Univ. of Nebraska Press, 1971. Pp. 95–136.

Berkowitz, L., Corwin, R., & Heironimus, M. Film violence and subsequent aggressive tendencies. *Public Opinion Quarterly,* 1963, *27,* 217–229.

Berkowitz, L., & Geen, R. G. Film violence and the cue properties of available targets. *Journal of Personality and Social Psychology,* 1966, *3,* 525–530.

Berkowitz, L., & Geen, R. G. Stimulus qualities of the target of aggression: A further study. *Journal of Personality and Social Psychology,* 1967, *5,* 364–368.

Berkowitz, L., & Rawlings. Effects of film violence on inhibitions against subsequent aggression. *Journal of Abnormal and Social Psychology,* 1963, *66,* 405–412.

Bryan, J. H., & Test, M. A. Models and helping: Naturalistic studies in aiding behavior. *Journal of Personality and Social Psychology,* 1967, *6,* 400–407.

Bryan, J. H., & Walbek, N. Preaching and practicing self sacrifice: Childrens' actions and reactions. *Child Development,* 1970, *41,* 329–353. (a)

Bryan, J. H., & Walbek, N. The impact of words and deeds concerning altruism upon children. *Child Development,* 1970, *41,* 747–757. (b)

Byrne, D. *The attraction paradigm.* New York: Academic Press, 1971.

Byrne, D., & Wong, T. J. Racial prejudice, interpersonal attraction, and assumed dissimilarity of attitudes. *Journal of Abnormal and Social Psychology,* 1962, *65,* 246–253.

Buss, A. Physical aggression in relation to different frustrations. *Journal of Abnormal and Social Psychology,* 1963, *67,* 1–7.

Cederblom, D., & Diers, C. J. Effects of race and strategy in the prisoner's dilemma (PD) game, *Journal of Social Psychology,* 1970, *81,* 275–276.

Dion, K. L. Determinants of unprovoked aggression. Unpublished doctoral dissertation, Univ. of Minnesota, 1970.

Dollard, J., Doob, L. W., Miller, N. E., Mower, O. H., & Sears, R. R. *Frustration and Aggression.* New Haven: Yale University Press, 1939.

Donnerstein, E., & Donnerstein, M. Variables affecting black aggression. *Journal of Social Psychology,* 1971, *84,* 157–158.

Donnerstein, E., & Donnerstein, M. White rewarding behavior as a function of the potential for black retaliation. *Journal of Personality and Social Psychology,* 1972, *24,* 327–333.

Donnerstein, E., & Donnerstein, M. Variables in interracial aggression: Potential ingroup censure. *Journal of Personality and Social Psychology,* 1973, *27,* 143–150.

Donnerstein, E., & Donnerstein, M. The effect of attitudinal similarity on interracial aggression. *Journal of Personality,* 1975, *43,* 485–502.

Donnerstein, E., Donnerstein, M., Simon, S., & Ditrichs, R. Variables in interracial aggression: Anonymity, expected retaliation, and a riot. *Journal of Personality and Social Psychology,* 1972, *22,* 236–245.

Donnerstein, M., & Donnerstein, E. Direct and vicarious censure in the control of aggression. Paper presented at *Southeastern Psychological Association,* New Orleans, 1973.

Donnerstein, M., Donnerstein, E., & Lipton, S. Modeling generality in the control of interracial aggression. Paper presented at *Southeastern Psychological Association,* Miami, 1975.

Donnerstein, M., & Donnerstein, E. Variables in interracial aggression: Exposure to aggressive interracial interactions. *Journal of Social Psychology,* 1976, in press.

Epstein, R. Aggression toward outgroups as a function of authoritarianism and imitation of aggressive models. *Journal of Personality and Social Psychology,* 1966, *3,* 574–579.

Farina, A., Chapnick, B., Chapnick, J., & Misiti, P. Political views and interpersonal behavior. *Journal of Personality and Social Psychology,* 1972, *22,* 273–278.

Feshbach, S. The function of aggression and the reputation of aggressive drive. *Psychological Review,* 1964, *71,* 257–272.

Gaertner, S., & Bickman, L. Effects of race on the elicitation of helping behavior: The wrong number technique. *Journal of Personality and Social Psychology,* 1971, *20,* 218–22.

Geen, R. G. Some effects of observing violence upon the behavior of the observer. In B. Maher (Ed.), *Progress in experimental personality research,* Vol. 8. New York: Academic Press, 1975.

Geen, R., & Berkowitz, L. Name-mediated aggressive cue properties. *Journal of Personality,* 1967, *34,* 456–465.

Genthner, R. W., & Taylor, S. P. Physical aggression as a function of racial prejudice and the race of the target. *Journal of Personality and Social Psychology,* 1973, *27,* 207–210.

Gillespie, J. F. Aggression in relation to frustration, attack, and inhibition. Unpublished doctoral dissertation, Univ. of Pittsburg, 1961.

Gilmore, J. B. Implications for a theory of contagion from an experiment invoking model self-censure. *Journal of Social Psychology,* 1971, *85,* 195–208.

Goranson, R. E. Media violence and aggressive behavior: A review of experimental research. In L. Berkowitz (Ed.), *Advances in experimental social psychology.* Vol. 5. New York: Academic Press, 1970. Pp. 2–33.

Harding, J., Proshansky, H., Kutner, B., & Chein, I. Prejudice and ethnic relations. In G. Lindzey, & E. Aronson, (Eds.), *The handbook of social psychology.* (2nd ed.). Vol. V. Reading, Massachusetts: Addison Wesley, 1969.

Heller, J. R. The effects of racial prejudice, feedback strategy, and race on cooperative-competitive behavior. Unpublished doctoral dissertation, Univ. of California at Berkeley, 1966.

Hendrick, C., Bixenstine, V. E., & Hawkins, G. Race versus belief similarity as determinants of attraction: A search for a fair test. *Journal of Personality and Social Psychology,* 1971, *17,* 342–349.

Hendrick, C., & Taylor, S. P. Effects of belief similarity and aggression on attraction and counteraggression. *Journal of Personality and Social Psychology,* 1971, *17,* 342–349.

Hokanson, J. E. Psychophysiological evaluation of the catharsis hypothesis. In E. Megargee & J. E. Hokanson (Eds.), *The dynamics of aggression.* New York: Harper, 1970. Pp. 74–86.

Honhart, B. B. An investigation of catharsis: Overt aggression and heart rate as functions of retaliation and arousal and opportunity for aggression. Unpublished doctoral dissertation, Univ. of Iowa, 1970.

Katz, I. Experimental studies of Negro-white relationships. In L. Berkowitz (Ed.), *Advances in experimental social psychology,* Vol. 5, New York: Academic Press, 1970. Pp. 71–119.

Kaufmann, H. Definitions and methodology in the study of aggression. *Psychological Bulletin,* 1965, *64,* 351–364.

Krebs, D. L. Altruism—an examination of the concept and a review of the literature. *Psychological Bulletin,* 1970, *73,* 258–302.

Leftcourt, H. M., Barnes, K., Parke, P., & Schwartz, F. Anticipated social censure and aggression-conflict as mediators of response to aggression induction. *Journal of Social Psychology,* 1966, *70,* 251–263.

Lipton, S. L. Observation of models and the potential for generalization. Unpublished M. A., Southern Illinois Univ., 1973.

McGuire, W. M. The nature of attitudes and attitude change. In G. Lindzey & E. Aronson

(Eds.), *The handbook of social psychology.* (2nd ed.) Vol. 3. Reading, Massachusetts: Addison-Wesley, 1969.

Megargee, E. I. The psychology of violence: A critical review of theories of violence. *National Commission on the Causes and Prevention of Violence, Task Force III: Individual acts of violence.* Washington, D.C.; U.S. Government Printing Office, 1969.

Mezei, L. Perceived social pressure as an explanation of shifts in the relative influence of race and belief on prejudice across social interactions. *Journal of Personality and Social Psychology,* 1971, *19,* 69–81.

Milgram, S. Liberating effects of group pressure. *Journal of Personality and Social Psychology,* 1965, *1,* 127–134.

Parke, R. D., & Walters, R. H. Some factors influencing the efficacy of punishment training for inducing response inhibition. *Monographs of the Society for Research in Child Development,* 1967, *32* (1, Serial No. 109).

Piliavin, I. M., Rodin, J., & Piliavin, J. M. Good samaritanism: An underground phenomenon. *Journal of Personality and Social Psychology,* 1969, *4,* 280–299.

Ring, K., & Farina, A. Personal adjustment as a determinant of aggressive behaviors toward the mentally ill. *Journal of Consulting and Clinical Psychology,* 1969, *3,* 683–690.

Rokeach, M. Belief versus race as determinants of social distance: Comment on Triadis' paper. *Journal of Abnormal and Social Psychology,* 1961, *62,* 187–188.

Rokeach, M., Smith, P. W., & Evans, R. I. Two kinds of prejudice or one? In M. Rokeach (Ed.), *The open and closed mind.* New York: Basic Books, 1960. Pp. 132–168.

Shortell, J., Epstein, S., & Taylor, S. P. Instigation to aggression as a function of degree of defeat and the capacity for massive retaliation. *Journal of Personality,* 1970, *38,* 313–328.

Simpson, G. E., & Yinger, J. M. Techniques for reducing prejudice: Changing the situation. In P. Watson (Ed.), *Psychology and race.* Chicago: Aldine, 1973.

Singer, J. L. The influence of violence portrayed in television or motion pictures upon overt aggressive behavior. In J. L. Singer (Ed.), *The control of aggression and violence,* New York: Academic Press, 1971. Pp. 19–60.

Waldman, D. M., & Baron, R. A. Aggression as a function of exposure and similarity to a nonaggressive model. *Psychonomic Science,* 1971, *23,* 381–383.

Walters, R. H., & Willows, D. C. Domitative behavior of disturbed and nondisturbed children following exposure to aggressive and nonaggressive models. *Child Development,* 1968, *39,* 79–89.

Weiss, W. Effects of the mass media of communication. In G. Lindzey, & E. Aronson (Eds.), *The handbook of social psychology.* (2nd ed.) Vol. 5. Reading, Massachusetts: Addison-Wesley, 1969. Pp. 77–195.

Wheeler, L., & Smith, S. Censure of the model in the contagion of aggression. *Journal of Personality and Social Psychology,* 1967, *6,* 93–98.

Wilson, L., & Rogers, R. W. The fire this time: Effects of race of target, insult, and potential retalitation on black aggression. *Journal of Personality and Social Psychology,* in press.

Wispe, L. G., & Freshley, H. B. Race, sex, and sympathetic helping behavior: The broken bag caper. *Journal of Personality and Social Psychology,* 1971, *17,* 59–65.

Wrightsman, L. S., O'Conner, J., & Baker, N. J. *Cooperation and competition: Readings on mixed-motive games.* Belmont, California: Brooks/Cole, 1972.

Yinger, J. M., & Simpson, G. E. Techniques for reducing prejudice: Changing the prejudiced person. In P. Watson (Ed.), *Psychology and race.* Chicago: Aldine, 1973.

Youssef, A. I. The role of race, sex, hostility, and verbal stimulus in inflicting punishment. *Psychonomic Science,* 1968, *12,* 285–286.
Zimbardo, P. S. The human choice: Individuation, reason, and order versus deindividuation, impulse, and chaos. In W. J. Arnold & D. Levine (Eds.), *Nebraska symposium on motivation, 1969.* Vol. 17. Lincoln: Univ. of Nebraska Press, 1970. Pp. 237–307.

The Environmental Psychology of Aggression

EDGAR C. O'NEAL

PETER J. MCDONALD

Introduction

Although belatedly, environmental quality has become a public concern as a result of a growing awareness of the potentially harmful effects of pollution, crowding, and radiation upon our bodily well-being. It is now also clear that behavioral deterioration may result from unfavorable environmental conditions (Calhoun, 1962), and a new discipline, environmental psychology (Wohlwill, 1970), has emerged to investigate behavior in its natural (or unnatural) settings. With regard to aggression, a number of possible environmental determinants, including heat, noise, and crowding, have been the subject of literary treatments and speculation (e.g., Ardrey, 1966; Lorenz, 1966). The purpose of this chapter is to examine the experimental evidence linking such environmental parameters to aggression. Before doing so, however, it is appropriate to propose a tentative list of mechanisms to account for causal links between the physical setting and aggression.

First, and perhaps most obvious, is the possibility that, in some cases, aggression may be instrumental to the reduction of an aversive quality of the environment or to freer access to appetitive resources. Or put in functional terms, aggression, especially in the face of environmental privation, may serve to enhance individual or species survival.

In addition, the stimulus properties of the environment may evoke inherited or learned aggressive behaviors. Frequently cited examples would include the presence of a territorial intruder (O'Neal, Caldwell, & Gallup, 1976) or of a weapon (Berkowitz, 1969). It has been variously suggested that such a stimulus may serve as an "ethological releaser" to aggressive behavior patterns (Berkowitz, 1969) or as a discriminative stimulus (Hanratty, O'Neal, & Sulzer, 1972).

A third way in which the environment may influence aggression is through the drive effects of an environmental condition such as noise, heat, or crowding. An arousing stimulus can serve to increase the probability of a prepotent aggressive response (Bandura, 1973) or increase responsiveness to aggressive cues (Berkowitz, 1969).

The environment may also provide barriers and physical limits that affect the probability of aggressive behaviors. Ten violent criminals housed in separate cells would have very little opportunity to assault each other, but a bloodbath would be the probable result of assigning them all to the same cell. Physical barriers often serve as society's ultimate safeguard against aggression when other controls are found to be less than effective deterrents. Confinement, isolation, and crowding are often the result of environmental constraints and frequently influence the likelihood of aggressive encounters.

In the case of aggression among humans, two additional processes may be cited which, in some situations, link environment with aggression. In an unfamiliar environment, especially in one that affords anonymity, norms that proscribe aggression may be less salient or their behavioral effects reduced (Zimbardo, 1969). The sanctions against norm violation (e.g., ruined reputation, social isolation, criminal apprehension) are not as strong as they are in a familiar setting or in one in which the individual's identity is known.

Finally, aggressiveness may be influenced by what an individual believes to be the influence of a given environmental condition, whether that belief is valid or not. For example, while theories relating lunar phase and violent crimes have largely been discredited (Pokorny & Jachimczyk, 1974), a given individual's belief in such a mythical relationship may well provide justification for an aggressive act. An individual otherwise inhibited about expressing his hostilities may react aggressively if he believes that a quality of the environment is "making" him do so.

In considering the effects of any one environmental parameter upon aggressiveness, it is probably a mistake to think simply in terms of only one of these mechanisms. Usually it is apparent that two or more are operative, and only a multifaceted approach is likely to produce models that allow for the type of predictions needed to solve social problems. All of these processes will be utilized in the following discussion, which will focus first on the effects of two physical parameters of the environment (heat and noise) upon aggression, and then on the effects of others' presence.

The Physical Environment and Aggression

Noise

Recently, noise levels in our cities have attracted the alarmed attention previously accorded only to air pollution and radiation (cf. Baron, 1970; Solomon, 1970). Noise of the intensities routinely encountered in urban living can produce deafness (Kryter, 1970), but psychological stress turns out to be related not so much to the intensity of noise as to its predictability and controllability (Glass & Singer, 1972). We often voluntarily expose ourselves to noise in intensities that cause permanent hearing loss (e.g., Dey, 1970). Physiological arousal, however, is produced by noise of intensity in excess of 60 dB (Kryter, 1970), whether or not the noise is predictable, controllable, or annoying (Glass & Singer, 1972). Apparently, after prolonged exposure, such arousal eventually diminishes.

The possibility that noise-induced arousal would increase aggressiveness was investigated by Geen and O'Neal (1969). Prior to the experiment, some care was taken to determine the intensity of white noise that would be stimulating but would not be reported as annoying (60 dB). The subjects were not angered in any way, but half were shown a brief segment from an aggressive boxing film and half, a clip from a nonaggressive sports film. They then read a standard solution to a human relations problem ostensibly written by an experimental accomplice posing as a subject in another experiment running concurrently. At this point, the experimenter instructed the subject to communicate his evaluation of the confederate's answer by giving him from 1 to 10 electric shocks. The subject could choose from among 10 "intensity" buttons in delivering the shock and was told to give more, severe shocks for a poor solution and fewer, mild shocks for a good solution. Earphones, "to mask out distracting outside noises," were worn by the subjects while evaluating the solution, and half the subjects heard the white noise while half heard nothing.

The amount of shock delivered (summation of intensities across number given) is presented in Table 1, and one can see that the noise

Table 1 Total Shock as a Function of Noise and Film Condition[a,b]

	Film condition	
	Aggressive	Nonaggressive
White noise	22.25$_a$	10.33$_b$
No noise	12.75$_b$	14.75$_{a,b}$

[a] Based on data from Geen and O'Neal, 1969.

[b] Cells having common subscripts are not significantly different at the .05 level by a Duncan multiple range test.

only increased the aggressiveness of those subjects who had seen the aggressive film. It is interesting to note that the simple number of shocks delivered—a measure that would seem to be sensitive to the motoric effects of activation or arousal—was reliably increased irrespective of film condition. The results of this experiment, then, suggest that noise can facilitate aggression, and the effect is more marked after exposure to aggressive cues.

A study reported by Knipmeyer and Prestholdt (1973) produced evidence supporting the Geen and O'Neal conclusions and extending their range of applicability. Knipmeyer and Prestholt's college student subjects believed they were testing a "passive resister" who was, in fact, an experimental stooge. The subjects were run in same-sexed groups of three and, for 3 min, were supposed to throw foam rubber balls at the victim, who was always of their own sex. The episodes were videotaped, and observers blind to experimental condition counted the number of balls thrown by each subject and rated his aggressiveness. During the test period, audio speakers in the room either produced 80-dB white noise, boxing-match crowd noise of approximately the same intensity, or were silent.

The total number of balls thrown by the subjects is presented in Table 2. The presence of environmental noise resulted in significantly more balls thrown by male and female subjects at the victim, an effect that held regardless of noise type. The same pattern of results was produced by the judge's ratings of the subjects' aggressiveness. In this study then, a somewhat more intense noise than that employed by Geen and O'Neal (1969) produced effects that were not at all dependent on the more aggressive cue content of the boxing-match noise.

There is evidence, however, that the noise–aggression relationship may be profoundly influenced by the person's attributions regarding the arousal produced by noise. Harris and Huang (1974) reported that subjects who were told to expect arousal following exposure to noise were less aggressively responsive to a verbal insult than were subjects led to expect other aftereffects of the noise. The investigators argue that this is the result of arousal-forewarned subjects misattributing their anger arousal to the noise.

In a very recent study, Konečni (1975) exposed subjects either to a 73-dB tone or a 97-dB tone after having been either insulted or not insulted. Subjects hearing the louder tone delivered more shocks to a confederate than did those hearing the softer tone, only if they had been angered. In interpreting his results, Konečni favors an explanation similar to Zillmann's (1971) "excitation transfer" position on arousal–aggression relationships; that is, angered subjects were able to label their noise-induced arousal as more anger and, therefore, aggressed more than noninsulted subjects. It is worth noting in passing that comparison of the Konečni results with those of studies mentioned earlier is very difficult because the tone used by Konečni in his lower intensity condition (73 dB) is substantially louder than the higher intensity noise employed in the other studies.

There are very few studies of noise–aggression relationships to report. Obviously, work needs to be done varying noise intensity systematically to determine its effects upon both angered and nonangered subjects. Also, the recent research reported by Mathews, Canon, and Alexander (1974) and by Sherrod and Downs (1974) suggests that noise may have "deindividuating" effects, a possible noise–aggression linkage yet to be explored. Finally, in considering the applicability of the studies reviewed in this section to outside-of-laboratory behavior, it is appropriate to point out that the most likely target of aggression, when someone is subjected to annoying noise, is the person perceived to be responsible for his discomfort. In the experimental studies, the subject has not been placed in the position where he is able either to stop the noise by

Table 2   Total Number of Balls Thrown as a Function of Noise Condition and Subject's Sex[a]

	Subject's sex	
Noise condition	Males	Females
White noise	84.3	80.7
Crowd noise	81.7	81.7
No noise	76.7	62.3

[a] Based on data from Knipmeyer and Prestholdt, 1973.

his hostile reactions or to retaliate against his real tormentor, the experimenter.

Heat

Of the possible environmental determinants of aggression, heat is perhaps most often implicated in popular accounts. A heat–aggression relationship is suggested by such expressions as, "hot under the collar," or "hot and bothered." A considerable body of descriptive evidence (e.g., Goranson & King, 1970; Robbins, Dewalt, & Pelto, 1972; Schwartz, 1968; U.S. Riot Commission, 1968) is consistent with the truism that high temperature facilitates the occurrence of aggression. A number of laboratory studies with animals (e.g., Berry & Jack, 1971; Greenberg, 1969, Ulrich & Azrin, 1962) also suggest heat as a reliable precursor of violence. Greenberg (1969), for example, found a positive relationship between ambient temperature and frequency of aggressive responding in mice for temperatures up to 95°F. Above this point, all forms of motor activity were severely reduced.

Two laboratory studies with human subjects (Griffitt, 1970; Griffitt & Veitch, 1971) also provide evidence indirectly supporting the view that heat increases aggression. In these studies, high ambient temperature led subjects to indicate a low level of liking for hypothetical strangers. If it is assumed that one is more likely to aggress against a disliked as compared to a liked target (cf. Baron & Kepner, 1970), the results of the Griffitt studies offer support for a heat–aggression link. In none of the aforementioned studies, however, has there been an experimental attempt to establish the effects of high ambient temperature upon overt aggression in humans or to identify possible mediators of a heat–aggression relationship.

It may be argued (cf. Baron & Bell, 1975) that high ambient temperature indirectly influences aggression via its arousal properties and the subsequent energization of dominant responses. Studies employing both physiological (e.g., Okuma, Funimori, & Hayashi, 1965) and behavioral (e.g., Provins & Bell, 1970) indices of arousal have documented that heat is arousing. In reference to the enhancement of dominant responses, Rohles (1967) found that high ambient temperature facilitated both verbal and physical aggression in prison parolees and juvenile delinquents but had no effect on the aggressive behavior of graduate students. Assuming that aggressive responses were more dominant for the prison parolees and juvenile delinquents than for the graduate students, these results suggest a possible arousal mediator in the heat–aggression link. Similarly, Baron and Lawton (1972) found that high ambient temperature facilitated aggressive responding only in those subjects who had previously been provoked and had observed an aggressive model. There was also a tendency, however, for high temperature to inhibit aggression in those angered subjects not exposed to the modeling influence.

Perhaps the most direct, albeit negative, evidence regarding the proposed heat–aggression relationship is that provided in three recent studies by Baron and his colleagues (Baron, 1972; Baron & Bell, 1975, in press). In the first (Baron, 1972), male subjects were either angered or not angered by a confederate prior to being given an opportunity to retaliate. Half of the subjects performed under normal temperature conditions; half performed under hot temperature conditions. It was expected that high ambient temperature would be most effective in facilitating aggression in those subjects who had been angered. The results for the shock intensity measure indicated that high ambient temperature actually inhibited aggression, both in angered and non-angered subjects. A similar pattern of results was obtained for the duration measure.

In the second study (Baron & Bell, 1975), male subjects were either provoked or not provoked by a confederate, were either exposed or not exposed to an aggressive model, and performed under either normal or hot temperature conditions. It was predicted that high temperature would facilitate aggression most in those subjects who were exposed to both the provocation and the aggressive model. As is evident in Table 3, however, high ambient temperature facilitated aggression in nonangered subjects but actually inhibited aggression in angered subjects. There was also a tendency, though not significant, for high temperature to inhibit aggression more in the angered subjects who had not observed the aggressive model than in those who had.

The third study (Baron & Bell, in press) yielded similar results; high ambient temperatures (warm and hot) increased the aggressiveness of nonangered subjects but reduced the aggressiveness of angered subjects. Furthermore, it was demonstrated that these effects could be mitigated if subjects were given a "cooling drink" before they administered shock to the victim.

Taken together, the results of the Baron studies would seem to cast some doubt on the applicability of the arousal model to the heat–aggression link. There are a number of features of the laboratory paradigm employed, however, that may account for the discrepancy between the results obtained and those expected from the arousal model.

For example, a number of studies (Epstein & Taylor, 1967; Green-

Table 3   Total Shock as a Function of Anger, Temperature Level, and Model[a,b]

	Cool temperature		Hot temperature	
	Aggressive model	No model	Aggressive model	No model
Angered	4.72	4.61	4.61	3.41
Not angered	2.86	2.10	3.38	3.05

[a] Based on data from Baron and Bell, 1975.
[b] Total shock is transformed shock intensity times duration.

well & Dengerink, 1973; Nickel, 1974) have indicated that, in the typical aggression paradigms, the perceived intent of a provocateur is a more reliable predictor of subsequent aggression than is the magnitude of the pain sustained. It could reasonably be argued that those subjects in the Baron studies who were provoked under high temperature conditions may not have perceived the provocation to be as intentional as those subjects who were provoked under normal temperature conditions. In the former case, the provocation could have been seen by the subject as due partly to the effects of the high temperature on the provocateur. In the latter case, the subject would not have been aware of an environmental determinant of the confederate's actions. The consequence of these differential attributions would have been a reduction in the level of aggression exhibited by angered subjects under high temperature conditions.

Another way to interpret the results of these laboratory studies dealing with heat and aggression involves the distracting and irritating properties of high ambient temperature. It seems possible to argue that the presence of an obtrusive aversive environmental condition, such as uncomfortably high temperature, when there is an opportunity to aggress, may distract the previously provoked person from the specifics of his earlier insult or injury. The result of such a shift in attention from the highly personalized provocation to a more impersonal discomfort (shared, it should be added, with the potential target of aggression!) would be to mitigate the magnitude of the counterattack. The annoying qualities of the high temperature could slightly increase the irritability of persons not otherwise angered, producing the elevation in aggression frequently observed in the hot but not angered of Baron's subjects.

The results of the laboratory work with heat and aggression in humans seems to indicate that sometimes high temperature can indeed increase aggressiveness, but the opposite is equally true: Increased heat may decrease aggression. Obviously, more research is necessary in order to specify exactly when high temperature can be expected to exert one influence rather than the other. Nevertheless, the relationship between high temperature and aggression is not the simple one that is suggested by some of the reports linking riots with the "long hot summer." The contribution of factors correlated with high temperature (e.g., more beer drinking, more unemployment) warrant closer attention.

The Social Environment and Aggression

Territoriality

The security of one's own domain is an increasing concern of urban dwellers, and invasion of private property is frequently the occasion for violence. The ubiquity of the trespass–retaliation norm is illustrated by the legendary schoolboy's taunt to "cross over this line," drawn with his toe in the dust. In many localities, the law is exceedingly ambiguous on the point of how to prosecute a homeowner accused of killing an intruder.

A very strong relationship between territorial invasion[1] and intraspecific aggression has also been inferred from naturalistic observations of animal—from ant (Wallis, 1964) to primate (Carpenter, 1958)—populations. The relationship has been interpreted by a number of popular writers (e.g., Ardrey, 1966; Storr, 1968) as evidence of an evolutionary basis for an impulse in humans to attack invaders. As intuitively appealing as this interpretation may be, there are a number of reasons why we cannot say unequivocally that human territorial aggression is inherited. First, territorial behavior has not been noted in every species. In a number of species, no evidence has been found of individual organisms responding aggressively to territorial invasion. While territorial defense is common in human beings, it is not seen in every culture (Alland, 1972). The issue is complicated by the fact that, in the animal literature, territoriality has two hypothetical orientations: object-centered territory (defense of a specific object irrespective of its location) and space-centered territory (defense of a geographic area with definite boundaries). Furthermore, each orientation has been selectively applied to different species. Second, informal norms and sometimes even legal codes support the notion of violent defense of hearth and home (Blumenthal, Kahn, Andrews, & Head, 1972). While the forma-

---

[1] Territorial invasion has been defined by Lyman and Scott (1967) as the unwarranted use, contamination, and/or alteration of the social meaning of an area on the part of a conspecific.

tion of these trespasser norms may possibly be attributed to some direct genetic influence, their effect would seem to provide adequate justification for aggression in many instances. In addition, there is a confounding of physical proximity with both invasion and aggression in animals, a confounding that does not necessarily obtain in humans because of advanced weaponry and burglar detection devices.

Very recently, a study was conducted at Tulane (O'Neal *et al.*, 1976) to investigate aggressive responses to territorial invasion in humans. In order to minimize the effect of a "thou shalt not trespass" norm, children were used as subjects, and pains were taken to employ a procedure that would not explicitly invoke the norm. The subjects were black; their race was not due to any consideration other than that they constituted the largest pool of first- and second-grade children available during the summer months.

The children were given instructions intended to induce possessiveness for a carpeted play area and were allowed to attach a name card to a chain strung along its boundary.[2] After the child was allowed to play with a toy in the area for a few minutes, the experimenter left the toy either inside or a few feet outside the carpeted play area before he led the child into an adjoining room to "play another game." In the new room, the child could press a button that would "hurt" a clown whom he could see advancing toward the play area.

The design was a 2 (male or female subject) $\times$ 2 (space invasion or no space invasion) $\times$ 2 (object invasion or no object invasion) factorial with 5 subjects per cell. In the space invasion conditions, the clown entered the carpeted area, and in the no-space invasion conditions he did not. Subjects in the object invasion conditions saw the clown play with the toy they had played with, while subjects in the no-object invasion conditions saw the clown play with another attractive toy. When the clown began playing with a toy, the child was given 10 opportunities (trials) to press the button. Each time the button was pressed the clown heard a click and shouted "Ow!"

The number, duration, and latency (number of trials before the child pressed the button for the first time) are presented in Table 4. The data are averaged across trials since there were no trial effects. While overall, males pressed the button more often, for longer periods of time, and did not wait as long to do so as the females, the sex variable reliably interacted with the other variables. Separate analyses for males and fe-

---

[2] The subjects' parents signed statements in advance indicating their consent to the experimental procedure, a procedure similar to that previously employed by Baron and Liebert (1972).

Table 4   Mean Number, Duration, and Latency of "Pain-Button" Depressions[a,b]

		Space invasion			No space invasion		
		Response measure			Response measure		
		Number	Duration	Latency	Number	Duration	Latency
Object invasion	Female	1.00_a	3.10_m	$.00_y$	$.73_a$	$.77_n$	$.21_y$
	Male	$.81_a$	2.04_{mn}	$.10_y$	$.70_a$	1.66_{mn}	$.19_y$
No object invasion	Female	$.71_a$	3.63_m	$.59_{xy}$	$.13_b$	$.09_n$	$.85_x$
	Male	$.82_a$	$.71_n$	$.43_{xy}$	$.91_a$	1.87_{mn}	$.03_y$

[a] Based on data from O'Neal, Caldwell, and Gallup, 1976.

[b] Subscripts in common within any one response measure indicate that the means are not significantly different at the .05 level by a Duncan multiple range test.

males revealed that the invasion manipulations frequently increased the number, duration, and reciprocal latency of the button presses in females, but they never reliably produced such differences in the male subjects. Moreover, for females, the number and latency reflected the most aggression in subjects exposed to both invasion manipulations and the least in those exposed to neither.

It is interesting to speculate as to why the females in the study were responsive to the invasions and the males were not. It could be, of course, that the females understood the instructions better than the males or that the button-pressing apparatus was similar to the toys frequently used by boys and, therefore, was "played with" rather than used as an instrument of aggression. Another possibility, however, is very provocative. If black families are indeed more often headed by a female (see Baughman, 1971), the female may more frequently be the one to insure the physical security of the home and cope with intruders; the behavior of the girls in this study could reflect sex-role socialization. To establish the validity of this latter interpretation would obviously involve comparisons of children from father-absent homes with other children, a comparison which was not possible in this study because of the small number of subjects. What is evident, however, is the strong possibility that the forms and extent of territorial aggression are largely determined by complex processes of socialization, the effects of which may obscure whatever inherited territorial aggressiveness exists in human beings.

Clues as to what may be some of the functional bases of territoriality in humans are provided in Oscar Newman's (1973) fascinating book, *Defensible Space.* Newman explores the relationship between crimes in public housing projects and aspects of their design, providing evidence that high-rise buildings, where surveillance of interior lobbies and hallways is difficult and which are surrounded by large expanses of undivided yards, are the site of the highest rates of crime. He argues that this relationship obtains because the conditions necessary for territoriality—a proprietary interest in the grounds, an ability to identify intruders, a possibility for surveillance—are absent. Indeed, much the same point has been made regarding the role of territoriality in animals. While animals usually fight when a territory is being established and occasionally when a stranger intrudes, one rarely observes fighting once the territory is established, especially when the territory is an area which the animal can continuously monitor (Eibl-Eibesfeldt, 1970).

It is tempting to make the provisional conclusion that territoriality leads to a reduction in hostility in animals and in humans and to a greater stability in interpersonal relations. Both Mack (1954) and Marine (1966) have reported instances in which the separation of neighborhood ethnic groups by clearly defined boundaries helped reduce conflict. In elementary school yards, a line painted down the middle frequently divides the area into "girls" and "boys," reducing conflicts which competing sex-role stereotyped demands for space (e.g., hopscotch versus marble shooting) provoke. Such territorial boundaries and "markers" would seem to play an especially important role in reducing conflicts when crowding is as great as it is in our inner-cities.

Crowding

The relationship between the proximity of others and aggression is not a simple one, and little clarity emerges from the limited literature in the area. Theoretically, there are a number of considerations that might lead one to propose that physical proximity to others would increase aggressiveness. The proximity of others may be aversive, and also aggressive "cues"—for example, eye contact, threatening gestures, invasion of personal space—would be more apparent. The arousal produced by others' presence (Zajonc, 1965) might enhance aggressive responses if they are dominant. Moreover, if someone is provoked, it may be easier for him to "get at" his tormenter, thus lowering the probability of any "cooling off" before retaliation.

There are obvious cultural differences in the extent to which simple population density is experienced as the subjective state of "crowding"—densities which in the United States are moderately associated with high rates of violent crime are exceeded in Tokyo without apparent social pathology. In addition, it is apparent from recent studies that proximity of others and tendency to aggress are not orthogonal; Kinzel (1970), for example, reported that criminals with a history of violent crimes preferred greater interaction distances than did other criminals in his sample.

Laboratory studies investigating the relationship between crowding and aggressiveness in humans have frequently found that increased density raised competitiveness and hostility in males but increased females' cooperativeness and liking for each other (e.g., Freedman, Levy, Buchanan, & Price, 1972). In a recent study of attitudes toward others in a large number of college classrooms, Schettino and Borden (in press) found increases in competitive attitudes in males to be associated with increases in density, but not numerosity. It should be noted that, in many previous studies that demonstrated a crowding–aggression relationship (e.g., Hutt & Vaizey, 1966), numerosity and density were confounded. Recent laboratory investigations have focused upon two frequent correlates of crowding in humans—audience effects and identity loss—and their influence on aggression.

Identity Loss

An individual who finds himself with a large number of other persons can experience a loss of identity and become immersed in the crowd. In light of the many instances of collective violence and mob behavior in our society, along with a growing trend toward urbanization and concomitant crowding, an analysis of the effects of the "crowd" on an individual's tendency to be aggressive is relevant. This analysis will stem primarily from the theoretical framework developed by Zimbardo (1969) to explain "deindividuation." Deindividuation refers to a hypothetical process in which individuals experience a loss of self-awareness, self-observation, and self-evaluation, along with a lack of sensitivity to social norms. Under these conditions, behaviors such as aggression, which are normally restrained by normative influences, become disinhibited. Although Zimbardo (1969) lists a number of antecedent conditions that can lead to a subjective state of deindividuation, the focus here will be on immersion in a group as a precursor to deindividuation and aggression. Within this context, two specific factors characteristic of immersion in a group, anonymity and diffusion of responsibility, seem particularly relevant. As a prelude to the subsequent discussion, two propositions indicating how the anonymity and diffusion of responsibility afforded by immersion in a crowd can affect aggression should be presented. First, to the extent that an individual becomes anonymous in a crowd, he is less likely to be sanctioned for any socially prohibited behavior in which he engages, because the sanctioning agents will have difficulty in identifying him. Second, to the extent that an individual can share responsibility with other group members, he is less likely to feel personally responsible for the negative consequences of any counternormative behavior in which he engages. When the individual is immersed in a group, either or both of these factors should serve to increase the probability that aggression will result. At this point, some experimental evidence bearing on these relationships will be examined in order to provide an understanding of the mechanics of crowd behavior.

ANONYMITY

A number of studies (e.g., Diener, Westford, Dineen, & Fraser, 1973; Zimbardo, 1969) have demonstrated that when individuals in a group are made anonymous, their aggressiveness increases. Furthermore, such individuals tend to be insensitive to victim characteristics indicating the relative appropriateness of their aggression (Zimbardo, 1969). Conversely, individuals exposed to similar anonymity manipulations and who subsequently aggress alone are less aggressive than their nonanonymous peers (Diener et al., 1973; Zimbardo, 1969). Presumably, the manipulation used to induce anonymity in subjects who are alone actually serves to increase their self-consciousness. For example, an individual wearing a hood and lab coat in a group of similarly attired individuals would probably perceive himself as anonymous since "everyone looks the same"; however, an individual wearing a hood and lab coat in a situation in which others were not similarly attired would no doubt feel conspicuous, self-conscious, and individuated.

Another factor that can mediate the relationship between anonymity and aggression involves the specific person or persons to whom one is unidentifiable. Thus, to maximally facilitate aggression, the anonymity should be from possible sanctioning agents (Dion, 1971) or the victim himself (Penner & Hawkins, 1971). If the individual is anonymous from others engaging in the same behavior or from others with favorable attitudes toward the behavior, aggression could possibly be inhibited. For example, Zabrack and Miller (1972) varied the anonymity of group members from each other, rather than from the experimenter or the victim. The groups were composed of either strangers or friends. Anonymity produced a decrement in aggressive responding, especially among groups composed of friends. Apparently, anonymity can mitigate the effects of social support and/or diffusion of responsibility in a group setting.

DIFFUSION OF RESPONSIBILITY

Diffusion of responsibility has been implicated as the mediator of bystander apathy in relation to helping behavior (see Latane & Darley, 1970). In addition to decreasing the likelihood of prosocial behavior, however, diffusion of responsibility should also increase the likelihood of antisocial behavior. As mentioned earlier, immersion in a crowd is one situation in which an individual would be less likely to feel personal responsibility for any of his actions, and, consequently, behaviors that are normally socially prohibited, to the extent that they are rewarding, should occur more frequently. A number of experimental studies bear on this issue. For example, Paloutzian (1972) found that decreased responsibility for aggression, by immersion of the individual in a group, significantly increased the amount of distracting noise that subjects delivered to the target person. Similarly, Diener, Dineen, Endresen, Beaman, and Fraser (1975) reported that individuals were more aggressive if they were told that the experimenter would take full responsibility for their actions than if they had to assume responsibility themselves.

Diffusion of responsibility is especially likely to occur in a situation in which the individual and the other group members are highly motivated to engage in the prohibited behavior. Mathes and Kahn (1975) exposed subjects, who were either alone or in triads, to either an insult or no insult. Presumably, insulted subjects should have been more motivated to seek revenge than noninsulted subjects. Results indicated that subjects who desired revenge and were in groups administered more severe fines to their provocateur than either single subjects who desired revenge or subjects in groups who had no reason to retaliate against the target person. Furthermore, subjects in groups felt less responsible for their punitive behavior than did subjects who were alone.

Finally, extensive research literature indicates that groups tend to make riskier decisions than individuals (e.g., Dion, Baron, & Miller, 1970). One possible explanation of the risky shift phenomenon implicates diffusion of responsibility as the crucial mediator. A recent study (Yinon, Jaffe, & Feshbach, 1975) employed a risky shift paradigm in investigating the relationship between group decision making and aggression. Both male and female unisex triads took greater risks than individuals of the same sex, even though the risky decision involved administering electric shock to a target person, a dependent measure typically employed in aggression studies.

In this section, immersion in a group has been shown to be a precursor to the subjective state of deindividuation, which, in turn, increases the likelihood that an individual will emit behaviors that are typically under normative control. Evidence relating two components of group behavior, anonymity and diffusion of responsibility, to aggression suggests that the crowd is a potent disinhibitor of socially prohibited acts and an important environmental determinant of aggression. There are also other factors characteristic of crowds that may contribute to collective or mob violence. For example, modeling and social comparison processes in a group situation could serve to make aggression more likely. Diener, Dineen, Westford, Beaman, and Fraser (1974) found that the presence of aggressive models within a group was an extremely potent facilitator of aggression by the individuals in the group. For a number of reasons then, immersion in a crowd appears to be a strong environmental determinant of aggression.

Audience Effects

The presence of individuals in a particular setting can be construed as an environmental stimulus that may affect the tendency of a person in that setting to behave aggressively. The focus in this section will be on what perhaps is the "simplest" role that individuals can assume in a given situation, namely, that of passive spectators or observers. Specifically, the relationship between audience presence and an actor's aggressiveness will be assessed.

The effects of the presence of spectators on an individual's behavior has generally been approached under the rubric of social facilitation theory. A substantial body of research has accumulated, but most studies have employed task performance measures rather than indices of aggression as dependent variables. There is some evidence, however, relating audience presence to aggression.

Before considering this evidence in detail, it will be informative to speculate about the possible mechanisms by which an audience might affect aggression. Social facilitation theorists (Cottrell, 1972; Zajonc, 1965) have suggested that the presence of an audience serves to increase an individual's arousal level, which, in turn, enhances the emission of dominant responses. Thus, to the extent that aggressive responses are dominant for an individual, the presence of others would be expected to facilitate aggression. At a more cognitive level, it could be argued that since aggression, at least in most situations, is socially prohibited, the presence of others would serve to reduce its occurrence, since an individual might anticipate a negative evaluation from the audience for engaging in a counternormative behavior. Conversely, to the extent that the audience is perceived as favoring aggression, individuals might engage in aggressive behavior in order to receive the approbation of the audience. Finally, the presence of others could serve as a cue, indicating the relative appropriateness or inappropriateness of aggressive behavior, with a resulting increase or decrease, respectively, in its occurrence. These mechanisms are by no means necessarily independent. In fact, any or all could be operative in a given situation. With these possible mechanisms in mind, some relevant empirical findings will now be examined.

Baron (1971) investigated the effects of audience presence and prior anger arousal on aggression. Male subjects were either angered or not angered by a confederate before being given an opportunity to retaliate. Subjects aggressed in the presence of an audience who either had or had not witnessed their earlier treatment by the confederate or with no audience present. The audience members were two men described as a professor and graduate student engaged in research at a nearby school. The presence of the early audience lowered aggression in angered subjects on both shock duration and intensity measures. Conversely, the late audience did not appear to affect the angered subjects, and the type of audience did not influence the aggressiveness of nonangered subjects. Although this pattern of results should have yielded anger-arousal $\times$ audience-presence interactions for the two measures, neither was significant. Post hoc comparisons, however, provided evidence that the inhibitory effect of the early audience on aggression in angered subjects was a reliable one.

Two recent studies (Borden, 1975; Borden & Taylor, 1973) have also examined the relationship between audience presence and aggression using a competition reaction-time paradigm (see Taylor, 1967). Although Borden and Taylor (1973) were primarily interested in the effect of social pressure (both aggressive and pacifistic) exerted by observers on aggression, a portion of their design included a comparison between alone and passive spectator conditions. The passive spectators were described as undergraduates who wanted to observe a psychology experiment. This comparison revealed that the presence of the spectators facilitated aggressive responding toward either an aggressive or a pacifistic opponent, although the effect was stronger when the opponent was pacifistic.

Borden (1975) examined the effects of the observer's cue value on aggression. In his first experiment, male subjects engaged in the competition reaction-time task in the presence of either a male or a female observer prior to continuing the task with no observer present. It was expected that aggression would be higher in the presence of the male than in the presence of the female observer, since sex should function as a cue indicating the relative appropriateness of an aggressive strategy. Results confirmed this prediction; subjects' shock settings were significantly higher in the male observer condition. Furthermore, on the subsequent alone trials, the subjects who had previously been observed by a male significantly reduced their aggressiveness, while subjects with the female observer showed no change after the observer departed. The second experiment was similar, except that the sex and values of the observers were orthogonally manipulated. Four conditions were created: aggressive male observer, pacifistic male observer, aggressive female observer, and pacifistic female observer. The observer's values were manipulated by means of a jacket patch indicating membership in either a karate club or S.A.N.E. (Society Against Nuclear Expansion) for the aggressive and pacifistic value groups, respectively. In each of these conditions, the observer also made comments appropriate to his/her group membership. Following the trials during which the subject performed in the presence of an observer, all subjects continued the task alone. Results indicated that subjects employed significantly higher shock settings in the presence of an aggressive observer than in the presence of a pacifistic observer, and the difference disappeared when they subsequently performed alone. Specifically, subjects in the aggressive observer groups substantially reduced their aggressiveness when the observer departed, whereas subjects in the pacifistic observer groups did not alter their shock settings when alone. In this experiment, the sex of the observer made no difference. Apparently, when the observer's values concerning aggression were made explicit, the implicit values indicated by sex were relatively unimportant determinants of aggression.

Before any conclusions are drawn concerning the relationship between audience presence and aggression, one other study should be mentioned. Harrell and Schmitt (1973) used a somewhat different paradigm in examining the effects of an audience on aggression. While subjects were performing a knob-pulling task to earn money, an aversive tone sounded every 60 sec. All subjects could escape or avoid the tone by either pressing a button with a force of 1.5 lb or hitting a padded cushion with a force of 20 lb. The investigators assumed that button pressing represented a nonaggressive response, while hitting the cushion was an aggressive response. Half of the subjects performed alone, while half performed in the presence of another person working on the same task. The coactor was a confederate who never made any aggressive responses. Results indicated that the presence of the coactor facilitated both the rate and the intensity of the punching response. Conversely, the button pressing response was used more frequently by subjects who performed alone. This reversal is not particularly surprising, since the two responses are mutually exclusive, and an increase in one should result in a decrease in the other. Finally, the presence of the coactor also facilitated the rate of knob pulling. In interpreting this study within the context of this discussion, three limiting factors should be discussed. First, the individual present in the audience condition served in the role of a coactor, rather than that of a passive spectator. The subject was aware of the coactor's performance since a panel indicated the earnings of each. Thus, the coactor may have been perceived by some subjects as a competitor, thereby limiting the applicability of the results to the issue under consideration here. Second, since the confederate was also required to escape and/or avoid his own aversive tone and since the authors did not specify whether or not the subject was able to hear the confederate's tone or how successful the confederate was in avoiding the tone, the differences between the coactor and alone conditions were possibly confounded with differences in the amount of aversive stimulation experienced in each situation. Third, there is some doubt as to whether punching a padded cushion to terminate an aversive tone qualifies as an "aggressive" response in terms of the more commonly accepted definitions of aggression. If the importance of these limitations is minimized, the Harrell and Schmitt study does provide evidence that the presence of another individual can facilitate aggression. We suggest, however, that these results be accepted only with caution.

What conclusions, then, can be drawn concerning the relationship between the presence of an audience and aggression? In reviewing the foregoing studies, it is evident that the presence of an audience sometimes facilitates aggression (Borden, 1975; Borden & Taylor, 1973; Harrell & Schmitt, 1973), sometimes inhibits aggression (Baron, 1971), and sometimes has no effect on aggression (Baron, 1971; Borden, 1975). We will now examine a number of factors that could account for these apparent discrepancies.

Whether or not the subject is provoked may be a determinant of the effects of the presence of an audience on aggression. Both the Baron (1971) and the Borden and Taylor (1973) studies employed some type of provocation manipulation. Recall that Baron (1971) found that the presence of an early audience inhibited aggression in angered subjects, but that the presence of a late audience had no effect on the aggressiveness of angered subjects. Neither type of audience was effective for nonangered subjects. Borden and Taylor (1973), however, found that the presence of an audience facilitated aggression against either an aggressive or a nonaggressive opponent. Obviously, the apparent discrepancy cannot be resolved in terms of the differential effects of an audience on provoked versus nonprovoked subjects. A comparison of the type of audience employed in each of these studies would perhaps be more enlightening. Baron's audience members were described as a professor and graduate student, whereas Borden and Taylor's audience members were described as undergraduate students who wanted to observe an experiment. It seems reasonable to assume that these two types of audiences differed on a number of dimensions. For example, the evaluative salience of the professor–graduate student audience was probably much greater than that of the undergraduate audience. The professor–graduate student audience was also probably perceived as less tolerant of aggression than was the undergraduate audience. In the Baron study then, the early audience may have been effective in inhibiting aggression because the angered subjects were concerned with the possibility of a negative evaluation for such behavior. This concern may have been especially important for these subjects because they were already motivated to behave aggressively and because the vengeful nature of the behavior was especially salient. Conversely, in the Borden and Taylor study, subjects who competed against an aggressive partner only faced the possible negative evaluation of "undergraduates" for engaging in socially prohibited behavior. Finally, Borden's subjects, both angered and nonangered, may have anticipated some approval from the undergraduate audience for aggressive behavior. The results of the more recent Borden (1975) study do provide rather clear-cut evidence that, to the extent that an audience is perceived as favoring aggression, subjects will engage in such behavior in order to gain audience approval.

In conclusion then, a number of factors that appear to influence the relationship between audience presence and aggression will be summarized in the form of three propositions. First, to the extent that an audience has evaluative salience for an individual, the individual will inhibit aggression in order to avoid a possible negative evaluation for having engaged in a socially prohibited behavior. This tendency will increase as a function of the individual's motivation (apart from that derived from characteristics of the audience) to behave aggressively. Second, to the extent that the audience is perceived, either implicitly or explicitly, as having favorable attitudes toward aggression, the individual will behave aggressively in order to gain the approval of the audience. This tendency will increase as a function of the reinforcement value of audience approval. Third, although the presence of others may have drive-inducing properties, the effects of audience-induced arousal on aggression will, to the extent that either of the first two propositions are applicable, be minimal.

Conclusions

The environmental psychology of aggression is a relatively new field in which a substantial number of questions remain unanswered. One issue that has surfaced once more in this chapter deals with the applicability of laboratory experimentation to an understanding of the same parameters as they exist in a nonlaboratory social context. Variables that are "pure" manipulations of one intended conceptual variable in the laboratory are isolated from other variables with which they are frequently correlated elsewhere.

It is ordinarily true that the subject's exposure to the environmental condition is rather brief in laboratory procedures. Subjects in the laboratory may be primarily reacting to the change in stimulation, rather than to the stimulation per se. Glass and Singer (1972) present evidence that the arousal effects of noise diminish fairly quickly, and it is possible that similar adaptation occurs to other environmental stressors. It is also possible that the irritating qualities of an environmental stressor may sometimes increase with time of exposure. In future laboratory studies, the time factor should be observed more carefully than it has been in the past.

It has frequently been the case that what was earlier assumed to be a simple one-to-one relationship between an environmental parameter and aggression becomes a considerably more complex relationship when cognitive factors are taken into account. For example, in the case of noise, high intensities may either decrease or increase aggression, depending on the individual's appreciation of his noise-induced bodily changes.

Finally, future research could profitably employ multifactor experimental paradigms to adequately assess the possible interrelationships among the environmental determinants of aggression. Furthermore, attention should be directed at investigating environmental factors as they exist in the "real world" by means of naturalistic studies employing unobtrusive measures.

REFERENCES

Alland, A. *The human imperative.* New York: Columbia Univ., 1972.

Ardrey, R. *The territorial imperative.* New York: Delta, 1966.

Bandura, A. *Aggression: A social learning analysis.* Englewood Cliffs, New Jersey: Prentice-Hall, 1973.

Baron, R. *The tyranny of noise.* New York: St. Martin's, 1970.

Baron, R. A. Aggression as a function of audience presence and prior anger arousal. *Journal of Experimental Social Psychology,* 1971, *7*, 515–523.

Baron, R. A. Aggression as a function of ambient temperature and prior anger arousal. *Journal of Personality and Social Psychology,* 1972, *21,* 183–189.

Baron, R. A., & Bell, P. A. Aggression and heat: Mediating effects of prior provocation and exposure to an aggressive model. *Journal of Personality and Social Psychology,* 1975, *31,* 825–832.

Baron, R. A., & Bell, P. A. Aggression and heat: The influence of ambient temperature, negative affect, and a cooling drink on physical aggression. *Journal of Personality and Social Psychology,* in press.

Baron, R. A., & Kepner, C. R. Attraction toward the model and model's competence as determinants of adult imitative behavior. *Journal of Personality and Social Psychology,* 1970, *14,* 335–344.

Baron, R. A., & Lawton, S. F. Environmental influences on aggression: The facilitation of modeling effects by high ambient temperatures. *Psychonomic Science,* 1972, *26,* 80–83.

Baron, R. A., & Liebert, R. Short-term effect of televised aggression on children's aggressive behavior. In J. Murray, E. Rubenstein, & G. Comstock (Eds.), *Television and social behavior.* Washington: U.S. Government Printing Office, 1972, Pp. 181–201.

Baughman, E. *The black society.* New York: Atherton, 1971.

Berkowitz, L. The frustration-aggression hypothesis revisited. In L. Berkowitz (Ed.), *Roots of aggression.* New York: Atherton, 1969.

Berry, R. M., & Jack, E. C. The effect of temperature upon shock-elicited aggression in rats. *Psychonomic Science,* 1971, *23,* 341–343.

Blumenthal, M., Kahn, R., Andrews, F., & Head, K. *Justifying violence.* Ann Arbor, Michigan: ISR, 1972.

Borden, R. J. Witnessed aggression; Influence of an observer's sex and values on aggressive responding. *Journal of Personality and Social Psychology,* 1975, *31,* 567–573.

Borden, R. J., & Taylor, S. P. The social instigation and control of physical aggression. *Journal of Applied Social Psychology,* 1973, *3,* 354–361.

Calhoun, J. B. Population density and social pathology. *Scientific American,* 1962, *206,* 139–148.

Carpenter, C. Territory: A review of the concepts and problems. In A. Roe & G. Simpson (Eds.), *Behavior and evolution.* New Haven: Yale Univ. Press, 1958.

Cottrell, N. B. Social facilitation. In C. G. McClintock (Ed.), *Experimental social psychology.* New York: Holt, 1972.

Dey, F. Auditory fatigue and predicted permanent hearing defects from rock-and-roll music. *The New England Journal of Medicine,* 1970, *282,* 467–469.

Diener, E., Dineen, J., Endresen, K., Beaman, A., & Fraser, S. Effects of altered responsibility, cognitive set, and modeling on physical aggression and deindividuation. *Journal of Personality and Social Psychology,* 1975, *31,* 328–337.

Diener, E., Dineen, J., Westford, K., Beaman, A. L., & Fraser, S. C. Effects of group presence, observers, and modeling on aggression. Paper presented at the meeting of the Western Psychological Association, San Francisco, April 1974.

Diener, E., Westford, K. L., Dineen, J., & Fraser, S. C. Beat the pacifist: The deindividuating effects of anonymity and group presence. *Proceedings of the 81st Annual Convention of the American Psychological Association,* 1973, *8,* 221–222.

Dion, K. L. Determinants of unprovoked aggression. (Doctoral dissertation, Univ. of Minnesota) Ann Arbor, Michigan: University Microfilms, 1971. No. 71–18, 716.

Dion, K. L., Baron, R. S., & Miller, N. Why do groups make riskier decisions than individuals? In L. Berkowitz (Ed.), *Advances in experimental social Psychology.* Vol. 5. New York: Academic Press, 1970.

Eibl-Eibesfeldt, I. *Ethology: The biology of behavior.* New York: Holt, 1970.
Epstein, S., & Taylor, S. P. Instigation to aggression as a function of degree of defeat and perceived aggressive intent of the opponent. *Journal of Personality,* 1967, *35,* 265–289.
Freedman, J., Levy, A., Buchanan, R., & Price, J. Crowding and human aggressiveness. *Journal of Experimental Social Psychology,* 1972, *8,* 528–548.
Glass, D., & Singer, J. *Urban stress.* New York: Academic Press, 1972.
Geen, R., & O'Neal, E. Activation of cue-elicited aggression by general arousal. *Journal of Personality and Social Psychology,* 1969, *11,* 289–292.
Goranson, R. E., & King, D. Rioting and daily temperature: Analysis of the U.S. riots in 1967. Unpublished manuscript, New York Univ., 1970.
Greenberg, G. The effects of ambient temperature and population density on aggression in two strains of mice. Unpublished doctoral dissertation, Kansas State Univ., 1969.
Greenwell, J., & Dengerink, H. A. The role of perceived versus actual attack in human physical aggression. *Journal of Personality and Social Psychology,* 1973, *26,* 66–71.
Griffitt, W. Environmental effects on interpersonal affective behavior: Ambient effective temperature and attraction. *Journal of Personality and Social Psychology,* 1970, *15,* 240–244.
Griffitt, W., & Veitch, R. Hot and crowded: Influence of population density and temperature on interpersonal affective behavior. *Journal of Personality and Social Psychology,* 1971, *17,* 92–98.
Hanratty, P., O'Neal, E., & Sulzer, J. The effect of frustration upon the imitation of aggression. *Journal of Personality and Social Psychology,* 1972, *21,* 30–35.
Harris, M., & Huang, L. Aggression and the attribution process. *Journal of Social Psychology,* 1974, *92,* 209–216.
Harrell, W. A., & Schmitt, D. R. Effects of a minimal audience on physical aggression. *Psychological Reports,* 1973, *32,* 651–657.
Hutt, C., & Vaizey, M. Differential effects of group density upon social behavior. *Nature,* 1966, *209,* 1371–1372.
Kinzel, A. Body buffer zone in violent criminals. *American Journal of Psychiatry,* 1970, *127,* 59–64.
Knipmeyer, J., & Prestholdt, P. The influence of environmental noise upon group aggression. Paper presented at the meeting of the Southeastern Psychological Association, New Orleans, April 1973.
Konečni, V. The mediation of aggressive behavior: Arousal level vs. anger and cognitive labeling. *Journal of Personality and Social Psychology,* 1975, *32,* 706–712.
Kryter, K. *The effects of noise on man.* New York: Academic Press, 1970.
Latane, B., & Darley, J. M. *The unresponsive bystander: Why doesn't he help?* New York: Appleton, 1970.
Lorenz, K. *On aggression.* New York: Harcourt, 1966.
Lyman, S., & Scott, M. Territoriality: A neglected dimension. *Social Problems,* 1967, *15,* 236–249.
Mack, R. Ecological patterns in an industrial shop. *Social Forces,* 1954, *32,* 118–138.
Mathes, E. W., & Kahn, A. Diffusion of responsibility and extreme behavior. *Journal of Personality and Social Psychology,* 1975, *31,* 881–886.
Marine, G. I've got nothing against the colored, understand. *Ramparts,* 1966, *5,* 13–18.
Mathews, K., Canon, L., & Alexander, K. The influence of level of empathy and ambient noise on the body buffer zone. *Proceedings of the APA Division of Personality and Social Psychology,* 1974, *1,* 367–370.
Newman, O. *Defensible space.* New York: Collier, 1973.

Nickel, T. W. The attribution of intention as a critical factor in the relation between frustration and aggression. *Journal of Personality*, 1974, *42*, 482-492.

Okuma, T., Funimori, M., & Hayashi, A. The effect of environmental temperature on the electrocortical activity of cats immobilized by neuromuscular blocking agents. *E.E.G. and Clinical Neurophysiology*, 1965, *18*, 392-400.

O'Neal, E., Caldwell, C., & Gallup, G. Territorial invasion and aggression in young children. Unpublished manuscript, Tulane Univ., 1976.

Paloutzian, R. F. Some components of deindividuation and their effects. (Doctoral dissertation, Claremont Graduate School) Ann Arbor, Michigan: University Microfilms, 1972. No. 72-30, 578.

Penner, L. A., & Hawkins, H. L. The effects of visual contact and aggressor identification on interpersonal aggression. *Psychonomic Science*, 1971, *24*, 261-263.

Pokorny, A., & Jachimczyk, J. The questionable relationship between homicides and the lunar cycle. *American Journal of Psychiatry*, 1974, *131*, 827-829.

Provins, K. A., & Bell, C. R. Effects of heat stress on the performance of two tasks running concurrently. *Journal of Experimental Psychology*, 1970, *85*, 40-44.

Robbins, M. C., Dewalt, B. R., & Pelto, P. J. Climate and behavior: A biocultural study. *Journal of Cross-Cultural Psychology*, 1972, *3*, 331-334.

Rohles, F. H. Environmental psychology: A bucket of worms. *Psychology Today*, 1967, *1*, 54-63.

Schettino, G., & Borden, R. Group size vs. group density: Where is the affect? *Personality and Social Psychology Bulletin*, in press.

Schwartz, D. C. On the ecology of political violence: The long, hot summer as a hypothesis. *The American Behavioral Scientist*, 1968, *11*, 24-28.

Sherrod, D., & Downs, R. Environmental determinants of altruism: The effects of stimulus overload and perceived control on helping. *Journal of Experimental Social Psychology*, 1974, *10*, 468-479.

Solomon, J. Aural assault. *The Sciences*, 1970, *10*, 26-31.

Storr, A. *Human aggression.* New York: Atheneum, 1968.

Taylor, S. P. Aggressive behavior and physiological arousal as a function of provocation and the tendency to inhibit aggression. *Journal of Personality*, 1967, *35*, 297-310.

Ulrich, R. E., & Azrin, N. H. Reflexive fighting in response to aversive stimulation. *Journal of the Experimental Analysis of Behavior*, 1962, *5*, 511-520.

United States Riot Commission. *Report of the National Advisory Commission on Civil Disorders.* New York: Bantam Books, 1968.

Wallis, D. Aggression in social insects. In D. Carthy & H. Ebling (Eds.), *The natural history of aggression.* New York: Academic Press, 1964.

Wohlwill, J. The emerging discipline of environmental psychology. *American Psychologist*, 1970, *25*, 303-312.

Yinon, Y., Jaffe, Y., & Feshbach, S. Risky aggression in individuals and groups. *Journal of Personality and Social Psychology*, 1975, *31*, 808-815.

Zabrack, M., & Miller, N. Group aggression: The effects of friendship ties and anonymity. *Proceedings of the 80th Annual Convention of the American Psychological Association*, 1972, *7*, 211-212.

Zajonc, R. B. Social facilitation. *Science*, 1965, *149*, 269-274.

Zillmann, D. Excitation transfer in communication-mediated aggressive behavior. *Journal of Experimental Social Psychology*, 1971, *7*, 419-434.

Zimbardo, P. G. The human choice: Individuation, reason and order, versus deindividuation, impulse and chaos. In W. J. Arnold & D. Levine (Eds.), *Nebraska symposium on motivation.* (Vol. 17). Lincoln: Univ. of Nebraska Press, 1969.

Observing Violence in the Mass Media: Implications of Basic Research[1]

RUSSELL G. GEEN

Introduction

In September of 1974, police in St. Louis arrested a young man for the murder of a couple in an isolated area outside the city (St. Louis *Globe-Democrat,* 20 September 1974). The victims had been shot in the head and stabbed several times. The suspect confessed that he had committed both murders, explaining that he had purchased the ammunition for his gun in order to rob someone. After making the purchase, and just before going to the place of the murder, he had stopped off at a drive-in theater and seen the movie *Open Season.* In this film, three Viet Nam veterans indulge in an annual ritual whereby they kidnap a young couple, then set them free to be hunted and killed; the film ends with the three killers themselves being hunted down and shot by a self-ordained avenger.

The St. Louis murder was one of many that have been reported in recent years showing a close temporal relationship between an act of violence and some portrayal of brutality in one of the mass media of

[1] The author's research cited in this chapter was supported by grants GS 2748 and GS 40171 from the National Science Foundation.

193

communication. The most widely reported of those was the killing of Evelyn Wagler, in Boston on October 2, 1973, by a gang of youths who first forced her to douse herself in gasoline and then set her afire. Police investigating the crime pointed out that a comparable burning had been shown on television only two nights earlier, strongly suggesting that the television program had, in some way, suggested or instigated the murder. These incidents, and others like them, illustrate a problem of considerable social significance—the possible influences that the mass media, especially television and cinema, have upon antisocial behavior. Even casual inspection of the cinema advertisement page of an urban daily paper indicates that a large proportion of motion pictures being shown today contain much that can be characterized as violence. As for television, even though some of the aggression portrayed has been toned down in intensity, the relative amount of time devoted to violence, such as in the numerous shows based on law-and-order themes, is still quite large. Furthermore, where statistics on the prevalence of aggressive displays are available, as in television programming, this conclusion is supported by data (Baker & Ball, 1969; Clark & Blankenburg, 1971; Gerbner, 1972).

We need more than statistics on television programming and a few anecdotes from newspapers, however, before we can draw any firm conclusions on the relationship between mass media violence and interpersonal aggression. To conclude with any accuracy that observation of violence in the media does or does not affect aggressive behavior, we must use the evidence of scientific investigations in which other sources of influence are controlled. In this chapter, evidence from such research is reviewed, and some of the theoretical constructions that have been placed on the data are discussed. Evidence comes from two sources: the highly controlled laboratory experiment and the less controlled investigation carried out under natural conditions.

Laboratory Studies

From the early 1960s until the present, an impressive number of laboratory experiments has been reported concerning the implications of observing violence for aggression in the observer. As was noted in the first chapter, "The Study of Aggression," several of these experiments were conducted within the framework of the emerging social learning theory, others reflectod various formulations of drive theory, and still others emphasized the importance of stimuli as elicitors of purely reactive behavior not mediated by cognition or volition. The findings of these studies were many and varied, but the overall conclusion is that the observation of violence does enhance, facilitate, elicit, or otherwise promote subsequent aggressiveness in the viewer. The important early studies have already been reviewed several times (e.g., Bandura, 1973; Berkowitz, 1965b; 1974; Goranson, 1970; Weiss, 1969) and will not be discussed in detail here. Instead, the emphasis will be on summarizing the theoretical explanations of the findings that have been offered and on more recent investigations carried out as tests of the several theories.

Imitation and Modeling

Much of the popular concern over the possible adverse effects of exposure to violence is motivated by fear that children will be the principal victims. The concern is customarily expressed as worry that children may learn antisocial behaviors from the media that would not otherwise be part of their behavioral repertoires. The inference that aggressive acts are learned through observation of violence committed by others is especially likely when the aggression takes some unusual or highly novel form that corresponds to an equally strange or novel action portrayed in the media. The murder of Evelyn Wagler, for instance, was suspected by Boston police of having been directly influenced by a television program because of the unusual nature of the crime; an incineration almost exactly similar to the one committed by the youths had been shown on the suspected program.

A large body of evidence has been gathered from laboratory experiments showing that children can learn aggression simply by observing it in others. Two basic processes are involved in such observational learning: acquisition, whereby the response becomes part of the observer's behavioral repertoire, and performance, whereby the observer acts out the newly learned response. Performance, of course, presupposes prior acquisition. As we shall see, however, acquisition does not guarantee performance; before an acquired response is performed other conditions must be met.

Studies on imitative learning use a basic methodology in which the child merely observes, but does not act out at the time of observation, the aggressive behaviors of a model. Later the child is tested for similar behaviors in the setting that the model had previously occupied. The victim is usually, but not always (e.g., Hanratty, O'Neal, & Sulzer, 1972), a large inflated clown doll. Performance of the observed aggressive acts (which are ordinarily novel and hitherto strange to the child) is taken as evidence that the child has acquired them without having previously performed them and thus, by definition, without having been rewarded for performing them. Simply by observing the act, the child is able to encode it, remember it, and bring it forth later when situational cues previously associated with it are reinstated (Bandura, 1973). What the child learns, therefore, is not a stimulus–response connection but rather a set of relationships among stimuli in the situation, including those emanating from the behavior of the model. Evidence for the acquisition through observation of novel aggressive behaviors has been demonstrated in several experiments (e.g., Bandura, Ross, & Ross, 1963a).

The acquisition of responses, including aggressive ones, through observation involves both imaginal and verbal representational systems. The child watching an aggressive model, for example, forms mental images of the aggressive behaviors and also verbalizes, at some overt or covert level, what he is seeing. Both the images and the verbalizations later facilitate memory of the observed event. An experiment by Gerst (1971), which did not involve aggression, gives a general illustration of the importance of verbal and imaginal mediators in observational learning. Prior to watching a model perform a series of motor responses, the subjects were told either to form mental images of the responses, to make concrete verbal descriptions of them, or to attach convenient verbal labels that summarized the essential nature of the responses. A group of control subjects was not instructed to form mental images or to verbalize. In both an immediate and a delayed test of recall of the modeled responses, the subjects who had formed one of the types of mediating responses reproduced more of the responses than did the control subjects. Overall, the formation of concise, summary labels mediated recall best of all.

Retention of observed modeled behaviors is, therefore, not a passive act but one involving active cognitive processes that foster the encoding and establishment of sequences in memory. Two such processes are the formation of summary codes for the model's behavior and rehearsal of the coded material. Bandura and Jeffery (1973) have shown that translation of observed acts into coded sequences that parallel familiar aggregates of numbers or letters (such as numbers that follow each other in serial order or letters that form words) followed by rehearsal of the sequences promotes recall more than did encoding without rehearsal and observation without encoding. Bandura, Jeffery, and Bachicha (1974) have shown that recall of modeled behaviors is especially enhanced by formation of codes that combine a simple translation of acts into symbolic letters and combination of those letters into acronyms that indicate the nature of the observed act (e.g., where the code TBSNSB represents the linguistic mnemonic *Tall boys stand near small boys*).

Because of the importance of encoding processes to observational learning, it is necessary that the observer pay a high degree of attention to the model. Bandura, Grusec, and Menlove (1966) demonstrated this in another study not directly relevant to aggression. Prior to watching a model perform several complex behaviors, children were instructed to watch attentively, to verbalize what they saw happening, or to count rapidly. Subjects who verbalized the model's responses later reproduced these responses better than those who merely watched. The latter, however, reproduced more responses than those who counted rapidly. The counting apparently distracted the child and reduced the attention that he paid to the model, thereby showing that when attention is divided observational learning suffers. Some evidence of the importance of attention in an aggression experiment has been reported by Parton and Geshuri (1971), who showed that a model is more likely to be imitated when carrying out aggression with vigor and intensity than when making the same responses in a more restrained way. Responses performed with intensity may engage and hold the viewer's attention better than less intense ones.

The responses that a child learns from observing aggressive models are, from the standpoint of the theory of observational learning, not simply generalized aggression but a set of specific motor responses demonstrated by the model. The child, moreover, does not learn simply that harm should be inflicted upon the victim. Children in an experiment by Dubanoski and Parton (1971) were shown a number of aggressive acts carried out against clown dolls. Some of the children saw these responses performed by a live human model, whereas the others saw the instruments of attack guided to their targets by invisible nylon threads. The latter treatment duplicated the former but eliminated the example of the model's precise motor responses. When the children later played with the same toys, it was found that those who had observed the live model hit and stab the dolls were more aggressive than those who had witnessed similar acts committed by free-floating objects.

Once acquired, modeled aggression tends to be persistent. Hicks (1965) tested children for imitative aggression both immediately after observation of the model and again 6 months later. Relative to children who had not seen the model, the ones who had been exposed previously made more imitative responses after the long lapse of time. Hicks later (1968) demonstrated retention of more than 60% of the model's aggressive acts 2 months after observation and 40% as long as 8 months afterward. A long-range modeling effect has also been reported among Kniveton (1973), who has shown imitative aggression among British preschool children 5 months after observation of the model.

As we noted earlier, acquisition of an aggressive response does not necessarily mean that the response will later be performed. Whether or not an acquired aggressive act will be acted out by the observer depends upon both the perceived consequences of the model's behavior for the model and the consequences of aggressing for the observer. If the observer sees that the model is punished for aggressing, he may inhibit overt aggression even though he has thoroughly learned the response and is capable of performing it (Bandura, Ross, & Ross, 1963b). What is more, whether a learned aggressive response is performed depends, to some extent, on whether the observer is rewarded for doing so. Both of these contingencies have been shown in a study by Bandura (1965). Children saw a film of a model carrying out aggression with the model being either rewarded, punished, or suffering no consequences at all for aggression. Children who observed a punished model subsequently had fewer imitative aggressive responses than did those who saw the model either rewarded or treated indifferently. Boys also manifested more aggression overall than did girls. Later, however, the experimenter offered each child a reward for performing the responses carried out earlier by the model. The addition of this incentive canceled out the effects on imitative aggression of reward and punishment to the model and also greatly reduced sex differences. Children of both sexes in all three treatment conditions had apparently learned the model's behaviors equally well. Reward served chiefly to facilitate performance of these learned responses.

Bandura (1973) has identified four interrelated types of subprocesses involved in learning through the observation of others. Restatement of these serves as a summary on the learning of aggression from aggressive models. The first set of processes is *attentional* and refers to the premise that a stimulus will be effective as a cue for modeling only to the extent that the observer is attending to it. The second set of processes has to do with *retention* and includes the forming of mental images, verbal labeling, symbolic coding, and rehearsal in memory. The third set is *motor reproduction* processes, which must be available to the observer before he can execute the behaviors observed in the model. Finally, *reinforcement and motivational* processes are involved since the child will not necessarily perform an acquired response unless he is motivated to do so, such as by the promise of a reward.

Reduction of Restraints against Aggressing

Observation of violence carried out by others may produce aggression in ways other than those involving the learning of novel responses. It may also promote an overall reduction of restraints against aggressing by showing the observer that aggression is permissible, or even desirable, in certain situations. In modeling experiments such as those described earlier, children who are exposed to aggressive models sometimes perform not only the model's specific responses but also more nonimitative aggression than children who are not exposed to the model. Bandura *et al.* (1963b) showed such an effect in an experiment in which children observed an aggressive model either in a realistic context or dressed as a cartoon character. Although children exposed to the aggressive "cartoon" model later performed fewer imitative aggressive responses than those who had seen the more realistic model, they committed just as many generally aggressive responses (imitative plus nonimitative) as the latter. The high incidence of nonimitative aggression in children who saw the cartoonlike figure suggests that such relatively unrealistic characterizations of violence may convey information that aggression is, in general, permitted and perhaps even fun. Other experiments with children have shown an increase in generalized aggression following exposure to violent programs similar to those seen on television (Steuer, Applefield, & Smith, 1971; Ellis & Sekyra, 1972).

Observation of aggression in experiments with adult subjects has been shown to elicit aggression by informing the observer that aggression is permitted and, thereby, reducing restraints against aggressing. Wheeler and Caggiula (1966) have shown that such behavior is a special case of behavioral contagion. When the subject is instigated to attack an antagonist, because of an attack, insult, or some other cause, the subject is initially inhibited by socialized restraints against violence. After observing a model attack the antagonist, however, the observer is emboldened to aggress on his own. In a subsequent study, Wheeler and Smith (1967) showed that censure of the aggressive model by the experimenter reinstates the subject's original inhibitions against aggressing, perhaps by informing the observer that such behavior was not sanctioned in that setting. Such censure of an aggressive model, however, while inhibiting aggression toward the initial frustrator, may provoke the subject to express hostility toward the person delivering the censure (Cohen & Murray, 1972).

Further evidence that inhibitions against aggressing are involved in modeling situations has been adduced by Bandura (1965), who has shown that punishment of an aggressive model can limit a child's willingness to perform the observed acts, and by Hicks (1968), who has found that a similar restraint can be imposed upon the child by the presence of an adult who utters verbal disapproval of the model's behavior. Furthermore, Baron (1971) has shown that adults experience a greater disinhibition of aggression by observing a single aggressive model than by seeing both an aggressive one and a nonaggressive one. Discrepant modeling cues probably elicit conflicting response tendencies, rendering the subject unable to determine which one signals the appropriate behavior.

Performance of modeled aggression is also affected by the subject's perceptions of the emotional state of the model, which can have either inhibiting or disinhibiting consequences for the subject. Powers and Geen (1972) commanded subjects to deliver shocks of progressively greater intensity to a confederate supposedly as punishment for the latter's errors on a task. Prior to this, the subject had observed another person in the same situation either obey the experimenter's orders to give 30 progressively stronger shocks or disobey the command to go beyond a certain moderate level. At the outset, the model appeared to be either calm or nervous. In half the conditions, the emotional state of the model remained constant over the entire session, but, in the other half, it changed, with the calm model becoming obviously more nervous and the nervous one becoming calmer. The results of the study (Figure 1) showed that observation of a disobedient model led to less obedient aggression than observation of an obedient one. Furthermore, when the model's apparent emotional state changed, the behavior of the observer was affected: A disobedient model who became nervous was imitated less than one who remained calm, whereas one who became calm elicited more imitative disobedience than one who remained nervous. Perhaps the subject inferred from the emotional consequences of disobedience for the model what type of emotions he himself might experience after disobedience. Observing that the experience had been calming for the confederate may have assuaged the subject's fears about how he would later feel in that situation; perceiving increased nervousness in the model may have motivated the subject to avoid that condition. In both cases the subject's overall level of restraint against aggression was affected.

An experiment by Drabman and Thomas (1974a) has shown that observation of filmed violence can do more than merely enhance momentary expressions of aggression; such observation may promote a general tolerance for aggression by others as well. Children in this study were given the responsibility for monitoring the play behavior of younger children. Half of the older children had been exposed previously to a violent cowboy film, whereas the other half had seen no film. At first, the younger children played amicably, but, as time went on, they became more and more destructive, eventually beginning to fight among each other. The investigators found that children who had

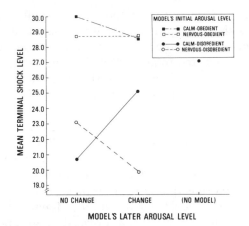

Figure 1. Mean intensity of terminal shock given by subjects in various modeling conditions (From Powers & Geen 1972).

earlier seen the violent movie allowed a longer amount of time to elapse before reporting the abusive behavior of the youngsters than did those who had seen no film. The majority of children who had seen the cowboy film did not report the actions of the others until they had erupted into fighting, whereas most of those who had seen no film reported the behavior of the little ones before it progressed to such a stage. In a subsequent study (Drabman & Thomas, 1974b), the same investigators showed that children exposed to an arousing but nonviolent film behaved in much the same way as did those who saw no film in the previous study. Overall, therefore, prior exposure to violence appears to have promoted a tolerant attitude toward fighting.

The information provided by the example of others aggressing may have an effect other than simply as a signal that aggression is permitted. It may initiate a restructuring of the observer's judgment of what constitutes an act of violence. For example, in the Drabman–Thomas experiments, the violent films shown to some of the children may have defined for these observers what are and what are not to be considered acts of aggression within the setting of the study. In terms of social judgment theory, the film may have caused the observers' anchor point on a hypothetical scale describing aggressive acts to shift in the direction of greater violence. Thus, a fight between the younger children that might have been defined as aggression prior to the witnessing of the movie could have been defined as relatively less "aggressive" after the film.

This conclusion is suggested by an experiment by Harrison and Pepitone (1972). In this study, subjects delivered slightly painful shocks to a rat as punishment for responses. Some of the subjects were informed that the shock apparatus they were using could also deliver a moderately strong shock (somewhat more intense than the slight ones the subjects were instructed to give), but that such shocks could not be given to the rat. Other subjects were told that their devices could deliver shocks of extreme intensity to the animal but were likewise forbidden to use such shocks. It was found that subjects in the condition characterized by a large discrepancy between the intensity of shocks delivered and those that were possible (but forbidden) gave the slightly intense shocks with greater frequency than subjects who perceived a small discrepancy between what was allowed and what was proscribed. The authors reasoned that the perception of an intense shock as an alternative, even though it could not be employed, caused subjects in the large-discrepancy condition to revise upward their anchor point for defining an effectively punitive shock. The slightly intense shock actually used was, therefore, contrasted to this upper value and was defined as less intense than it would have been had the anchor point been lower, as it was for subjects in the small-discrepancy condition. Subjects in the large-discrepancy condition, therefore, compensated by giving the permitted shocks more often. Observing fighting by others may act in a similar way to bring about a shift in the observer's judgment of when a given act is to be defined as aggression.

Impulsive Aggression

Berkowitz (1971) has described the effects of observed violence on aggression in terms of "impulsive," or reactive, behavior. Briefly stated, this point of view holds that aggressive behaviors may simply be elicited by appropriate stimuli. As examples of such reactive violence, Berkowitz (1974) has noted that relatively few homicides are the result of premeditated determination to kill but are, instead, "spontaneous acts of passion" carried out quickly and impulsively. At best, the only expectancy that seems to characterize such behaviors is a general idea that they will, in some way, hurt the victim. Aggression of this type, Berkowitz has proposed may be elicited by observation of violence carried out by others or, in some cases, by the mere presence of the instruments of violence.

An early test of the impulsive aggression hypothesis was an experiment by Berkowitz and LePage (1967). Male subjects were either attacked or treated with (less hostility) by a confederate, and afterward they were allowed to give electric shocks to the latter. As they delivered the shocks, some of the subjects sat beside a table on which lay a rifle and a hand gun; the remaining subjects were not exposed to weapons. The behavior of the subjects revealed an interaction between provocation and the presence of weapons: Subjects who had been attacked retaliated against the confederate with a greater number of shocks in the presence of weapons than in their absence. Subjects who had not previously been attacked were uniformly less punitive than those who had been attacked, failing to manifest any differences in aggressiveness as a function of presence or absence of weapons. Berkowitz and LePage concluded that objects of violence are stimuli for aggression in subjects who have first been aroused to aggress, as the hypothesis of impulsive aggression would predict.

Subsequent investigations of the "weapons effect" have yielded conflicting evidence. Tannenbaum (1971) showed subjects a sexually arousing movie that was periodically interrupted by insertion of brief glimpses of weapons and to which, in addition, sections of aggressive verbal commentary had been added. Subjects given this treatment were later more aggressive than others who had seen either a silent version of the movie or one containing the aggressive commentary but no pictures of weapons. Leyens and Parke (1973) have also shown that photo-slides of weapons elicit greater subsequent aggression in viewers than slides depicting neutral items. Fischer, Kelm, and Rose (1969) have also reported that exposure to different types of knives can also elicit aggression in previously angered subjects.

By contrast, a number of studies have failed to find evidence supporting the weapons effect (Buss, Booker, & Buss, 1972; Ellis, Weinir, & Miller, 1971; Page & Scheidt, 1971). Commenting on failures to replicate the findings of his study with LePage, Berkowitz (1974) has conceded that the weapons effect may be a relatively weak one that can be masked by situational variables that create strong inhibitions against aggressing. The study by Ellis et al. (1971) suggests such a conclusion. In the experiment, male subjects who had not been shocked by a confederate gave significantly fewer shocks when weapons were present than when they were absent. By contrast, subjects who had previously been given eight shocks later gave slightly, though not significantly, more shocks in the presence of weapons than when no weapons were present. These data suggest that the presence of weapons elicits restraints against aggression under normal circumstances. To elicit aggression in angered subjects, the presence of weapons must overcome the mitigating effects of these restraints. The finding of no significant differences as a function of weapons among angered subjects must, therefore, be evaluated with respect to the opposite effect of the weapons among nonangered subjects.

A more recent investigation by Turner and Simons (1974) further indicates the attenuating effects of inhibitions against aggressing upon the elicitation of aggression by weapons. In this study, male subjects were exposed to weapons as they delivered shocks to a confederate that had previously angered them in a close replication of one of the levels of the Berkowitz–LePage experiment. Prior to entering the laboratory, the subject had been approached by a confederate posing as the subject previously run. This confederate created one of three levels of sophistication in the subject. To some subjects, he said that weapons were involved and were probably intended to influence the subject (high sophistication) and, to others, that some sort of deception was probably involved (medium sophistication). To still others he said only that he had just been in the experiment (low sophistication). After the subject had entered the laboratory, the experimenter then induced either a high level of evaluation apprehension, by informing him that the procedure would indicate whether or not he was "maladjusted," or a low level of apprehension, by giving a less threatening introduction to the experiment.

The results of the study, shown in Table 1, indicate that both the level of sophistication induced in the subject and the degree of evaluation apprehension led to main effects: Both sophistication regarding the true nature of the procedure and apprehension led to a reduction in the intensity of the subject's retaliation. Furthermore, the least aggression was found in subjects who were both highly sophisticated and highly apprehensive; this combination led to even less aggression than was found in subjects who were low in sophistication and apprehension and who, moreover, were not exposed to weapons. The findings of this study suggest that evaluation apprehension made subjects anxious, and that this anxiety interfered with and inhibited aggressive behavior. Possibly the sophistication treatment also created differential anxiety: Self-reports of anxiety were significantly higher in the medium sophistication condition and slightly higher in the high sophistication condition than in the low sophistication group. Sophistication may have bred suspiciousness, an expectancy that che experimenter was being devious, and consequent anxiety.

Inhibitions arising from personality variables may also inhibit weapon-elicited aggression. Fraczek and Macaulay (1971) found that only males who had scored low on a measure of emotionality were more aggressive in the presence of weapons. Highly emotional men tended to manifest less aggression when weapons were present. The authors argued that highly emotional men were made anxious by the sight of weapons and, thus, inhibited aggression. We must conclude, therefore,

Table 1   Mean Number of Shocks Administered in the Experimental Treatments[a,b]

Evaluation apprehension	Subject sophistication			
	Low	Medium	High	$\bar{X}$
Low	6.15a	5.30ab	4.38bc	5.28_I
High	4.77bc	4.25bc	3.42c	4.14_{II}
$\bar{X}$	5.46_A	4.78_{AB}	3.90_B	
No weapons	5.18ab	—	—	

[a] From Turner and Simons (1974).
[b] Means which share a subscript in common are not significantly different at the .05 level by a Duncan multiple range test. Comparisons are to be made only among subscripts of the same typescript. Each cell mean is based on 11 subjects.

that any attempt to confirm or deny the possibility that weapons elicit aggression must include proper controls for both situational and personality variables that might predispose the person toward counteraggressive restraints.

Bandura (1973) has proposed that the weapons effect is due to a lowering of restraints against aggression elicited by the sight of instruments of violence. Thus, the subject, by seeing guns prominently displayed, may conclude that aggression is acceptable behavior under the circumstances. This explanation is somewhat supported by the discovery of Buss *et al.* (1972, Experiment III) that subjects who fired a gun after shocking one victim were later more punitive toward a second victim than others who did not fire a gun between the first and second shock sessions. Consistent with Bandura's suggestion, this finding may indicate that the subject who fired a gun judged such behavior to be acceptable. It may also support Berkowitz's general point of view. Perhaps the presence of weapons does elicit covert and fractional aggressive responses (that become explicit when the subject is permitted to use the weapon), and perhaps it is these responses that subsequently reduce inhibitions against aggression. The finding that aggression facilitates further aggression has been reported in other contexts (e.g., Geen, Stonner, & Shope, 1975). Therefore, the disinhibition of aggression associated with the presence of weapons may not be due to the information that weapons provide about the suitability of aggression but rather to the covert aggressive reactions that they elicit.

Most experiments that have shown a relationship between the observation of violence and aggression have involved some treatment whereby the observer is first aroused or angered. Several such treatments have been used. Physical attacks, verbal insults and badgering, frustrative interference, and failure at a ego-involving task have all been shown to be strong antecedents of aggression in subjects who later observe violence (e.g., Berkowitz & Geen, 1966, 1967; Geen, 1968; Berkowitz & Alioto, 1972; Hanratty *et al.* 1972). Berkowitz (1969) has summarized the effects of the various treatments by proposing that each produces general arousal which, in turn, intensifies aggressive responses to the observed violence. In a test of this idea, Geen and O'Neal (1969) found that subjects stimulated by white noise shocked a fellow subject more intensely than did subjects not exposed to the noise after viewing a violent film. Following the presentation of an arousing but nonviolent film, however, noise had no effects on aggressive behavior. Thus, even a purely physical stimulus served as an antecedent of aggression provided that some act of violence had previously been seen. A study by Christy, Gelfand, and Hartmann (1971) tends to support this notion by showing that induced competition enhances the imitation of both aggressive and nonaggressive models, regardless of whether subjects succeeded or failed at the competitive task. They concluded that competition, by producing arousal, exacerbates the emission of situationally relevant imitative behavior.

Reactive aggression is promoted by certain features of the observed violence. When witnessed aggression is especially associated with the potential victim of the subject's attack, the subject behaves more aggressively than when there is no such association. In several studies, it has been shown that an angered subject is more likely to retaliate against an antagonist when the latter is associated with the victim of an observed beating than when he is not. The association can be a clear one, created by referring to the subject's victim as a boxer (Berkowitz, 1965a), or a fairly subtle one based on either first or last names that are identical to those of characters in the violent film (Berkowitz & Geen, 1966; Geen & Berkowitz, 1966, 1967). More recently, Turner and Berkowitz (1972) have shown that, when subjects were instructed to empathize and identify with the winning boxer in a filmed fight, they later behaved more aggressively than subjects who were merely told to watch the film or to identify with a fight judge. Similar findings have been reported by Leyens and Picus (1973). Such findings suggest that identification with the aggressor, or covert role taking, enhances reactive aggression.

Berkowitz (1974) has explained reactive aggression in terms of classical conditioning and stimulus generalization, so that "reported or portrayed violence in the mass media is associated with other violent scenes the individual has encountered previously—there is a response-mediated stimulus generalization—and these stimuli, in turn, can evoke a range of aggressive responses [pp. 105–106]." Scenes of violence in the mass media have some generalized similarity to other stimuli associated with violence in the person's life history and ultimately come to act as conditioned stimuli for aggression. In a more recent theoretical analysis of impulsive aggression, Berkowitz (1974) has pointed to reinforcement for aggression as another important element in the process. If, in the person's lifetime, stimuli become associated not only with fighting but also with reinforcement for such behavior, they are especially likely to become elicitors of similar behaviors later on. This has been demonstrated in an experiment by Swart and Berkowitz (cited by Berkowitz, 1974).

After first being either insulted or treated without hostility by an experimental confederate, male subjects shocked the confederate each time a discriminative stimulus, a light, came on. On some of the trials, a neutral stimulus, a tone, followed the light. On two-thirds of all trials, the shock was followed by the conspicuous tripping of a shutter on a box located near the subject. Half the men were informed that the shutter tripping indicated that their victim had been hurt by the shock, whereas half were told that it was irrelevant to the other man's condition. It was assumed that a signal informing the subject of pain being inflicted upon his adversary (when the latter had been insulting) would reinforce the aggression that had produced the pain (cf. Feshbach, Stiles, & Bitter, 1961).

After a series of 70 trials under these conditions, the subject was instructed to deliver shocks to another person, a second confederate, each time the light or the tone came on. Inspection of the results of the study, shown in Table 2, indicates that the discriminative stimulus evoked shocks of longer duration, relative to the neutral stimulus, when it had originally been paired with pain inflicted upon a provocateur. An internal analysis of the data further revealed that some of the subjects in all conditions had increased the duration of shocks given in response to the light (relative to the tone) during the original 70 trials, whereas others had decreased the duration of shocks given during the same period. When the data on duration of shocks given to the second confederate were broken down according to whether the subject had increased or decreased shock duration earlier, the effect of prior reinforcement is demonstrated even more clearly. Those who increased shock duration during the original trials, and who may, therefore, be considered to have shown positive reinforcement effects over those trials, gave much longer shocks to the light stimulus (relative to the tone) later on than did those who showed negative reinforcement effects (38.0 versus −27.5). Overall, the experiment showed that stimuli

Table 2 Differences in Duration of Shocks Given to Second Confederate
(After S^D—After Neutral Stimulus)[a,b]

	Pain cue signal	Signal not as pain cue
Insulted subjects		
Positive reinforcement effect in training	38.0	2.3
Negative reinforcement effect in training	− 27.5	− 27.3
	10.5	− 25.0
Noninsulted subjects		
Positive reinforcement effect in training	− 45.0	7.8
Negative reinforcement effect in training	− 10.1	− 4.7
	− 55.1	− 3.1

[a] From Berkowitz (1974)

[b] Positive scores indicate that the shocks were longer to the S^D then to the neutral stimulus. Data are in milliseconds. The subjects showing a "positive reinforcement effect" displayed a gain in the relative duration of shocks to S^D from the start to the completion of the initial training. There are five men in each group. The mean of 38.0 is significantly different from all others by planned comparisons.

associated with reinforced aggression subsequently became more potent elicitors of aggression than stimuli not associated with reinforced aggression.

To summarize briefly the reactive aggression hypothesis, we should note again, as we did at the beginning of this section, that the major emphasis is the impulsive and irrational nature of some aggressive acts. As we have seen, such outbursts may be triggered by stimuli that have acquired strong associations with violent behavior, especially when such behavior has had reinforcing outcomes. Among such stimuli may be those emanating from the mass media of communication. Arousal states produced by frustration, attack, or other such antecedents may serve primarily to activate and intensify responses to these stimuli.

Observed Violence and Arousal

Displays of violence, such as those in the mass media, may be a potent source of emotional arousal, as anyone knows who has ever experienced physiological change while watching an aggressive movie or television program. These conditions of heightened arousal may activate aggressive responses to provocations, such as interpersonal attacks or insults (Tannenbaum, 1972), or summate with arousal produced by the provocation itself (Doob & Climie, 1972; Doob & Korschenbaum, 1973).

Zillmann (1971) used this general line of reasoning to account for the results of an experiment in which male subjects were shown either an aggressive or an erotic film subsequent to aggressing against a provocateur. The erotic film, which showed a man and a woman engaged in precoital activity, had previously been shown to be more arousing physiologically than both a violent prizefight film and a third film having neither aggressive nor sexual meaning. When shown to previously angered subjects, the erotic movie was followed by higher levels of retaliatory aggression than either of the other films. The erotic material had been carefully prepared to eliminate all hints of violence and to stress the romantic side of sexual activity and, thus, did not provide cues for aggressive responses. Zillmann concluded that excitation elicited by the films was still present in a residual form at the time of the subject's attack upon his antagonist, and that this excitation transferred to, and summated with, aggressive arousal elicited by the provocation. Meyer (1972b) has also reported data showing that a sexual stag film provokes greater aggression among angered males than a more neutral one, but he differed from Zillmann in finding that a violent movie was followed by greater aggression than was the erotic one. The films used in the two studies were different, however, so precise comparisons are impossible.

The "excitation-transfer" principle described earlier and the hypothesis on reactive aggression outlined in the previous section both lead to the prediction that an angered person would behave more aggressively after seeing an enactment of violence than after witnessing a neutral and nonarousing activity. The hypotheses differ in their explanations for this prediction, with one stressing the aggression-eliciting properties of violence and the other the arousal that violence produces. Zillmann and Johnson (1973) conducted an experiment in which they sought to test the predictive accuracy of the two hypotheses. After being provoked by a confederate, the subject was shown either a scene from a violent western movie, a historical travelogue, or no movie at all. Prior to provocation and again after the film had been shown, the subject was instructed to deliver some electric shocks to the confederate; various measures of physiological arousal were likewise taken on both occasions. Therefore, the study contained two features not found in previous studies on observation of violence: a no-film condition that represented a zero-treatment control against which the effects of both the violent and the nonviolent films could be tested and a before-after measure of aggression and arousal.

Among previously provoked subjects, observation of the nonarousing film led to a general decrease in arousal, measured by both blood pressure and skin temperature, relative to subjects who saw no film.

Provoked subjects who observed the violent film revealed a maintenance of arousal at levels close to those produced by the provocation. Table 3 shows the change in intensity of shocks from the pre-provocation series to the series given just after the film. The data reveal that subjects who saw the violent film were not significantly more aggressive than those who saw no film, and that subjects who saw the neutral film were less aggressive than those in the no-film condition. Zillmann and Johnson concluded that previous studies that lacked the no-film condition and showed more aggression following the violent film than the control were actually demonstrations of reduced aggression due to the latter. Therefore, they argue that "reactive aggression" is not a suitable explanation for data such as those reported in the preceding section. Instead, they propose that the presentation of a nonarousing film following provocation distracts the attention of the observer from the injury that has been done to him. Presumably a violent film should also produce such an attentional shift. The violent film, however, also keeps the individual's arousal level relatively high so that considerable residual excitation is carried over to the situation in which the subject delivers his second retaliatory set of shocks. The angry subject may, in the presence of violent stimuli, be reminded of his own grievance toward the confederate, or, as Zillmann and Johnson put it, exposure to films "which reiterate the individual's acute motivational state apparently can help sustain the level of physiological excitation for some time. It thus appears that aggressive materials potentially extend the time in which the severely provoked individual is motivated to engage in aggressive activities [p. 275]."

We shall return to this idea of "reinstatement of motive state" later. First, though, the Zillmann–Johnson study requires some comment. In the no-film control condition, the subject delivered the second series of shocks almost immediately after being provoked, whereas, in the two film conditions, an additional 5.5 min intervened, this being the running time of each film. The authors purposely omitted from their design a condition in which the subject would have waited 5.5 min without seeing a film (the most obvious sort of control) on the grounds that the long enforced inactivity could be frustrating or could give the subject time to cope with his anger, in either case introducing behavioral confounding. While admitting that they could not control for elapsed time, the authors used the before–after measure of aggression in order to have some common basis for measurement among subjects who witnessed violence and those who did not. What they showed in their study, then, is that angry subjects, who are forced to wait for more than 5 min before counterattacking and who observe a violent movie in the interim, are as punitive as those who are allowed to retaliate immediately. Such a finding does not rule out the possibility of reactive aggression. Perhaps, exposure to the violent film did elicit impulsive aggressive responses that were powerful enough to withstand a long waiting period during which time subjects not exposed to violence experienced a cooling of emotion. Elicited aggression could, in other words, have overpowered a contrary tendency to become less aggressive because of a gradual decrease in hostility. Use of a no-film condition that compelled the subject to wait for 5.5 min but still kept him occupied (such as by solving a puzzle or making baskets) might have obviated this problem. Finally, the use of a nonviolent but arousing film as an added control would have allowed a better test of how much of the effects was due to residual excitation and how much to violence of the cowboy movie.

In the typical experiment on observation of aggression, the subject is exposed to a relatively short presentation, seldom more than 5–10 min in duration. Such studies do not allow for any conclusions concerning possible effects of lengthy exposure to violence or influences that previous history of such exposure may have upon reactivity to short presentations. History of exposure could, however, be an important individual difference variable. Controlling for this variable through random sampling and assignment of subjects to conditions could be obscuring some strong effects of observation of violence upon arousal, as shown in a study by Cline, Croft, and Courrier (1973). In this experiment, children between the ages of 5 and 12 were classified in terms of how many hours per week they watched television, groups designated as "high" or "low" viewers were thereby created. All children were shown a composite movie made up of a violent boxing episode, an arousing but nonviolent skiing sequence, and a humorous slapstick scene. The children's reaction during the showing of the film revealed that prior exposure to television reduced the arousal potential of the violent scene. Children who had received a high degree of exposure to the medium

Table 3 Mean Changes of Shock Intensity Over All 18 Responses[a,b]

Provocation	Communication condition		
	No exposure	Neutral film	Aggressive film
Minimal	−1.067[a]	−.978[a]	−1.511[a]
Extreme	1.749[b]	−.542[a]	1.547[b]

[a] From Zillmann and Johnson (1973).

[b] Differences between means were analyzed by the Newman–Keuls method. Cells having different superscripts differ significantly at $p < .05$.

showed less increase in skin conductance and blood volume pulse amplitude while observing the violent portions of the film than those who had had less exposure. No comparable differences between the two conditions were observed in response to the nonviolent portions of the film. This finding suggests that prolonged exposure to television is associated with habituation to violence but not to otherwise exciting material. Perhaps this was due to the high probability that highly exposed children had seen considerable violence, given the nature of much current television programming.

Research on the arousing effects of mass media violence, therefore, shows that such programming does have fairly strong short-term influences. At the least, the observation of violence tends to sustain arousal levels at a level attained prior to observation, in contrast to nonviolent presentations that promote a decline in activation. Arousal elicited by a display of violence may carry over to, and summate with, arousal associated with instigation to aggression.

Maintenance of Aggressive Motivation

Zillmann and Johnson (1973), as was mentioned earlier, proposed that violent films, by reminding the angered subject of the attack recently inflicted upon him, keep him aroused for a period of time during which his anger might otherwise dissipate. The fact that subjects who have observed violence are more aroused at the time of retaliation accounts for their greater aggressiveness. In this section, a variant of the Zillmann–Johnson hypothesis will be proposed, in which the idea of reiteration of motives will be applied to a wider range of potential motivational states. This hypothesis, which has obvious features in common with some of the other points of view reviewed in this chapter, proposes that the person who observes violence makes a comparison between his motivational state and that of the actors in the observed event and uses cues from the latter as information concerning appropriate behavior for himself. Thus, the subject in a typical aggression experiment is not certain how he should behave, he is unsure of the appropriateness of his motivational and emotional states to the situation, he is largely inhibited in aggressing, and he is susceptible to cues from his surroundings regarding the suitability of his motives and emotions and the relative desirability of possible behaviors.

In such a situation, the subject who has just been attacked, insulted, or otherwise provoked by another person is aware of several factors. He has just been attacked, in all probability he perceives the attack as unjustified, he is angry and prepared to retaliate, but he is also cognizant

of social restraints against open aggression. He then observes a television show or a movie in which aggression is committed in a context that
not only makes it permissible, but perhaps even highly desirable. This
type of presentation may remind the subject, and keep him reminded,
of his motive to retaliate. It may set an example that informs the subject that retaliatory aggression is a proper response following unjustified
provocation, and it may also keep him aroused at a level previously
reached because of the provocation. Arousal may be a conditioned
response to cues that have been associated with fighting in the past, in a
way suggested by Berkowitz's general point of view. It may also be a
consequence of reduced inhibitions against aggressing: As the subject
becomes less restrained, he may become excited at the impending prospects of getting even with his antagonist.

An anecdote recently reported in the news illustrates the hypothesis
proposed here. It describes the emotional response of Greek citizens to a
film portrayal of punishment being meted out to persons associated
with the now-overthrown military government.

> After the junta's iron-fisted rule, Greece is now savoring the political and cultural
> freedoms of a revived democracy. But the new-found liberties, rather than mellowing
> the desire for retribution, seem to have inflamed it. Released from rigid censorship,
> almost every art form has been used to launch direct or indirect attacks on the junta.
> The French-Algerian film Z—based on the 1963 assassination of a popular left-wing
> member of the Greek Parliament and banned by the junta when it was released in
> 1969—is now being shown in Athens for the first time. In the past five weeks a record
> 500,000 have seen it. When the film's hero, a young tenacious prosecutor, penetrates
> an official cover-up and indicts six police officials for complicity in the murder, the
> audience almost invariably responds with a frenzy that verges on blood lust [*Time*
> Magazine, 3 February 1975, p. 40B].

From the premises stated here, we might expect that the more similar
the motives of the subject are to those of the actors in the observed violence, the greater will be the arousal, the loss of inhibition, and the consequent aggression of the subject. We would expect, therefore, in the
typical experiment in which the subject is provoked, retaliatory aggression to be greater when the subject perceives the aggressor in an observed presentation to be likewise motivated by a desire for revenge.
The results of several experiments support this expectation. Hoyt
(1970) reported that a boxing movie elicited more aggression in viewers,
all of whom had first been provoked by a confederate, when the action
was described as revenge by the winning fighter than when the winner
was said to be defending himself. In a related study, Meyer (1972a)
found similar effects when a true-to-life display of violence was shown.
Subjects retaliated against a confederate after seeing a newsreel in

which a Vietnamese guerrilla is stabbed to death by soldiers. The killing was described to some subjects as vengeance for atrocities inflicted by the guerrilla upon civilians and to others as the cold-blooded murder of a prisoner of war. Still others saw the film without comment. Subjects who had been told that the execution was justified as revenge for atrocities were more punitive toward their antagonist than subjects in either of the other conditions.

Geen and Stonner (1973) further tested the possibility that observation of aggression defined as revenge elicits greater aggressiveness in angered viewers than seeing the same acts defined in other terms. Some subjects were informed that a prize fight shown in a videotape was motivated by the winning boxer's desire for vengeance, others were told that the fight was simply professional boxing without hostility, and still others had no introductory statements. Half of the subjects were given a chance to give electric shocks to the confederate after seeing the tape, and finally all subjects gave a verbal report of how restrained they had felt as they delivered the shocks. The results of the study show that both aggressive behavior and restraints against aggressing were influenced by an interaction between the two independent variables (Tables 4 and 5). Subjects who had been attacked were more aggressive than nonattacked ones after both had seen a display of vengeful aggression, but the opposite was found after professional fighting had been observed. Reports of restraint tended to parallel the aggressive behavior; generally lower restraints against aggressing were reported in conditions characterized by the highest shock intensities.

The finding that subjects who had not been attacked by the confederate shocked with greater intensity and were also less inhibited about aggressing after seeing professional violence than after observing revenge is consistent with the viewpoint that subjects are influenced by the comparability of their motives to those of aggressing actors. Sub-

Table 4 Mean Intensities of Shocks[a,b]

	Treatment	
Film context	Attack	No attack
Vengeance	6.88_a	4.14_b
Professional	$5.57_{a,b}$	5.74_a
Control	$5.34_{a,b}$	$4.72_{a,b}$

[a] From Geen and Stonner, 1973.

[b] Cells having common subscripts are not significantly different at the .05 level by a Duncan multiple range test.

Table 5 Mean Ratings of Restraint Over Shocking[a,b]

Film context	Treatment	
	Attack	No attack
Vengeance	$56.8_{a,b}$	76.0_a
Professional	69.3_a	43.6_b
Control	$60.2_{a,b}$	66.7_a

[a] From Geen and Stonner, 1973.

[b] High scale score represents high level of expressed restraint. Cells having common subscripts are not significantly different at the .05 level by a Duncan multiple range test.

jects in the nonattacked condition had no obvious motive to shock the confederate, who had done nothing to provoke them. They did, however, have a reason to give shocks—the experimenter had commanded them to give a shock each time the confederate supposedly made an error on the task. Even subjects who had not been provoked were, therefore, not free to refrain from aggressing against the confederate. Presumably the aggression they committed was not founded on hostility but was instead instrumental to the attainment of a goal unrelated to aggression—the approval of the experimenter. These subjects may have experienced fairly strong restraints against aggressing that were partly overcome by the reminder, provided by the example of professional violence, that aggression may sometimes be carried out in the absence of hostility when some other motive exists.

In a subsequent study, Geen and Stonner (1972) showed that the portrayal of an unsuccessful attempt at revenge fails to produce lowered restraints against aggressing and also elicits less aggression than depiction of a successful act of revenge. As in the first study, one group of subjects was attacked by a confederate and another group was treated less provocatively. The prize fight tape was then shown with some subjects being told that it represented vengeance sought by the winner (a man named Dunne in the story) and others being told that the fight was merely professional. A third group was told that vengeance was sought by the man (named Kelly in the story) who eventually *loses* the fight. A fourth group was told that Kelly was seeking revenge and was further informed that in the original film, not shown in the experiment, the man eventually does go on to win the fight. Subjects then shocked the confederate.

The results (Table 6) shows that when provoked subjects are shown an example of an unsuccessful attempt at revenge (i.e., Kelly fails), they are less aggressive than after seeing a successful attempt at revenge by either boxer. Self-reports of restraint taken after the experiment again parallel the shock intensity data, with conditions marked by high shock intensities uniformly showing relatively low levels of reported restraint. Being shown a failing attempt at revenge apparently informs the subject that vengeance is not always attained and may actually lead to even more injury—a lesson that prompts discretion in the subject as he comtemplates his own retaliation. Furthermore, as in the earlier study, nonprovoked subjects were more punitive after observing professional violence than after seeing either successful or unsuccessful attempts at revenge.

A third study by Geen and Stonner (1974) showed that, in addition to lowering restraints against aggressing, the observation of vengeful aggression also maintained the arousal of angered subjects at a relatively high level. In this study, four groups of previously attacked and nonattacked subjects were used. All saw a videotape of a scene from a western movie in which a small band of gunmen fight and overcome a larger group of attackers. The fighting was described, by means of a narrative read before the showing of the tape, as motivated either by a desire for revenge on the part of the gunfighters, as services rendered by these men for payment, or as an act of unselfish altruism. Subjects in a fourth group saw the tape without commentary. As Table 7 shows, the combination of prior attack on the subject and the description of the fight as vengeance elicited the most aggression when the subject later shocked the confederate.

Measurement of blood pressure was made at three points during the procedure: before the attack on the subject, immediately after the attack, and just after the showing of the tape (before the subject shocked the confederate). Subjects in the eight conditions did not differ in mean blood pressure at the beginning of the experiment, but subjects who

Table 6   Mean Intensities of Shocks Given by Subjects[a,b]

	Treatment	
Film context	Attack	No attack
Vengeance–Dunne	$6.29_{a,b}$	4.72_c
Vengeance–Kelly	$6.63_{a,b}$	4.87_c
Professional	$5.16_{b,c}$	6.82_a
Vengeance–Kelly fails	4.94_c	4.91_c

[a] From Geen and Stonner, 1972.

[b] All cells having common subscripts are not significantly different at the .05 level by a Duncan multiple range test.

Table 7 Mean Intensities of Shocks Given by Subjects[a,b]

Film narrative	Treatment of subject by confederate	
	Attack	No attack
Vengeance	5.29$_a$	2.58$_c$
Professional	3.67$_b$	2.69$_{b,c}$
Altruistic	3.39$_{b,c}$	2.63$_{b,c}$
No narrative	2.66$_{b,c}$	2.36$_c$

[a] From Geen and Stonner, 1974.

[b] Cells having common subscripts are not significantly different at the .05 level by a Duncan multiple range test.

were attacked experienced a greater rise in pressure at the time of the second measurement than those who were not attacked. Table 8 presents the change in blood pressure that occurred from before to after the tape was shown for subjects in all eight conditions. In every condition except the attack–vengenace, the subjects showed a decrease in pressure, probably due to normal tendencies toward homeostatic control of vascular processes. The attack–vengeance treatment offset this normal return toward baseline pressure and kept subjects at a level slightly higher than that experienced as a result of the attack. Recall that Zillmann and Johnson (1973) also found that observation of fighting by angered subjects produced a maintenance of vascular arousal at the immediate postattack level. Interestingly, the violent scene used in that experiment showed the aggression of a group of gunmen following the cold-blooded murder of one of their friends—a story that could easily have led the observer to attribute the violence to a desire for revenge.

Table 8 Mean Changes in Mean Arterial Pressure from before Movie to after Movie (mm Hg)[a,b]

Film narrative	Treatment of subject by confederate	
	Attack	No attack
Vengeance	1.45$_a$	−2.20$_b$
Professional	−4.00$_{b,c}$	−2.55$_{b,c}$
Altruistic	−5.30$_c$	−3.42$_{b,c}$
No narrative	−5.35$_c$	−2.50$_{b,c}$

[a] From Geen and Stonner, 1974.

[b] Cells having common subscripts are not significantly different at the .05 level by a Duncan multiple range test.

The postexperimental measure of restraint against aggressing also revealed the weakest restraint in the attack-vengeance condition. Thus, the presentation of vengeful aggression to angry subjects appears to serve at least two purposes: It keeps the subjects aroused and also weakens their inhibitions against being aggressive. Possibly the two processes have combined effects. Reduction of restraints may permit the expression of responses that are intensified by the high level of arousal maintained by the violent scene.

Whether violence seen in mass media settings is perceived as real or as fantasy is another variable that influences its potential as an antecedent of aggression. As noted earlier, real violence does act as a stimulus for aggression in much the same way as the fictitious displays usually used in experiments (Meyer, 1972b). The question we are posing here is whether real violence has effects that are different from those of fantasy material. We could reason, from our point of view, that an observer might perceive the behavior of a real aggressor to be more consistent with the aggression that he himself is motivated to commit against his antagonist than the unreal acts of a person in a play.

Studies that have contrasted the impact of real violence with that of fiction within the same experiment have shown that the realistic portrayals are stronger elicitors of aggression. Feshbach (1972) showed children a film of a campus riot composed of footage from both newsreels and fictional television drama. Some children were told that the scene showed a real riot and others that it portrayed a fictitious one. When the children later ostensibly gave bursts of aversive noise to an experimental accomplice, those who had seen an apparently real riot used higher intensity settings than those who had seen the fictitious riot. Berkowitz and Alioto (1973) have also shown that subjects provoked by a confederate gave shocks of greater duration to him after seeing a sequence from a war movie that was described as actual combat than after seeing the same material labeled as part of an enactment of real fighting. Thomas and Tell (1974) have reported comparable results with a movie of two people fighting over a traffic mishap.

The experimental evidence indicates that observation of real violence does lead to greater aggressiveness in both children and adults. One reason for this has been suggested by Geen and Rakosky (1973), who found that subjects who see a videotape of a prizefight staged by two professional actors and are explicitly reminded that the fight is not real do not manifest as much arousal (in terms of skin conductance) as others who are not given this reminder. Calling a person's attention to the fictitious nature of violence may dissociate that event from the real world in which the person lives and thereby render it less relevant to any aggressive motives that he may have. Violence that is regarded as unreal may also have fewer associations with aggression in the viewer's past and, hence, be a weaker stimulus for conditioned aggressive responses than real violence. It may, in other words, be perceived as less violent than the latter.

In a subsequent study, Geen (1975) further demonstrated the importance of arousal as a mediating variable in the relationship of realistic observed violence to aggression. Subjects were shown a short videotaped scene in which two men get into a fight over a minor accident in a parking lot. Some subjects were informed that the fight had actually occurred, some were told that it had been staged by actors, and some were shown the film without any explanation of its meaning. Subjects then gave electric shocks to a confederate who had earlier either attacked them or treated them without provocation. Subjects who had been attacked gave shocks of highest intensity after seeing the fight and being told that it was real (Table 9).

Measures of blood pressure and palmar sweat were taken at three points in the experiment: at baseline, after the attack on the subject, and after the showing of the videotape. The attack treatment produced a significant increase in blood pressure but no change in the PS measure. Blood pressure then returned to near-baseline levels in every condition but one: that in which previously attacked subjects had seen a display of real violence. Furthermore, shock intensity and blood pressure change during the showing of the tape were positively correlated in all conditions, with the highest correlation in the attack-real violence condition. This suggests that the aggressive behavior of the subjects may have been due, in part, to arousal levels that either declined or remained high during the viewing of the videotape. Finally, palmar sweat was found to increase significantly during the showing of real violence in both attacked and nonattacked subjects. This finding may indi-

Table 9   Mean Intensities of Shocks Given to Confederate[a,b]

	Treatment of subject	
Narrative condition	Attack	No attack
Real violence	7.15_a	$2.40_{c,d}$
Fictional violence	$4.70_{b,c}$	1.90_d
No story	4.80_b	$2.43_{c,d}$

[a] From Geen 1975.

[b] Cells bearing common subscripts are not significantly different at the .05 level by a Duncan multiple range test.

cate that real violence is more emotionally involving for the subject than its fictitious counterpart. Palmar sweat has been found by Stotland (1969), for example, to be a fairly reliable concomitant of empathy reactions, by which an observer becomes vicariously involved in the suffering of another person.

The "Symbolic Catharsis" Hypothesis

Finally, we must note a widely cited experiment that points to a conclusion opposite to the one drawn by most investigators cited here. In this study (Feshbach, 1961), male subjects were either instigated to aggress against an experimenter by the latter's insulting remarks or were treated in a nonhostile way. Later, all subjects watched either a segment of a fight movie or a control film; afterward they responded to a two-part, self-report questionnaire. In one part, the subject made some ratings of the insulting experimenter, and, in the other, he wrote out free associations to a set of verbs that had been determined beforehand to be high in aggressiveness connotations. Feshbach found that subjects who had been insulted and had then seen the boxing movie were *less* hostile in their ratings of the experimenter than insulted men who had seen the neutral movie and also made fewer hostile word associations to the aggressive verbs. This difference between the move conditions was not found among men who had not been insulted, and Feshbach was led to conclude that insulted subjects who watched the violent movie were thereby able to experience "hostility catharsis" in a vicarious and symbolic way.

The fact that Feshbach's is the single laboratory study thus far to report a diminution of aggression following observation of violence prompts us to consider how it may have differed from those of other investigators. Goranson (1970) has suggested that, by showing a film of violence without any preliminary explanation of why the bloody fight was justified, Feshbach may have created aggression anxiety in his subjects. Therefore, the low level of aggression found in insulted men who had seen the boxing movie could be attributable to an elevation of inhibitions caused by a combination of their own anger and their witnessing the "senseless" violence of the movie. Still another possible explanation is suggested by a recent experiment by Zillmann, Johnson, and Hanrahan (1973), who argue that a reduction in aggression following a violent film may occur when the story has an eventual ending that is happy for the main protagonist. Male subjects were shown the same fight senquence as that originally used by Feshbach, but edited so as to have two different endings. Males in one group saw the story end with the defeat of the film's hero, but those in another condition saw a version in which the hero wins the fight and is later reunited with his old sweetheart. This "happy ending" version is the one used by Feshbach. Subjects who saw the happy finale experienced a more profound reduction in emotional arousal (blood pressure and heart rate) just prior to the film's ending than did subjects shown the sadder climax to the story. In addition, subjects who saw the happy ending were less aggressive toward an antagonizing confederate than were those who saw the other ending, a finding which is entirely consistent with Zillmann's general hypothesis regarding the role of film-mediated arousal in aggression. Zillmann and his colleagues propose that a happy ending allows the dissipation of tensions that accumulate over the course of the fight because of the tribulations of the hero. Thus, Feshbach may not have demonstrated symbolic catharsis, but rather tension reduction in response to the movie's favorable ending.

Perhaps the most obvious way in which Feshbach's study differed from the studies of most other experimenters cited in this chapter is that it involved the expression of verbal hostility and not physical aggression. Possibly the observation of violence in others promotes a dissipation of hostility (roughly defined as an internal emotional or arousal state) while at the same time eliciting aggressive behavior in one of the ways reviewed in the previous section. This possibility has been considered in a study by Manning and Taylor (1974). After first being either verbally insulted or treated neutrally by a confederate, subjects were shown either an aggressive or an exciting but nonviolent movie. Each subject was subsequently (1) given a chance to shock the confederate and (2) required to identify objects depicted on slides shown on a tachistoscope. Each slide was a superimposition of some "violent" stimulus (such as a riot scene or a gun fighter) upon a "nonviolent" one (such as a flute or an ice skater). It was assumed that hostility will manifest itself under such conditions in the subject's identifying the composite as the violent stimulus.[2] As predicted, angered subjects who had seen the violent film identified the stimulus as aggressive less often than similarly angered men who had seen the neutral film. Aggressive behavior did not vary with the treatment conditions. Manning and Taylor then concluded that the "vicarious catharsis" hypothesis applied to the emotion of hostility but not to aggression.

[2] This assumption is strengthened by the finding of Petzel and Michaels (1973) that subjects who score high in hostility on the Buss–Durkee scale are more likely to report seeing a violent stimulus than a neutral one when the two are paired in a binocular rivalry presentation.

Summary on Laboratory Research

From the preceding review, it is obvious that research on effects of observing violence has changed considerably since the early experimental studies were reported more than a decade ago. No longer do investigators ask the simple question "Does observing violence in the mass media make the observer more aggressive?" Instead, the emphasis in research has shifted to a search for moderator variables, an understanding of which will better enable us to answer the question "Under what specific conditions is the observation of violence likely to increase the aggressiveness of the viewer?" As we have seen, many such variables have been discovered: The consequences of the violence to its perpetrator, the degree of association between the violence and reinforcement for aggression in the observer's past, the extent to which the violence is consistent with the observer's own condition are among three that have received the most attention. Some of the theorizing on observation of violence, especially that of Berkowitz and his associates, has emphasized constructs and variables derived from classical conditioning, generalization, and other aspects of the psychology of learning and motivation. Other points of view give greater attention to the observation of violence as essentially an information processing phenomenon in which the observer makes some fairly subtle evaluations of what the witnessed violence means, how relevant it is to him, and so forth. At the present time, we are unable to come to a final conclusion as to which of these points of view is the most accurate.

Field Studies

The data from the laboratory on the effects of observing violence represent the outcome of highly controlled and contrived conditions. Even when experimental deceptions are successfully implemented and demand characteristics of the situation controlled, the experimental investigator is left with findings that may have little to do with behavior in natural life settings. We must, therefore, wonder whether the observation so commonly made in laboratory studies—that the observation of violence generally facilitates aggresssion—has any general applicability to human behavior outside the laboratory.

Obviously, the best way to test the external validity of laboratory findings is to extend their hypotheses to naturalistic studies. Such studies, however, do not provide a simple and complete solution to the problem. While field research does have the aura of authenticity about it, it necessarily lacks the precision of control that can be found in laboratory research. Thus, where the laboratory study loses external validity for the sake of control, the field study loses internal validity for the sake of generalizability. The happy medium between the two has not yet been attained in research on aggression in the media, and the student of the subject is left with the task of reconciling the problem of internal and external validity by assigning his own weights to the two types of evidence.

Studies Supporting Laboratory Evidence

Early attempts to discover whether a link exists between observation of violence in the media and aggressive behavior failed to show any such connection (Himmelweit, Oppenheim, & Vince, 1958; Schramm, Lyle, & Parker, 1961). More recently, however, several reports have appeared that at least suggest a relationship of the type found in laboratory studies.

Berkowitz (1971) has reported data relating the incidence of spectacular acts of violence (the sort reported in the communications media) to statistics on aggressive crime. After first obtaining FBI figures on crimes of violence for each month of the period 1960–1966 in 40 American cities, Berkowitz and Macaulay (cited by Berkowitz, 1971) determined the average monthly number of such crimes. Using this average as a base, they then calculated the deviation from the monthly average for each month from January, 1960 to December, 1966. A dramatic deviation in the direction of a higher rate of violent crime followed the assassination of President Kennedy in November, 1963. The rate then remained fairly stable until the summer of 1966, following the widely reported mass murders committed by Richard Speck (July, 1966) and Charles Whitman (August, 1966).

Of course, we must beware of the principle learned in every introductory statistics course: Correlation is not causation. Many factors are involved in violent crime besides the hypothesized one of observation of violence. Nevertheless, Berkowitz' data point to a correlation that *could have been predicted* by someone familiar with evidence from the laboratory. Other investigators have pointed out the same coincidence of sensational crimes and increases in antisocial behavior. Siegel (1969) noted that within one week of the showing on television of a movie called *The Doomsday Flight,* in which a person plants a bomb on an airliner, 13 bomb threats had been telephoned to airline offices—twice the number reported in the entire month before the broadcast. Bandura (1971) has also cited figures suggesting a relationship between airline hijacking and the amount of new coverage given to hijack attempts.

Somewhat less speculative than the material reviewed above are the results of a natural experiment carried out by Goldstein and Arms (1971). Male spectators were interviewed before and after the 1969 Army–Navy football game, with males in a control condition interviewed before and after a gymnastics meet between Army and Temple. Both sets of interviews included a self-report scale of hostility. Change scores showed that hostility after the football game was more intense than it had been before the game, regardless of which team the respondent supported. The increase in hostility was, therefore, not caused by anger over seeing the supported team beaten. No changes in hostility were found among men who watched the gymnastics meet. Possibly the aggressive nature of the football game made the event a powerful stimulus for hostile reactions.

Recall that, in an earlier section, we discussed laboratory evidence pertinent to the "weapons effect", and we reached the conclusion that, under some conditions, the presence of weapons may elicit aggression. Evidence for the weapons effect in a field experiment has been reported by Turner, Layton, and Simons (1975) in a study of aggression in drivers, with aggression defined as horn honking at a pickup truck that obstructed traffic at a signal light. In one condition, the truck bore an empty gun rack, plainly visible through the rear window, in another, it bore a rack holding a rifle and, in addition, a bumper sticker reading "Vengeance," and, in a third, it bore a weapon plus a more innocuous bumper label. When the driver of the pickup was invisible because of a drawn curtain, frustrated motorists were more likely to blow their horns in the presence of a rifle and a violent bumper sticker than in the other conditions. Turner and his associates interpret their data as an analogue of laboratory studies in which potentially violent stimuli are invested with either a violent or nonviolent meaning by associated stimuli, (e.g., the earlier discussion of the maintenance of aggressive motivation). The sticker reading "Vengeance" presumably led the observer to perceive the rifle as an instrument of violence (rather than a piece of sporting goods) and thus made it a suitable stimulus for an aggressive response.

A series of field experiments conducted by Harris and her colleagues have shown that verbally aggressive models tend to be imitated in natural settings. In one study (Harris, 1973), one experimental confederate bumped and jostled another in a crowded setting in full view of an unsuspecting subject selected at random to be a witness to the incident. The second accomplice replied with either a verbally aggressive harangue or with a polite response. Shortly thereafter, the experimenter, who had been trailing the subject, bumped into the latter from behind. It was found that subjects who had previously witnessed an aggressive model responded with verbal aggression of their own significantly more than did subjects who had witnessed a nonaggressive one. The study was later successfully replicated (Harris, 1973) in a cafeteria with "line jumping" serving as the instigator. Still another study (Harris, Liguori, & Joniak, 1973) revealed imitation of an aggressive model who verbally berated a confederate for dropping some bundles in a crowded store, but not of an altruistic one who helped the confederate retrieve his packages.

Eron and his colleagues have inferred a causal relationship between observation of violent television programs in childhood and aggressiveness of behavior in young adulthood by using correlational methods. Eron's work grew out of a study of third graders in a single school district in 1960, in which they ascertained, among other things, both the overall aggressiveness of the children and their preference for violence and aggression in their television viewing (see Eron, Walder, & Lefkowitz, 1971). Longitudinal data were also obtained on the aggressiveness and television preferences of over 400 of the original 875 young people 10 years later (Eron, Lefkowitz, Huesmann, & Walder, 1972). Aggressiveness in the third graders was ascertained from peer and parental ratings and from the child's self-report, whereas aggressiveness a decade later was based on peer and self-ratings only. Using a cross-lagged correlation analysis, Eron et al., (1972) showed that the preference for TV violence manifested by boys in grade 3 was significantly correlated with their aggressiveness 10 years later (referred to as grade 13). Aggressiveness in third grade, however, was not correlated with preference for televised aggression in grade 13. The investigators conclude from these correlations that watching violent TV in childhood influences aggressiveness in young adulthood.

Studies Not Supporting Laboratory Evidence

In a field experiment of impressive scope, Milgram and Shotland (1973) attempted to test the hypothesis that a person who has been frustrated by nonpayment of a promised reward is more likely to commit an antisocial act similar to one recently seen on television than a frustrated person who has not witnessed the modeled act. They predicted, in other words, a finding consistent with those of many laboratory experiments. With the aid of a major television network, Milgram and Shotland filmed a special hour-long episode from the series *Medical Center*. In this episode, a young man is fired from his job at a hospital. Later he expresses his anger against the physician who fired him by smashing several public donation boxes of a charity supported by the doctor. The film ends in one of two ways. In one version, the young thief is caught and sent to prison; in the other, he commits his antisocial act with impunity. A third film was also made in which the young man responds to being fired with the prosocial response of donating money to charity.

Subjects in the prototype experiment, recruited by public advertisement in New York, were promised a free transistor radio for reporting to a theater to judge a television presentation. Upon arriving at the theater, the subjects saw either one of the three versions of the foregoing program or a neutral film showing no hostility or aggression. Some time later, the subject reported, at a stated time, to an office where he was to receive his radio. The subject found the office unoccupied and bearing a notice informing callers that no more radios were to be given away. Among the furnishings in the office was a charity donation box obviously full of money and with a dollar bill dangling noticeably from the slot. Hence, we have this situation: The subject has been exposed (in two of the four conditions) to an angry model who commits an antisocial act. Will the frustrated subject also react by committing theft of either the entire box of money or at least of the "dangling dollar"?

The results of the study yielded only the barest suggestion of an effect in the predicted direction. Men who had seen the film of antisocial behavior with punishment were slightly more likely to commit theft than those who had seen the nonhostile neutral film, but the trend did not even approach significance. A series of replications and extensions, some of which involved televising the experimental films to entire urban populations in New York and St. Louis, likewise failed to yield any evidence that the observation of antisocial behavior on TV in realistic surroundings influences the incidence of modeled crime. Obviously the methodological problems involved in experimental research on the scale attempted by Milgram and Shotland are immense, and further refinements of their approach may ultimately bear empirical fruit. For the time being, however, the only conclusions that can be inferred from their data is that a case for the faciliation of aggression by displays of antisocial behavior has not been made.

The only large-scale field study that has reported results that conflict with most of the laboratory data is that of Feshbach and Singer (1971). In this study, an attempt was made to control the television viewing of samples of adolescent boys enrolled in private schools and in homes for the underprivileged. Within each sample, some of the boys were allowed to watch only programs that had been defined a priori as violent, and the others were allowed to watch only nonviolent shows. Over a 6-week period of controlled viewing, supervisory personnel at the institutions rated each boy's physical and verbal aggression. In addition, a number of personality tests were administered at the beginning and end of the 6-week period. Among these were a fantasy aggression measure based on responses to pictures and a peer rating device by which the overall aggressiveness of each child was judged by his classmates (Eron *et al.,* 1971). In general, the type of TV program shown to private school boys was found to be unrelated to aggressiveness. Among children in the boy's homes, however, those given a steady diet of televised violence showed *less* aggression against their peers than those who were restricted to watching nonviolent programs. In addition, the aggressiveness of boys shown only violence declined week by week at a significantly more rapid rate than did the aggressiveness of boys shown only the neutral programs.

Television viewing was also related to aggressive fantasy behavior, but in a way inconsistent both with the data on aggressive behavior and with the hypothesis that observation of violence fosters a vicarious and symbolic "catharsis" of hostility (Feshbach, 1961). Whereas exposure to nonviolent programs was associated with a decline in physical aggression themes in fantasy, exposure to violence was accompanied by a maintenance of the preexperimental level of these themes. In other words, by the end of the study, boys exposed to violent television were *higher* in fantasy aggression than those shown the control programs, a finding one would not expect if watching violent TV allows a "draining off" of aggressive drive. To reconcile their data on fantasy aggression with that on overt aggressive behavior, Feshbach and Singer proposed that aggressive fantasy "enables the child . . . to delay and control the immediate expression of impulses [p. 152]." Therefore, "Assignment to the aggressive TV diet provides an opportunity for extensive cognitive supports and, excluding the effects of other processes, a decrement in the acting out of aggressive tendencies can be anticipated [pp. 153–154]." This hypothesis differs from the notion of symbolic catharsis in that it does not treat aggressive fantasy as a substitute for overt aggression but rather as an inhibitor of it. The violent TV programs, by enhancing the formation of aggressive fantasies, promoted the control of physical and verbal aggression, at least in the residents of the boys' homes.

Other data cast some doubt on the idea of the control value of fantasy. Most important is the finding that, although violent TV led to reduced aggression in residents of a boys' home who were initially low in fantasy aggression, the opposite was found in private school boys who were initially high in fantasy activity. In other words, private school boys who were strong aggressive fantasizers behaved more aggressively after seeing violent television than after watching the neutral fare. If observing violence produces aggressive fantasy behavior, which in turn controls the expression of aggression, strong fantasizers should become extremely controlled and nonaggressive because the fantasies elicited by TV should strengthen the ones already present. Therefore, the absence of control in the private school boys is puzzling. Feshbach and Singer explain the absence of a cognitive-control effect in these children by proposing that they possess cognitive capacities superior to those of boys' home residents and are, thus, able to form their own fantasies without the aid of TV. If this were so, however, we would expect that boys from the two samples would have differed in pre-experimental levels of fantasy aggression, and the authors nowhere report such a difference.

The data raise some serious questions about the authors' interpretation of their findings. The Feshbach and Singer study was also marred by several procedural and methodological problems. No attempt was made, for example, to control or measure the aggressiveness of content in the two types of programs allowed. Children in the control condition sometimes watched violent programs during the 6-week period, on one occasion following demands on the supervisors that they be allowed to watch a particular program from the forbidden list. The ratings of aggressiveness were made by personnel who knew the nature of the programs that the children were watching and could have been influenced in their ratings by this knowledge. In light of these problems and of the uncertain nature of the data relating fantasy aggression to actual violence, we must reserve judgment on the meaning of the Feshbach–Singer findings.

The notion of symbolic catharsis is also implicit in another study to emerge from the longitudinal work of Eron and his associates described earlier. In this study, Lefkowitz, Eron, Walder, and Huesmann (1973) showed that, among *girls* in both grade 3 and grade 13, aggressive behavior was correlated with a preference for watching violent contact sports (such as football and hockey) on TV. No such correlation was found for boys. The interpretation of these data by the authors was *opposite* to that of the cross-lagged correlation study: It was argued that aggressive tendencies in the girls caused their preference for watching aggressive sports. Because of sex-role demands, girls in our society are encouraged not to express aggression as directly as boys do and, thus, turn to violence in the mass media as a way of vicariously experiencing aggression. One should note that this argument is quite similar to the symbolic catharsis notion proposed by Feshbach (1961): Observation of violence is assumed to satisfy some need to express aggression that is otherwise not allowed an outlet. Presumably this need is satisfied by watching violence on the TV screen.

On balance, the available and published data from field studies on the relationship of observation of violence to aggression provide some support for laboratory findings on the subject. Witnessing of aggression, both real and in fiction purveyed by the mass media, has been shown to be correlated with subsequent aggressive behavior. The data are, admittedly, not overwhelming in quantity or in conclusiveness, but the trend is clearly present. Moreover, there is no conclusive case for the hypothesis that the observation of violence leads to a reduction of aggression.

Summary and Conclusions

1.   Laboratory experiments conducted under controlled conditions have shown consistently that the observation of violence by others, both live and in mass media displays, facilitates aggression in the observer. This finding has been explained by various investigators as evidence of (1) modeling and imitation of aggression, (2) disinhibition of aggressive impulses by the modeled behavior, (3) the elicitation of aggressive actions that have become conditioned to modeled behaviors during the observer's lifetime, and (4) an increase in arousal produced by the observation of aggression which activates dominant responses, including aggressive ones.

2.   The meaning that is ascribed to violence carried out by others affects the incidence of aggression after viewing. Justified violence elicits more aggression than unjustified violence, in general, and violence that is justified as legitimate vengeance facilitates aggression more than that warranted for other reasons. Variables associated with the meaning of violence have been shown to influence aggression by affecting the viewer's level of arousal and his tendencies to restrain aggressive impulses. Real violence engenders greater aggression in the observer than fictional or faked fighting and also produces stronger arousal.

3.   The evidence from field studies is more equivocal than that from laboratory experiments. The investigations that have yielded significant findings tend to corroborate the experimental studies, with only one major piece of work indicating that observation of media violence suppresses aggressive behavior. The common criticism of laboratory studies—that they are unrealistic and that their findings are invalid in the external world—is not justified by the bulk of the data collected thus far in the field.

4.   The conclusion appears justified that observation of violence, such as that shown in movies and on television, contributes to aggressive behavior. This is not to say that it is the most important contributor to aggression; other influences upon the person, such as the value system of his primary reference group, the pressures of those around him toward behavioral conformity, his perceptions of the value of aggression, and the availability of weapons, all undoubtedly affect his level of aggressive behavior (Singer, 1971). In children, for example, it has been shown that, whereas television viewing contributes to aggression, it is not as important an influence on the child as the attitudes of his family toward violence (Dominick & Greenberg, 1971). Nevertheless, even though observation of violence may be only one contributor to aggression it may also, especially in aroused or angered persons, be a particularly powerful one for at least a short period of time (Doob & Climie, 1972).

REFERENCES

Baker, R. K., & Ball, S. J. *Violence and the media: A staff report to the National Commission on the Causes and Prevention of Violence.* Washington, D.C.: Government Printing Office, 1969.

Bandura, A. Influence of models' reinforcement contingencies on the acquisition of imitative responses. *Journal of Personality and Social Psychology,* 1965, *1*, 589–595.

Bandura, A. Social learning theory of aggression. In J. F. Knutson (Ed.), *Control of aggression: Implications from basic research.* Chicago: Aldine-Atherton, 1971.

Bandura, A. *Aggression: A social learning analysis.* Englewood Cliffs, New Jersey: Prentice-Hall, 1973.

Bandura, A., Grusec, J. E., & Menlove, F. L. Observational learning as a function of symbolization and incentive set. *Child Development,* 1966, *37,* 499–506.

Bandura, A., & Jeffery, R. W. Role of symbolic coding and rehearsal processes in observational learning. *Journal of Personality and Social Psychology,* 1973, *26,* 122–130.

Bandura, A., Jeffery, R., & Bachicha, D. L. Analysis of memory codes and cumulative rehearsal in observational learning. *Journal of Research in Personality,* 1974, *7,* 295–305.

Bandura, A., Ross, D., & Ross, S. A. Imitation of film-mediated aggressive models. *Journal of Abnormal and Social Psychology,* 1963, *66,* 3–11. (a).

Bandura, A., Ross, D., & Ross, S. A. Vicarious reinforcement and imitative learning. *Journal of Abnormal and Social Psychology,* 1963, *67,* 601–607. (b).

Baron, R. A. Reducing the influence of an aggressive model: The restraining effects of discrepant modeling cues. *Journal of Personality and Social Psychology,* 1971, *20,* 240–245.

Berkowitz, L. Some aspects of observed aggression. *Journal of Personality and Social Psychology,* 1965, *2,* 359–369. (a).

Berkowitz, L. The concept of aggressive drive: Some additional considerations. In L. Berkowitz (Ed.), *Advances in experimental social psychology.* Vol. 2. New York: Academic Press, 1965. Pp. 301–329. (b).

Berkowitz, L. The frustration-aggression hypothesis revisited. In L. Berkowitz (Ed.), *Roots of aggression: A reexamination of the frustration-aggression hypothesis.* New York: Atherton Press, 1969. Pp. 1-28.

Berkowitz, L. The contagion of violence: An S-R mediational analysis of some effects of observed aggression. In W. J. Arnold & M. M. Page (Eds.), *Nebraska symposium on motivation, 1970.* Lincoln: Univ. of Nebraska Press, 1971. Pp. 95-135.

Berkowitz, L. Some determinants of impulsive aggression: The role of mediated associations with reinforcements for aggression. *Psychological Review,* 1974, *81,* 165-176.

Berkowitz, L., & Alioto, J. T. The meaning of an observed event as a determinant of its aggressive consequences. *Journal of Personality and Social Psychology,* 1973, *28,* 206-217.

Berkowitz, L., & Geen, R. G. Film violence and the cue properties of available targets. *Journal of Personality and Social Psychology,* 1966, *3,* 525-530.

Berkowitz, L., & Geen, R. G. Stimulus qualities of the target of aggression: A further study. *Journal of Personality and Social Psychology,* 1967, *5,* 364-368.

Berkowitz, L., & LePage, A. Weapons as aggression-eliciting stimuli. *Journal of Personality and Social Psychology,* 1967, *7,* 202-207.

Buss, A. H., Booker, A., & Buss, E. Firing a weapon and aggression. *Journal of Personality and Social Psychology,* 1972, *22,* 296-302.

Christy, P. R., Gelfand, D. M., & Hartmann, D. P. Effects of competition-induced frustration on two classes of modeled behavior. *Developmental Psychology,* 1971, *5,* 104-111.

Clark, D. G., & Blankenburg, W. B. Trends in violent content in selected mass media. In G. A. Comstock & E. A. Rubinstein (Eds.), *Television and social behavior, Volume 1. Content and control.* Washington, D.C.: U.S. Government Printing Office, 1971. Pp. 188-243.

Cline, V. B., Croft, R. G., & Courrier, S. Desensitization of children to television violence. *Journal of Personality and Social Psychology,* 1973, *27,* 360-365.

Cohen, R., & Murray, E. J. Censure of vicarious aggression as an instigation to subsequent aggression. *Journal of Consulting and Clinical Psychology,* 1972, *39,* 473-477.

Dominick, J. R., & Greenberg, B. S. Attitudes toward violence: The interaction of television exposure, family attitudes, and social class. In G. A. Comstock & E. A. Rubinstein (Eds.), *Television and social behavior, Volume 3. Television and adolescent aggressiveness.* Washington, D.C.: U.S. Government Printing Office, 1971. Pp. 314-335.

Doob, A. N., & Climie, R. J. Delay of measurement and the effects of film violence *Journal of Experimental Social Psychology,* 1972, *8,* 136-142.

Doob, A. N., & Korshenbaum, H. M. The effects on arousal of frustration and aggressive films. *Journal of Experimental Social Psychology,* 1973, *9,* 57-64.

Drabman, R. S., & Thomas, M. H. Does media violence increase children's toleration of real-life aggression? *Developmental Psychology,* 1974, *10,* 418-421. (a).

Drabman, R. S., & Thomas, M. H. Exposure to filmed violence and children's tolerance of real life aggression. Paper read at Annual Convention of American Psychological Association, 1974. (b).

Dubanoski, R. A., & Parton, D. A. Imitative aggression in children as a function of observing a human model. *Developmental Psychology,* 1971, *4,* 489.

Ellis, G. T., & Sekyra, F. The effect of aggressive cartoons on the behavior of first grade children. *Journal of Psychology,* 1972. *81,* 37-43.

Ellis, D. P., Weinir, P., & Miller, L. Does the trigger pull the finger? An experimental test of weapons as aggression-eliciting stimuli. *Sociometry,* 1971, *34.* 435-465.

Eron, L. D., Lefkowitz, M. M., Huesmann, L. R., & Walder, L. O. Does television violence cause aggression? *American Psychologist,* 1972, *27,* 253–263.

Eron, L. D., Walder, L. O., & Lefkowitz, M. M. *The learning of aggression in children.* Boston: Little-Brown, 1971.

Feshbach, S. The stimulating versus cathartic effects of a vicarious aggressive activity. *Journal of Abnormal and Social Psychology,* 1961, *63,* 381–385.

Feshbach, S. Reality and fantasy in filmed violence. In J. P. Murray, E. A. Rubinstein, & G. A. Comstock (Eds.), *Television and social behavior: II. Television and social learning.* Technical Report to the Surgeon General's Scientific Advisory Committee on Television and Social Behavior. Washington: Department of Health, Education, and Welfare, 1972. Pp. 318–345.

Feshbach, S., & Singer, R. D. *Television and aggression.* San Francisco: Jossey-Bass, 1971.

Feshbach, S., Stiles, W. B., & Bitter, E. The reinforcing effect of witnessing aggression. *Journal of Experimental Research in Personality,* 1967, *2,* 133–139.

Fischer, D. G., Kelm, H., & Rose, A. Knives as aggression-eliciting stimuli. *Psychological Reports,* 1969, *24,* 755–760.

Fraczek, A., & Macaulay, J. R. Some personality factors in reaction to aggressive stimuli. *Journal of Personality,* 1971, *39,* 163–177.

Geen, R. G. Effects of frustration, attack, and prior training in aggressiveness upon aggressive behavior. *Journal of Personality and Social Psychology,* 1968, *9,* 316–321.

Geen, R. G. The meaning of observed violence: Real vs. fictional violence and consequent effects on aggression. *Journal of Research in Personality,* 1975, in press.

Geen, R. G., & Berkowitz, L. Name-mediated aggressive cue properties. *Journal of Personality,* 1966, *34,* 456–465.

Geen, R. G., & Berkowitz, L. Some conditions facilitating the occurrence of aggression after the observation of violence. *Journal of Personality,* 1967, *35,* 666–676.

Geen, R. G., & O'Neal, E. C. Activation of cue-elicited aggression by general arousal. *Journal of Personality and Social Psychology,* 1969, *11,* 289–292.

Geen, R. G., & Rakosky, J. J. Interpretations of observed violence and their effects on GSR. *Journal of Experimental Research in Personality,* 1973, *6,* 289–292.

Geen, R. G., & Stonner, D. The context of observed violence: Inhibition of aggression through displays of unsuccessful retaliation. *Psychonomic Science,* 1972, *27,* 342–344.

Geen, R. G., & Stonner, D. Context effects in observed violence. *Journal of Personality and Social Psychology,* 1973, *25,* 145–150.

Geen, R. G., & Stonner, D. The meaning of observed violence: Effects on arousal and aggressive behavior. *Journal of Research in Personality,* 1974, *8,* 55–63.

Geen, R. G., Stonner, D., & Shope, G. L. The facilitation of aggression by aggression: Evidence against the catharsis hypothesis. *Journal of Personality and Social Psychology,* 1975, *31,* 721–726.

Gerbner, G. Violence in television drama: Trends and symbolic functions. In G. A. Comstock & E. A. Rubinstein (Eds.), *Television and social behavior, Volume 1. Content and control.* Washington, D.C.: U.S. Government Printing Office, 1972. Pp. 28–187.

Gerst, M. Symbolic coding processes in observational learning. *Journal of Personality and Social Psychology,* 1971, *19,* 7–17.

Goldstein, J. H., & Arms, R. L. Effects of observing athletic contests on hostility. *Sociometry,* 1971, *34,* 83–90.

Goranson, R. E. Media violence and aggressive behavior: A review of experimental research. In L. Berkowitz (Ed.), *Advances in experimental social psychology.* Vol. 5. New York: Academic Press, 1970.

Hanratty, M. A., O'Neal, E. C., & Sulzer, J. L. Effect of frustration upon imitation of aggression. *Journal of Personality and Social Psychology*, 1972, *21*, 30–34.

Harris, M. B. Field studies of modeled aggression. *Journal of Social Psychology*, 1973, *89*, 131–139.

Harris, M. B., Liguori, R., & Joniak, A. Aggression, altruism, and models. *Journal of Social Psychology*, 1973, *91*, 343–344.

Harrison, M., & Pepitone, A. Contrast effect in the use of punishment. *Journal of Personality and Social Psychology*, 1972, *23*, 398–404.

Hicks, D. J. Imitation and retention of film-mediated aggressive peer and adult models. *Journal of Personality and Social Psychology*, 1965, *2*, 97–100.

Hicks, D. J. Effects of co-observer's sanctions and adult presence on imitative aggression. *Child Development*, 1968, *39*, 303–309.

Himmelweit, H. T., Oppenheim, A. N., & Vince, P. *Television and the Child*. London: Oxford Univ. Press, 1958.

Hoyt, J. L. Effect of media violence "justification" on aggression. *Journal of Broadcasting*, 1970, *16*, 455–464.

Kniveton, B. H. The effect of rehearsal delay on long-term imitation of filmed aggression. *British Journal of Psychology*, 1973, *64*, 259–265.

Lefkowitz, M. M., Eron, L. D., Walder, L. O., & Huesmann, L. R. Preference for televised contact sports as related to sex differences in aggression. *Developmental Psychology*, 1973, *9*, 417–420.

Leyens, J. P., & Parke, R. D. Aggressive slides can induce a weapons effect. Unpublished manuscript, Univ. of Louvain, 1973.

Leyens, J. P., & Picus, S. Identification with the winner of a fight and name mediation: Their differential effects upon subsequent aggressive behavior. *British Journal of Social and Clinical Psychology*, 1973, *12*, 374–377.

Manning, S. A., & Taylor, D. A. The effects of viewed violence and aggression: Stimulation and catharsis. *Journal of Personality and Social Psychology*, 1975, *31*, 180–188.

Meyer, T. P. Effects of viewing justified and unjustified real film violence on aggressive behavior. *Journal of Personality and Social Psychology*, 1972, *23*, 21–29. (a).

Meyer, T. P. The effects of sexually arousing and violent films on aggressive behavior. *Journal of Sex Research*, 1972, *8*, 324–331. (b).

Milgram, S., & Shotland, R. L. *Television and antisocial behavior: Field experiments*. New York: Academic Press, 1973.

Page, M. M., & Scheidt, R. J. The elusive weapons effect: Demand awareness, evaluation apprehension, and slightly sophisticated subjects. *Journal of Personality and Social Psychology*, 1971, *20*, 304–318.

Parton, D. A., & Geshuri, Y. Learning of aggression as a function of presence of a human mode, response intensity, and target of the response. *Journal of Experimental Child Psychology*, 1971, *11*, 491–504.

Petzel, T. P., & Michaels, E. J. Perception of violence as a function of levels of hostility. *Journal of Consulting and Clinical Psychology*, 1973, *41*, 35–36.

Powers, P. C., & Geen, R. G. Effects of the behavior and the perceived arousal of a model on instrumental aggression. *Journal of Personality and Social Psychology*, 1972, *23*, 175–183.

Schramm, W., Lyle, J., & Parker, E. B. *Television in the lives of our children*. Stanford, California: Stanford Univ. Press, 1961.

Singer, J. L. The influence of violence portrayed in television or motion pictures upon overt aggressive behavior. In J. L. Singer (Ed.), *The control of aggression and violence*. New York: Academic Press, 1971. Pp. 19–60.

Steuer, F. B., Applefield, J. M., & Smith, R. Televised aggression and the interpersonal aggression of preschool children. *Journal of Experimental Child Psychology,* 1971, *11,* 442–447.

Stotland, E. Exploratory studies of empathy. In L. Berkowitz (Ed.), *Advances in experimental social psychology.* Vol. 4. New York: Academic Press, 1969. Pp. 271–314.

Tannenbaum, P. H. Emotional arousal as a mediator of erotic communication effects. *Technical Report of the Commission on Obscenity and Pornography,* Vol. 8. Washington, D.C.: U.S. Government Printing Office, 1971.

Tannenbaum, P. H. Studies in film- and television-mediated arousal and aggression: A progress report. In G. A. Comstock, E. A. Rubinstein, & J. P. Murray (Eds.), *Television and social behavior: V. Television's effects—further explorations.* Technical Report to the Surgeon General's Scientific Advisory Committee on Television and Social Behavior, 1972. Pp. 309–350.

Thomas, M. H., & Tell, P. M. Effects of viewing real versus fantasy violence upon interpersonal aggression. *Journal of Research in Personality,* 1974, *8,* 153–160.

Turner, C. W., & Berkowitz, L. Identification with film aggressor (covert role taking) and reactions to film violence. *Journal of Personality and Social Psychology,* 1972, *21,* 256–264.

Turner, C. W., & Simons, L. S. Effects of subject sophistication and evaluation apprehension on aggressive responses to weapons. *Journal of Personality and Social Psychology,* 1974, *30,* 341–348.

Turner, C. W., Layton, J. R., & Simons, L. S. Naturalistic studies of aggressive behavior: Aggressive stimuli, victim visibility, and horn-honking. *Journal of Personality and Social Psychology.* 1975, *31,* 1098–1107.

Weiss, W. Effects of the mass media of communication. in G. Lindzey & E. Aronson (Eds.), *Handbook of social psychology.* Vol. 5. Reading, Massachusetts: Addison-Wesley, 1969.

Wheeler, L., & Caggiula, A. R. The contagion of aggression. *Journal of Experimental Social Psychology,* 1966, *2,* 1–10.

Wheeler, L., & Smith, S. Censure of the model in the contagion of aggression. *Journal of Personality and Social Psychology,* 1967, *6,* 93–98.

Zillmann, D. Excitation transfer in communication-mediated aggressive behavior. *Journal of Experimental Social Psychology,* 1971, *7,* 419–434.

Zillmann, D., & Johnson, R. C. Motivated aggressiveness perpetuated by exposure to aggressive films and reduced by exposure to nonaggressive films. *Journal of Research in Personality,* 1973, *7,* 261–276.

Zillmann, D., Johnson, R. C., & Hanrahan, J. Pacifying effect of happy ending of communications involving aggression. *Psychological Reports,* 1973, *32,* 967–970.

The Study of Aggression: Conclusions and Prospects for the Future

DAVID M. STONNER

Introduction: The Problem of Definition

Although the title of this chapter may imply that psychologists are currently in a position to make some equivocal statement on human aggression, the literature on aggression indicates that this is not the case. While there is little agreement as to the causes of aggression and the manner in which it can best be controlled, there is agreement that aggression constitutes a social problem of considerable magnitude. Rising statistics on acts of violence and their costs to society fail to offer much solace to those concerned about aggression as a social problem.

This lack of definitive answers does not reflect a disinterest on the part of researchers. During the decade ending in 1973, the number of articles on aggression listed in the *Psychological Abstracts* was more than three times the total number listed in the previous three decades. The formidable task of sifting through the more than 1200 articles on aggression that have appeared since 1970, comparing procedures, evaluating results, and reaching conclusions about our current knowledge of the subject is beyond the scope of this chapter. This review will focus instead upon some recent approaches to the study of human aggression, examine some possible resolutions of theoretical and definitional problems, and suggest some fruitful lines of future research.

One problem that has haunted research on aggression has been that of definition. Attempts to define aggression have ranged from classificatory schemes of a unitary nature (e.g., Dollard, Doob, Miller, Mowrer & Sears, 1939) to those which subdivide aggression responses into discrete categories. The basis of categorization may be stimulus situations (Moyer, 1971), mode of delivery (Buss, 1971), harm intent (Weiss, 1969), or coercive power (Tedeschi, Smith, & Brown, 1974) to name just a few. Each of these approaches has advantages, yet none foreshadows a general consensus of what constitutes aggression. Finally, any conclusions we may draw about the definitions of aggression currently being offered will be valuable only to the extent that they offer an externally valid explanation of the nature of aggression beyond the laboratory.

Because aggression is a social problem, any definition of aggression will have value implications, if not to the researcher then at least to much of his audience. However, the variety of possible behaviors which we may label aggressive and the limitations of investigating many of these in laboratory situations forces us to make careful distinctions between aggressive responses as a dependent measure in the laboratory and aggression as a social problem. For much of the remainder of this chapter, I will use the rather unorthodox approach of allowing as a definition of aggression "the response measure as operationalized by the researcher," postponing discussion of a unitary definition until later on.

An Aggression Paradigm

Perhaps the most widely used research paradigm in aggression research is some variation of those used by Buss (1961) and Berkowitz (1965). This paradigm places the subject in a position of administering noxious stimulation (typically electric shock) to another subject under the guise of a learning or evaluation experiment in which errors are punished or negative evaluations administered by the delivery of the noxious stimulation. In actuality, the learner in the experiment (or the person being evaluated) is a confederate of the experimenter and receives no noxious stimuli. The measure of aggression is the number, intensity, duration, or latency of shock that the subject thinks he is administering.

A number of criticisms have been leveled at the artificiality, ethics, and demand characteristics (Schuck & Pisor, 1974) of this approach, as well as the possibility that, from the subject's perspective, shocking another person in this context may be seen as altruistic (Baron & Eggleston, 1972; Tedeschi *et al.*, 1974). That is, a subject may be administering the noxious stimuli out of a sincere desire to encourage learning on the part of the confederate, rather than from any aggressive motives. The problems of demand characteristics (the subject's behaving in a manner that he feels is consistent with the experimenter's hypothesis), the effects of artificiality, and the problem of possible altruistic motivation can all be dealt with through existing methodological refinements. Demand characteristics and artificiality that may arouse suspicions in the subject can be detected through postexperimental interviews and simulations, as discussed by Orne (1970). Altruism as the motivation for administering shock can be effectively eliminated by using an evaluation rather than a "teacher–learner" paradigm (Baron, 1974a,b; Berkowitz & Geen, 1966).

The problem of ethics, however, is not so easily dismissed. Both the gross deception necessary to produce analogues of aggressive behavior in the laboratory and the possible effects on a subject's self-esteem that may accompany reflection on his aggressive behavior after the experiment present ethical problems. Miller (1972) reviews some of the ethical problems inherent in deception research, all of which are a source of concern to the investigator engaged in aggression research.

The reliance on a single paradigm for testing hypotheses about aggression poses a number of obvious difficulties, including artificial internal validity, which may result from paradigm-specific investigation. Unfortunately, the use of alternative approaches, particularly using adult populations, has, until recently, been infrequent (e.g., Goldstein, Davis, & Herman, 1975; Zillmann & Bryant, 1974). Despite these problems, the Buss–Berkowitz paradigm remains the basis for a large component of our current understanding of human aggression. Its value has been in generating hypotheses that can then be tested in more natural settings. The finding of Williams, Meyerson, Eron, and Semler (1967) that children who show more aggression in the laboratory are also rated as more aggressive by their peers offers some external validity to the Buss–Berkowitz paradigm. In addition, the "weapons effect" (Berkowitz & LePage, 1967), which indicated that exposure to aggressive stimuli (guns) resulted in increased aggression in the laboratory, has been replicated in the field experiment by Turner, Layton, and Simons (1975), reviewed in Geen's preceding chapter.

The laboratory paradigm has the further advantage of robustness with regard to internal validity (Goranson, 1970). Findings across laboratories, experimenters, and variations in methodology that indicate consistent patterning of responses (Goldstein *et al.*, 1975) and consistent interactions between stimulus conditions and amount of aggression displayed account for much of the widespread use of this paradigm. One additional limitation of the paradigm is its popularity. It will require a considerable amount of effort to establish an alternative approach to the laboratory study of aggression that can serve as a validation check for findings generated from the Buss–Berkowitz paradigm. This, plus the dearth of extensive external validity, tends to lessen the impact of aggression research as being not only *laboratory specific* but also potentially *paradigm specific*.

The Use of Arousal in Aggression Theory

By its very nature, aggressive behavior lends itself to some application of an energizing concept perhaps more than any other social behavior. Aggression is often typified by vigorous behavior, heightened emotionality, and responses of an intensity (hitting, shouting, etc.) which seem to set aggression apart from many other behaviors. Although definitions of aggression typically include responses that occur under apparently low levels of emotionality, these often have the appearance of being added as an afterthought. From our everyday observations, it seems only natural that the study of aggression include the study of an emotional state that accompanies it. The concept of an energization of responses has been introduced into most theories of aggression, including ethological, drive, frustration–aggression, and attribution models as well as the social learning model. In spite of the popularity of the arousal construct in theories of aggression, there is disagreement as to exactly what it refers to or how necessary it is in a conceptualization of aggression (Tedeschi *et al.*, 1974). From our common sense observations as well as from a large number of laboratory investigations reported in earlier chapters, however, one might conclude that the construct is one that will be used for some time to come. Although we are aware of acts of "aggression" that occur with very little emotionality, the bulk of recent aggression research has not explored these situations.

Since the previous chapters have dealt with a variety of experiments that implicitly use an energization conceptualization of aggression, this section will deal with some measurement problems inherent in energization formulations as well as some recent investigation which may have some implications for an arousal conceptualization in a social learning model of aggression.

The Arousal Measure

Inherent in much of the research on aggression is the concept of an emotional state that potentiates aggressive responses. This emotional state may be induced by the presentation of noxious noise (Geen & O'Neal, 1969), negative evaluations of a subject's performance on a task (Baron, 1974a,b; Berkowitz, 1965), frustration (Dollard et al., 1939), high ambient temperatures (Baron, 1974b), or any of a broad class of arousal producing stimulation, including direct stimulation of brain centers associated with emotional behaviors (Mark & Ervin, 1970). While arousal is a useful concept in describing internal states associated with behaviors labeled as emotional, many problems of measurement have yet to be overcome.

A logical approach to the interaction between arousal and aggression might assume a linear relationship between arousal level and probability of aggression. Baron and Bell (1975), however, found that angered subjects who were placed in an uncomfortably hot environment (92°F.) actually showed a decrease in aggression. Similar results were obtained in an extension of this experiment (Baron & Bell, in press) which also indicate that a momentary decrease in the high negative affect (angry and hot) subjects, obtained by giving them a cooling drink, resulted in increased aggression. Baron and Bell (in press) suggest that the interaction between affect and aggression is a curvilinear relationship, which increases in aggression occurring up to some optimal point of negative affect and then decreases. Although this interpretation may be valid, some alternative interpretations on the source and appropriateness of arousal will be offered in the section on attribution.

The measurement of arousal is typically achieved by either asking the subject for his analysis of his emotional state following the manipulation used to induce arousal or by taking physiological measures that reflect sympathetic nervous system activation. The first approach has the problem of contaminating arousal with a label that is provided by the experimenter. The rather diverse meaning of arousal, as used by the psychologist, is often shared by the subject, so that the question "How aroused do you feel right now?" is subject to such varied interpretation as to be of questionable value. If the experimenter provides a label (e.g., "How angry do you feel right now?"), he may be providing the subject with a label for an emotional state which had never occurred to the subject and which may interact with subsequent behavior.

Alternatively, various methods of indirectly measuring sympathetic nervous system activation are used, either alone or in concert with self-reports. Although various problems with individual differences in reactivity exist for any single measure (i.e., heart rate, blood pressure, electrodermal activity), the use of multiple measures can offset this limitation. A final problem with the measurement of physiological indices of arousal is the possible contribution of the measurement to the arousal. Stopping an experiment to record heart rate or blood pressure may in itself prove arousing, particularly to a subject who has just been insulted and wishes to maintain an outward appearance of calm. With the advent of self-contained telemetry devices for monitoring physiological activity, this problem too may be effectively overcome.

Among the various methods that have been used to assess physiological "arousal" in the context of aggression research, perhaps the most popular has been blood pressure (e.g., Geen & Stonner, 1973; Hokanson & Burgess, 1962; Hokanson, Burgess, & Cohen, 1963; Scarpetti, 1974; Schill, 1972). Results in these experiments typically indicate a relationship betweeen "arousal" (which is induced by an experimental manipulation) and increased systemic pressure. It is generally assumed that increased systemic pressure is the result of an increase in sympathetic activation (Alexander, 1970). A problem with blood pressure as a measure of arousal is that it is influenced by multiple factors (Guyton, 1966, pp. 342). For example, increased contraction of skeletal muscles can increase the mean systemic pressure more than threefold. Multiple measures of arousal are seldom taken during an aggression experiment, but, given the complexities of the psychophysiological interpretation of arousal (Duffy, 1972; Lang, Rice, & Sternbach, 1972), a single indicator of arousal has definite limitations.

Zillmann and Bryant (1974) found that sympathetic nervous system arousal induced through exercise also facilitated the expression of aggressive responses in subjects who were exposed to the insulting confederate after the exercise session. Increases in long-term humoral activation appear to have had residual effects which later increased aggression, regardless of the source of activation.

One problem with Zillmann's approach is his measure of sympathetic activation, which involves the multiplication of heart rate and mean arterial pressure. Since these two measures are not independent, somewhat inflated sympathetic activation values may be obtained as arousal increases. The use of multiple measures, however, is an appropriate step in any arousal formulation.

Additional validation of Zillmann's sympathetic arousal formulation might be obtained through the assessment of urine or blood catecholamines which provide a reliable indicant of sympathetic activity. The discrepancies between Baron and Bell's (1973) finding that sexual arousal obtained by presenting slides of nude females inhibits later aggression and Zillmann's (1971) finding of facilitation of aggression following exposure to an arousing erotic film is possibly due to the nature of the stimuli used. Wenger, Jones, and Jones (1956) suggest that the initial phases of sexual arousal may be dominated by the parasympathetic nervous system, which is followed by dominance of the sympathetic nervous system with increased sexual arousal. To the extent that parasympathetic dominance is incompatible with sympathetic arousal, the suggestion of Wegner *et al.* may explain this discrepancy.

Arousal in a Social Learning Model of Aggression

Bandura (1973), in a thorough review of the literature, has outlined the social learning position on aggression. He suggests that arousal will facilitate aggression to the extent that aggression is a dominant response and the situation indicates that aggression will lead to positive consequences. Although a number of recent studies support this contention (e.g., Konecni, 1975; Scarpetti, 1974; Stone & Hokanson, 1969; Zillmann & Bryant, 1974), evidence to the contrary is presented by Baron (1971), who found that, when retaliation for aggression was almost certain, aggressive responses were not significantly lowered in angered subjects. Bandura suggests that extreme levels of anger arousal may delay the concern over negative consequences under these circumstances. Specific instances of aggression of this type may be best explained in terms of a model of impulsive aggression proposed by Berkowitz (1974). The exact nature of the interaction between arousal and its effects on the perceived consequences of aggression is an area deserving of more attention.

Scarpetti (1974) showed that a social learning model was applicable to both the learning of new responses to aggression as well as arousal changes following the responses. Subjects classified as repressors initially preferred "friendly" responses toward an aggressor, while those classified as sensitizers initially preferred to respond aggressively to aggression. When subjects were reinforced for their nonpreferred responses during conditioning trials, not only did the type of response shift, but the arousal pattern following the response also shifted. Initially, rapid arousal reduction followed the preferred response; after counterconditioning, short latency arousal reduction followed the initial nonpreferred response.

The exact nature of the relationship between repression-sensitization and autonomic responsiveness is unclear (e.g., Buck, Miller, & Caul, 1974) and appears to be highly determined by situational factors. It is clear that the typical emotional response pattern of an individual has implications for further research directed at understanding the arousal–aggression relationship.

Several other recent studies on the nature of the relationship between arousal and aggression have implications for the social learning model. Zillmann and Bryant (1974), for example, found that sympathetic activation that resulted from exercise facilitated the expression of aggressive responses in angered subjects but facilitated the expression of prosocial (noxious stimulation reduction) responses in nonangered subjects. This implies that arousal may function to increase the output of nonaggressive responses in a situation in which they are dominant responses. Scarpetti's (1974) finding that nonpreferred responses were followed by longer latency arousal reduction might suggest that this arousal would facilitate the expression of the dominant (preferred) response on trials following a nonpreferred response. Although trial by trial data are not available, Scarpetti reported that repressors, whose preferred mode of responding is nonaggressive, tended to give a significantly increasing number of aggressive responses across baseline trials. Scarpetti (1974) speculates that this may be due to the repressor reverting to previously well-learned cultural role demands concerning the appropriate manner in which a male deals with aggression.

A very important aspect of the arousal–aggression relationship is the interpretation of an arousal state by the individual. This aspect of arousal will be discussed in a subsequent section on attribution. First, however, I will explore some of the more biological aspects of arousal and aggression. The social psychologist has become interested in the measurement of physiological responsivity because of its possible utility in providing information about an arousal component of aggression. By manipulating "social" situations and observing the effect on physiological variables and concomitant aggressive behavior, he has attempted to understand the pattern and impact of these interactions. A different approach has been taken by another group of investigators who manipulate the physiology of the individual and attempt to assess the consequences of this manipulation on social behavior. The following section deals with some of the recent investigations of the latter approach.

The Physiology of Aggression

Research dealing with possible brain centers that control the onset and inhibition of aggression has burgeoned during the past decade. The results of these explorations have led some investigators to conclude that the time is near when violence in our society may be significantly reduced by the use of surgical techniques (Delgado, 1969; Mark & Ervin, 1970) or the use of aggression inhibiting drugs (Moyer, 1971). Most of these investigators work on the logical assumption that there exist aggression centers in the brain of man which correspond to those already located in other primates. Indeed, some investigations indicate that the major centers of the brain in man that are associated with aggression have been located in the limbic system (Clemente & Chase, 1973; Hitchcock, Laitinen, & Vaernet, 1972; Laitinen & Livingston, 1973; Mark & Ervin, 1970).

Surgical Treatment of Aggression

An excellent review of the history and current status of surgical techniques for the control of aggression is to be found in Valenstein's (1973) book. Valenstein contends, contrary to some of the researchers in the area, that, because of the number of specific structures that have been implicated in aggressive behavior, the possibility of accurately locating and effectively treating each of these is extremely remote. In addition, there appear to be structures in the human brain other than the limbic system that may function to duplicate, augment, or inhibit the specific areas related to aggression. This redundancy appears to argue against the existence of a "locus of aggressive behavior" in the brain which is amenable to treatment through surgery.

Further problems arise in the assessment techniques used to measure pre- and postoperative levels of aggressive behavior. In many cases, aggressive behavior is associated with epileptic seizures, and, when more conservative treatments of the epilepsy fail, it is surgically treated. Surgical amelioration of the epileptic seizures is often accompanied by a cessation of aggressive outbursts. Unfortunately, many of the reported cases are with patients of less than average IQ or behavior disturbances not clearly tied to epilepsy. Because of this restricted patient population, it is often difficult to detect any intellectual or emotional alterations of behavior (other than the possible cessation of seizures and accompanying aggression) that may result from the operation. In addition, the exact function of eliminating seizure-related aggressive responses is poorly documented. Is the postoperative patient unable to respond aggressively (or even assertively) under *any* circumstances? In a case reported by Moyer (1969a), one patient was postoperatively unable to show anger. Although this finding is not necessarily a common one, a criterion for establishing an appropriate level of assertiveness is necessary in order to assess the effectiveness (or overeffectiveness) of the surgical technique.

The number of structures implicated in aggressive behavior (including the cingulate gyrus, temporal lobes, amygdala, posterior hypothalamus, thalamus, fornix, and upper mesencephalon) presents a problem in the use of surgery to decrease aggression. In a case reported by Mark and Ervin (1970), a patient who showed no neurological symptoms associated with hyperaggressiveness, was found to have abnormal brain wave patterns only upon the implantation of electrodes in the hippocampus. The authors suggest that many cases of aggression and violent outbursts are due to brain damage that may not be detected through routine neurological examinations. They estimate that from 10 to 15 million Americans have brain damage and that an "appreciable" percentage of acts of personal violence are committed by these individuals. Unfortunately, in stressing the possible biological considerations underlying aggressive behavior, Mark and Ervin feel compelled to minimize the social aspects. They propose that, although exposure to violent television may have some impact on aggression, this does not explain why Boston and Montreal, which share access to violent television programming, have such disparate rates of assaultive crimes. The vague implication is that Boston's (8 to 1) higher assault rate is due to some biological factor (brain damage?) rather than assorted social factors, which combine with any effects of televised violence.

Any suggestion that the occurrence of aggression and violence is more closely tied to brain damage than to social factors seems implausible. Valenstein's conclusion that, although some violence is certainly attributable to biological factors, it would be unfortunate to assume that violence is "mainly the product of a diseased brain rather than a diseased society [1973, p. 353]," seems much more plausible. While the necessity of continuing research on the possible effects of brain damage on aggressive behavior is obvious, greater precision in diagnosis, rather than surgical technique, appears to be the most rewarding approach.

Drug Effects on Aggression

Moyer (1969a, 1969b, 1971) reviews a number of studies of the effects of various drugs that have been used to decrease clinical signs of aggressive and hyperactive behaviors. Moyer (1969b) further suggests that, at some point in the future, antihostility drugs may be added routinely to a population's drinking water. A question of more popular social concern is the effect of social drugs that may function to increase aggression. As is suggested in Dengerink's review in this volume, the use of alcohol and subsequent aggression has been the focus of surprisingly little empirical research (Shuntich & Taylor, 1972). Although a number of correlational studies have strongly implicated alcohol use in the commission of crime (Shupe, 1954; Violent Crime, 1969; Wolfgang & Strohm, 1956), there is little data to indicate a direct causal relationship between alcohol consumption and aggression, and at least one study (Bennett, Buss, & Carpenter, 1969) indicated no such relationship at all.

Teger, Katkin, and Pruitt (1969) found evidence that supported the hypothesis that the type of alcohol consummed was important in risk-taking behavior. Ingestion of high congener (e.g., bourbon) beverages lead to increased risk-taking when compared to similar amounts of low congener (e.g., vodka) beverages. Shuntich and Taylor (1972) similarly found that the ingestion of bourban increased the likelihood of aggression, but an extension of this study (Taylor & Gammon, 1975) indicated that vodka, a low congener beverage, had an even greater effect on enhancement of aggressive responses. The authors interpreted these results as indicating that it is not the congener content, but rather the speed with which the alcohol is absorbed by the blood that affects aggressive behavior. Small doses of alcohol seemed to have an inhibitor effect on aggression, perhaps, as the authors suggest, because of the depressive effects on the cerebral cortex which increase social apprehension. Larger doses may function to incapacitate the cortical control over the emotional centers of the brain, leading to boisterous emotional behavior and aggression.

Because of the highly social nature of alcohol, it may be difficult to separate the physiological effects from the social learning effects of alcoholic consumption on aggression. Similar problems exist with other social drugs. Zimbardo (1969) has suggested that amphetamines may function to increase agitation, impulsiveness, and possible violence. Substantiation of this hypothesis is consistent with the previously noted arousal interpretations of aggressive behavior. Marihuana was found by the Commission on Marihuana and Drug Abuse (1972) to have no causal relationship with violent or aggressive behavior. The report stated that "If anything, marihuana generally serves to inhibit the expression of such behavior [p. 73]." Evidence leading to the same conclusion has been published by Tinklenberg and Woodrow (1974).

Hormones and Aggression

In their review of the literature on sex differences in aggression, Maccoby and Jacklin (1974) conclude that males are more aggressive than females as a function of biological factors as well as social learning influences. They point to evidence (Joslyn, 1973) that indicates that female rhesus monkeys given testosterone injections show increases in aggression and upward displacements in social dominance hierarchies. Untreated males in the experimental situation showed a decrease in aggression and sexuality when compared to males in a nonexperimental social group. Rose, Haladay, and Burnstein (1971) found that males in a rhesus monkey colony, who were at the top of the dominance hierarchy, had higher plasma testosterone levels than more submissive males. Rose *et al.* (1971) suggest that the causal relationship is influenced in the direction from dominance to testosterone levels. That is, shifts in dominance result in shifts in testosterone levels rather than the reverse. They note that the male with the highest testosterone levels (most dominant) engages in fewer aggressive behaviors than some of his less dominant cagemates. The evidence appears to implicate testosterone in the formation and stabilization of dominance hierarchies in primates, but the relationship between dominance hierarchies, testosterone levels, and aggression is still uncertain. Given the potential fluidity of any social hierarchy in man, extrapolation from animal studies must be tentative.

Although Maccoby and Jacklin (1974) base part of their argument for a biological sex difference in aggression on the fact that "males are more aggressive than females in all human societies for which evidence is available [p. 242]," the social learning contribution to sex differences in aggression may certainly account for much of this difference. Mulvihill and Tumin (1969) report that, in societies where male and female roles are more nearly equal, the crime rate for females is also more nearly equal to that of males. Although the exact contribution of hormonal effects to aggressive behavior may prove extremely elusive (due to the different socialization pressures exerted on high-testosterone females or low-testosterone males), there is fairly strong evidence that male hormones do affect aggression in some manner.

Chromosomal Anomalies and Aggression

The early reports on the possible aggressive behavior patterns in males with an extra Y chromosome (Jacobs, Brunton, Melville, Brittain, & McClairmont, 1965) have recently undergone much closer scrutiny. Shah (1970) reviewed the available literature and concluded that, while there is evidence of a greater prevalence of XYY males in various institutional populations than would be expected by chance, there existed no evidence that an extra Y chromosome was causally related to (or even a major element in) this finding. The causal link again may vary because of early socialization, but the fact remains that many

XYY males do manage to function outside of institutions. In addition, when matched with inmates with normal chromosome constitutions, they were not found to be any more aggressive.

Attribution Theory and Aggression

A number of implications for a model of aggression are contained in the rather broad theoretical arena labeled "attribution theory." Growing out of Heider's (1958) approach to the manner in which people ascribe causality and dispositional properties, attribution theory has been expanded and elaborated on by a number of theorists (Jones & Davis, 1965; Kelley, 1967, 1971). Some of the issues relevant to aggression which have been examined within an attribution framework are the labeling of emotional states, the perception of intentionality, the application of traits verus situational factors in describing behavior, and the labeling of behavior as aggression. Kelley (1967) alludes to the number of times researchers have unknowingly employed attributional concepts without reference to their origins in Heider's formal theory. It is not difficult, however, to see the relevance of a number of principles of "attribution theory" to much of the current research on aggression.

Attribution and Arousal

In a previous section on the concept of arousal in aggression research, a number of investigations in which arousal was found to increase aggression under certain conditions were cited. An attribution interpretation of arousal emphasizes the emotional label that is applied to the arousal as well as the subject's considerations concerning the source of the arousal. In laboratory investigations of aggression, these attributions have been shown to have an impact on the degree of aggression which a subject exhibits. Berkowitz, Lepinski, and Angulo (1969) manipulated their subjects' perceived arousal through false feedback and found that subjects who perceived their arousal as being inappropriately high reacted with lowered aggression toward the confederate. Similarly, the studies by Baron and Bell (1975), which were discussed in the section on arousal, indicated that extremely uncomfortable environmental conditions lead to decreased aggression in angered subjects. The attribution of extreme discomfort to a single source (the victim) may have seemed inappropriate, and only when the discomfort was decreased was the victim reconsidered as the source of arousal, which was then relabeled anger.

Perhaps one of the most widely cited examples of an attributional process in the labeling of emotions is the classic experiment carried out by Schachter and Singer (1962) in which drug-induced arousal states were interpreted by uninformed subjects as emotional states resulting from situational factors. The work of Zillmann and his associates (Zillmann, 1971; Zillmann & Bryant, 1974; Zillmann, Katcher, & Milavsky, 1972) indicates that arousal from a variety of sources, including erotic films and physical exercise (independent of one another), may be misattributed by a subject and serve to intensify a previously established emotional state.

A series of experiments by Baron and his associates (Baron, 1974a,b; Baron & Bell, 1973) investigated the effects of sexual arousal on aggression. If arousal as a generalized activation of emotion includes sexual arousal, then it would be logical to assume that such arousal would facilitate aggression. Baron's results, however, consistently indicated that moderate increases in sexual arousal, obtained by male subjects viewing pictures of nude females, resulted in a decrease in aggression. Baron suggests two possible reasons for his unexpected results. The first deals with the previously mentioned finding by Berkowitz *et al.* (1969) which indicated that a subject who perceives his arousal level as inappropriately high may reassess his emotional state to conform with the situation. Thus, angered subjects who are also exposed to erotic stimuli may find the increased arousal too high to label as anger and redefine their feeling more in terms of the situation. Alternatively, Baron suggests that the order of presentation may be crucial in the labeling of emotions. The most recent label would result from arousal induced earlier, such that, when the subject is first angered and then sexually aroused, his internal state is interpreted as sexual arousal. If the reverse order were followed, increased anger would be the resulting label.

The previously mentioned studies dealing with the effects of sexual arousal on subsequent aggression may also be explained within an attributional framework. The attribution of emotions assumes that there is a unitary emotional response that will be labled according to situational factors. While this interpretation has been shown to be a valuable one in a variety of experiments, it may be fruitful to reexamine this assumption with regard to aggression. The neurophysiological evidence that implicates brain structures as being causally related to "rage" behavior seems to indicate that stimulation of certain structures of the brain results in emotional behavior which is not misattributed. Although it is true that the intense stimulation of a localized section of the brain used in his research may never occur outside of the laboratory, it is also true that such stimulation does not result in attributions to environmental stimuli. Such stimulation has also never been reported as being fear or euphoria.

From a practical point of view, studies of the labeling of an emotional state and the subsequent behavior conforming to that label will probably constitute the most feasible line of research on emotion for some time to come. It may be premature however, to assume that, simply because we have been unable to differentiate emotions reliably, discriminable emotional states do not exist. Future technological advances might allow for the nonsurgical measurements of electrical patterns in localized parts of the brain. Such technology may offer information about emotional states that are functionally distinct, and thus unlikely to be misattributed.

Attribution and the Label of Aggression

As was mentioned in the introduction, criticism of definitions of aggression used by various investigators has followed theoretical and empirical attempts at definition with a degree of certainty exceeded, perhaps, only by death and taxes. This section will deal with a recent criticism of aggression as a psychologically useful term, and attempt to point out some shortcomings of any definition of the term.

Tedeschi et al. (1974) have recently argued against the concept of aggression as a descriptive or classificatory term for human behaviors. As noted earlier, a wide variety of responses have been used by various investigators as dependent measures of aggression. Tedeschi et al. contend that the problem with many studies of aggression is that the *intent* to aggress is never established. Using an attribution model, they suggest that the label "aggression" is applied whenever an observer perceives nonnormative, offensive, and intentional coercion being applied by an actor. Coercion is the use of threats and punishments to gain compliance. Threats may be any combination of contingent or noncontingent detrimental action and implicit–explicit requests. Four types of punishment may result from noncompliance with a threat (noxious stimulation, resource deprivation, expected gain deprivation, or social punishment). An example of a *contingent explicit* threat with noxious stimulation punishment, might be "if you don't give me your money, I'll blow you head off."

Aggression, within this model, becomes most closely related to the observer's perception of intent on the part of the actor and the legitimacy, degree of provocation, and the violation of equity perceived. Tedeschi et al. (1974) are aware that the actor will seldom ascribe aggressive intent to his actions. Evidence that investigators use their own criteria for what constitutes aggression is seen by Tedeschi *et al.* in the manner in which the researchers implicity introduce their own value systems into aggression research.

The problem in assessing "intent" on the part of the subject in an aggression experiment is an exceedingly difficult one. The experimenter must, as Tedeschi *et al.* (1974) suggest, rely on an "inference drawn from the circumstances and behavior [p. 541]." Typically it is the experimenter, rather than the subject, who makes this inference (for seldom do even the most honest among us label our own behaviors as hostile or aggressive). In a typical aggression experiment, the subject may be told that he is delivering noxious stimulation to another person as part of a learning or social evaluation experiment. He may well respond to queries about why he used a particular level of punishment by saying that he felt that the particular level "helped" the other subject learn more. The naive, one-time observer may attribute altruism to the subject for this response, as may the subject himself (Baron & Eggleston, 1972). The observation by the experimenter that subjects across experimental conditions make similar attributions leads him to very different conclusions. The experimenter notes that subjects who are exposed to certain manipulations (e.g., violent films, models, arousal, etc.) tend to use higher intensity noxious stimulation in their "altruistic" efforts. This leads the experimenter to label this behavior as more aggressive than the "low intensity altruism" exhibited by those subjects not exposed to the situational difference. Consistent with the attribution model of Kelley (1967), the experimenter may be wrong, but his faith in his attribution of aggression is strengthened as he observes similar results occurring over time, across modalities, and with concurring data from other sources.

In one sense, the Tedeschi *et al.* (1974) definition of coercion as the use of threats and punishments to gain compliance contrasts sharply with other approaches to dealing with the concept of aggression. The broad categorization used makes coercion applicable to any attempt to influence another person. Virtually any social interaction thus becomes a potential coercion. Teaching is coercive to the extent that explicit requests (to fulfill course requirements) are made, and punishments (disapproval or deprivation) are specified. Social greetings may be seen as coercive to the extent that they carry an implicit request for compliance (a reply) and a nonspecific (but probably social) punishment for noncompliance. Readers of Uncle Remus may readily identify social greetings as coercive. Br'er Fox's attribution of unfriendliness to the Tar Baby, however, seems to offer us little in the way of clarifying the parameters of the situations that lead to the infliction of harm. The fact that most of us would label Br'er Fox's behavior as aggression follows the Tedeschi *et al.* model but still leaves us in the dark as to why the interaction leads to fisticuffs.

The observer is seldom in a position to determine all of the events leading to an "aggressive" interchange. The actor, as noted before, is an unreliable source of information, as anyone knows who has ever asked two fighting boys the question "Who started it?" Laboratory investigations offer some control over the instigation but little over intent. The criticism that aggression research has typically ensured that the subject respond in an aggressive manner by providing no alternative to aggression (in the form of alternative coercive responses) has been a valid one but is becoming less so. For example, the Zillmann and Bryant (1974) investigations mentioned earlier indicate that aroused, insulted subjects used less positive reinforcement than aroused, noninsulted subjects.

The Tedeschi *et al.* (1974) reformulation of aggression in terms of attributions and equity is broad enough to cover virtually all instances of behavior that are typically called aggressive. However their answer to the question "Why do men use coercive power against one another as an offensive strategy?" is, in many respects, unsatisfactory. Coercion, Tedeschi *et al.* feel, "is used as a mode of influence when other means are perceived as unlikely to be successful [p. 553]." As mentioned earlier, however, virtually any social interaction can be viewed as coercive given the breadth of the definition used. The question, as asked by the more traditional researchers, is "Who, and under what circumstances, resorts to infliction of harm against others?" Often the observer will be uncertain as to exactly which behavior an actor is attempting to influence, and many times the actor himself will be unable to assess accurately his reason for aggressing.

As Tedeschi *et al.* (1974) point out, however, the reformulation will provide new questions concerning aggression research. If socialization provides some hierarchy for coercive responses, (requests, bargaining, threats, punishments, etc.), the research employing the coercion model might be directed to the circumstances under which this hierarchy short-circuits, such that aggression (as harm infliction) results. As noted earlier, this is apparently the direction taken by a number of recent investigations of aggression (Goldstein *et al.,* 1975; Scarpetti, 1974; Zillmann & Bryant, 1974). Although these studies have been cast in terms of approaches other than "coercion," they address themselves to some of the criticisms raised by Tedeschi and his associates.

Tedeschi *et al.,* (1974) state that there are no clear criteria for identifying an aggressive response. The same criticism, however, is as easily leveled at a definition of coercion. The implication is that the scientist should use the model of everyman in defining aggression. An attributional analysis seems somehow out of place here, inasmuch as Kelley (1967) sees attribution theory as everyman's attempt to use systematic scientific methods in determining causality.

Finally, Tedeschi et al.'s (1974) claim that the value connotations implicit in the use of the term aggression can be avoided by substituting the rubric coercive power appears untenable. In this view, the administration of noxious stimuli does not represent an aggressive act if the behavior is performed as a means of restoring equity. Whether or not an observer labels the act aggression or not will depend on his perspective.

The concept of equity has strong value implications of its own, and whether or not a more value-free approach is to be gained through this model is open to question. Furthermore, restoration of equity may occur either behaviorally or psychologically (Walster, Berschied, & Walster, 1973), and, inasmuch as equity enters into the attribution of aggression, confusion abounds. As an example, take an instance of mugging. The actor (mugger) may not consider his behavior aggressive if he is merely attempting to restore equity caused by a social system that fails to reward his inputs appropriately. The victim may restore psychological equity by saying that it was stupid to resist, or that he was lacking in common sense to be out alone on a dark street. An observer would generally attribute "aggression" to the behavior of the mugger, but may, if psychologically astute, realize that this is not aggression, but merely restoration of equity on the part of the mugger, who had no intent to harm. The mugger, who had no intent to harm at the outset of his endeavor, was forced to do so because of the "illegitimate" resistance on the part of the victim. The question then becomes one of recruiting "value-free" observers to assess the legitimacy and violation of equity in aggression-type interactions.

There is little doubt that, in all psychological research, there are implicit value systems (cf. Gergen, 1973). Two questions arise with regard to "values" in aggression research: First, can social psychological research ever be value free? Second, would such a state of affairs be desirable? If psychology continues to use, as a model for its investigations, the model used by the "hard" sciences (cf. Schlenker, 1974), the problem of values will be dealt with in the application of findings rather than in their basic relationships. The physicist can investigate the concept of friction in a value-free environment. To the engineer, friction is "good," if it applies to tire tread design, but "bad," if it applies to engine wear. The question of appropriate models for social psychology will be considered in the following section.

Future Directions in Aggression Research

In a paper presented at a conference on research paradigms and priorities, Walster and Walster (1974) took an intriguing look at what we may expect from social psychology in the year 2000. One of their hypotheses about the future is that a general theory of behavior, which will integrate many of the currently fashionable mini-theories, may well be a reality by the year 2000. Of course, predicting the future direction of any activity is a fascinating endeavor which contains the additional incentive of being viewed in one's old age as a person with remarkable foresight (if one's predictions are proven accurate) or merely being relegated to the section of the library reserved for old issues of *Popular Mechanics* if one's guesses prove not to be so correct.

With this gain–loss ratio in mind, I cannot help but attempt to forecast part of the future of aggression research prior to the aforementioned general model of behavior becoming a reality. Some aspects of the future of current aggression research can be dealt with in a fairly straightforward manner. Certainly, the rapid advances being made in the neurophysiology and neurochemistry of behavior will continue. Whether or not the more optimistic speculations of some researchers (e.g., Delgado, 1969; Mark & Ervin, 1970; Moyer, 1969a) on localizing and neutralizing aggression centers in the brain will have a large impact on aggression research other than in cases of pathological rage is doubtful (Valenstein, 1973). I have some confidence however, that the more general approach to interactions between physiological reactions and environmental stimuli may offer a more profitable line of investigations of aggression in nonpathological populations. The exact nature of future research in aggression (as well as all of social psychology) may well be shaped by the current controversy as to the most appropriate "model" for inquiry in the field of social psychology.

The Historical Nature of Social Psychology

Danto (1968) criticized philosophies of history on the grounds that in the process of identifying stable patterns of events which repeat themselves, information is provided which makes it possible to alter the cycle. In a similar vein, Gergan (1973) has suggested that social psychology is a reflection of current history rather than an investigation that will yield predictive laws. When evidence supporting a social psychological theory becomes available to the public, it becomes possible for people to respond in a manner that negates the theory. The motivation to negate psychological laws comes from man's desire to retain autonomy, and theories become statements of contemporary relationships rather than transhistorical laws. The researcher in aggression is well aware of this problem. When campus rumors about aggression research are widespread, subjects become suspicious about the truth of the experimenter's "cover story" and often act in such a way as to negate the effects of the manipulations.

Schlenker (1974), in a defense of the more traditional "psychology-as-science" approach, contends that, when such information becomes available, it does not invalidate previous findings but only removes a previously controlled variable (naivety) from the experimental situation. Much as a leak in a vacuum may seem to negate an experimental finding in a physics experiment, foreknowledge of a hypothesis may seem to invalidate a social psychological relationship. An awareness of the "leak" in either case merely provides the experimenter with information about one condition under which a "law" will not offer prediction.

The position that the reader takes will, to a large degree, reflect the type of indoctrination he has received. The two approaches, however, are not necessarily mutually exclusive. As Gergen (1973) points out, the more closely a social phenomenon is tied to a physiological phenomenon, the more historically durable it will be. My own predilections about the nature of aggression, as the reader is aware, place the phenomenon toward the historically durable end of the continuum. This does not invalidate any assumptions made within the broader (but potentially less predictive) approaches which are of a more "social" nature. As Hendrick (1974) points out, however, "Intrusive variables in ongoing social phenomena may ultimately be uncontrollable, at least to a degree sufficient to allow precise tests of predictions [p. 17]."

Essentially, the problem posed by viewing social psychology as either a science or a historical endeavor may have a minimal impact on aggression research. Although the debate between the two approaches will continue (this is only a prediction), its outcome, in terms of the direction of future research on aggression, will have its maximum impact on the "pure" versus "applied" nature of research.

The Future of Experimentation in Aggression Research

Gergen (1973) suggests that the value of social psychology does not lie in perfecting general laws of behavior, but rather in application to social problems of immediate concern. This call for application of social psychology is an echo of McGuire's (1973) previous suggestion that social psychology should address itself to social issues rather than to tests of hypotheses generated by theories. McGuire forecasts the demise of the experimental paradigm that rests on manipulating independent variables in the laboratory (or the field) and observing their effects on dependent variables, while controlling for factors with an effect that might be extraneous to the hypothesis. The social psychologist, he feels, has been engaging in stage manipulations that are mere demonstrations of obvious linear relationships; the time has come for the researcher to turn away from belaboring the obvious and toward sorting out the complexities of the real world. Although McGuire's suggestions include a variety of approaches to social psychological investigation which will undoubtedly be valuable in aggression research, his rather dismal outlook for the future of traditional laboratory and field experimentation suggests that the age of *experimental* social psychology is in its waning years.

Walster and Walster (1974) suggest that the best predictions about the future can be made by observing long-term trends in the past, and they have little doubt that experimentation will continue as a major force in social psychology. Whether the more traditional experimental approach qualifies as "long term," as the Walsters suggest, is, of course, a matter of conjecture. Regardless of the role experimentation will play in the future, more complex statistical analysis of data is seen as a certainty. The biggest controversy about the future of social psychology concerns the manner in which these data will be collected. McGuire (1973) suggests that multivariate time series designs will be applied to "real world" observations and archival data, with increasingly sophisticated statistical techniques being used to infer causality from correlations. Such an approach would have a major impact on aggression research in that the topic does not readily lend itself to observational studies and, while rich archival data on some aggressive behaviors are available (e.g., police reports, newspapers), much information necessary for current formulations of aggression behavior (e.g., stimulus cues, arousal levels, previous modeling exposure), as well as the proposed correlational approaches, may never be available. On this issue, I must cautiously cast my lot with the traditionalists.

Perhaps the greatest impact on the future of aggression research will not be the result of the philosophical paths we choose to follow in terms of our definition of the role of social psychology as a science nor the role of experimentation per se, but rather the result of social psychologist's finally being forced to come to grips with the ethical problems of aggression research. Having done research in aggression, I am aware of the ethical problems that arise. Although care is taken to assure the subject, that he was not administering harm to another subject that indeed his responses were being measured in order to enable us to better understand human interactions, and that the deception was necessary for a "noncontaminated" study of aggression, the problem of ethics has not been resolved. The issue of informed consent, criticisms that deception, even in the pursuit of a "higher good" cannot be tolerated, and growing public skepticism of social psychological research, which has the potential of degrading subjects, will all have an impact on future aggression research.

The ethical problems in aggression research are not insurmountable, but they are subject to growing public scrutiny. If current approaches are to be used in the future, psychologists must give evidence (as I believe they have) of growing concern over these problems. The problem, however, could be rephrased to ask, "If the social psychologist has the means to investigate the problems of growing social concern, do not ethics demand that he attempt to find solutions to these problems?"

Conclusions

In the preceding pages, I have attempted to point out some of the inconsistencies in the recent literature on aggression as well as some directions that aggression research may take in the future. Specifically, the nature of arousal in aggression has been a focal point in this chapter, both from a physiological and a cognitive perspective. While reliance on either formulation for a complete answer to the relationship between arousal and aggression is unlikely to provide a totally acceptable answer, I feel that an understanding of the interaction between the two will be of immeasurable value in aggression research.

Little attention has been paid here to the nature of aggression as a social problem, nor to the direct application of research findings to the control of aggression. Probably no area of social psychology will feel the increasing public pressure for social scientists to "solve problems now" more than that of aggression research. Given the current knowledge of the causes and control of aggression, there are some who feel that the means are available to vigorously apply this knowledge to prevent man from destroying himself. Others recoil at the implication for control over nonaggressive behaviors which the application of our current knowledge would necessarily have. The answer lies in broadening our empirical base of knowledge about aggression continuously such that the choices available and the repercussions of these choices can be constantly reassessed. Only in this way can we find a "cure" for aggression that is not more deadly than the disease itself.

REFERENCES

Alexander, A. A. Psychophysiological concepts of psychopathology. In N. S. Greenfield & R. A. Sternbach (Eds.), *Handbook of psychophysiology.* New York: Holt, 1970.

Bandura, A. *Aggression: A social learning analysis.* Englewood Cliffs, New Jersey: Prentice-Hall, 1973.

Baron, R. A. Exposure to an aggressive model and apparent probability of retaliation from the victim as determinants of adult aggressive behavior. *Journal of Experimental Social Psychology,* 1971, *7,* 343–355.

Baron, R. A. The aggression inhibiting influence of heightened sexual arousal. *Journal of Personality and Social Psychology,* 1974, *30,* 318–322. (a)

Baron, R. A. Sexual arousal and physical aggression: The inhibiting influence of "cheesecake" and nudes. *Bulletin of the Psychonomic Society,* 1974, *3,* 337–339. (b)

Baron, R. A., & Bell, P. A. Effects of heightened sexual arousal on physical aggression. *Proceedings, 81st Annual Convention, APA,* 1973.

Baron, R. A,, & Bell, P. A. Aggression and heat: Mediating effects of prior provocation and exposure to an aggressive model. *Journal of Personality and Social Psychology,* 1975, *31,* 825–832.

Baron, R. A., & Bell, P. A. Aggression and heat: The influence of ambient temperature, negative affect, and a cooling drink on physical aggression. *Journal of Personality and Social Psychology,* in press.

Baron, R. A., & Eggleston, R. J. Performance on the "aggression machine": Motivation to help or harm? *Psychonomic Science,* 1972, *26,* 321–322.

Bennett, R. M., Buss, A. H., & Carpenter, J. A. Alcohol and human physical aggression. *Quarterly Journal of Studies on Alcohol,* 1969, *30,* 870–877.

Berkowitz, L. The concept of aggressive drive: Some additional considerations. In L. Berkowitz (Ed.), *Advances in experimental social psychology.* Vol. 2. New York: Academic Press, 1965. Pp. 301–329.

Berkowitz, L. Some determinants of impulsive aggression: Role of mediated associations with reinforcements for aggression. *Psychological Review,* 1974, *81,* 165–176.

Berkowitz, L., & Geen, R. G. Film violence and the cue properties of available targets. *Journal of Personality and Social Psychology,* 1966, *3,* 525–530.

Berkowitz, L., & LePage, A. Weapons as aggression eliciting stimuli. *Journal of Personality and Social Psychology,* 1967, *7,* 202–207.

Berkowitz, L., Lepinski, J. P., & Angulo, E. J. Awareness of own anger level and subsequent aggression. *Journal of Personality and Social Psychology,* 1969, *1,* 293–300.

Buck, R., Miller, R. E., & Caul, W. F. Sex, personality, and physiological variables in the communication of affect via facial expression. *Journal of Personality and Social Psychology,* 1974, *30,* 587–596.

Buss, A. H. *The psychology of aggression.* New York: Wiley, 1961.

Buss, A. H. Aggression pays. In J. L. Singer (Ed.), *The control of aggression and violence.* New York: Academic Press, 1971. Pp. 7–18.

Clemente, D. C., & Chase, M. H. Neurological substrates of aggressive behavior. *Annual Review of Physiology,* 1973, *35,* 329–356.

Danto, A. C. Analytical philosophy of history. Cambridge: Cambridge Univ. Press, 1968.

Delgado, J. M. R. *Physical control of the mind.* New York: Harper, 1969.

Dollard, J., Doob, N., Miller, N. E., Mowrer, O. H., & Sears, R. R. *Frustration and aggression.* New Haven: Yale Univ. Press, 1939.

Duffy, E. Activation. In N. S. Greenfield & R. S. Sternbach (Eds.), *Handbook of psychophysiology.* New York: Holt, 1972.

Geen, R. G., & O'Neal, E. C. Activation of cue-elicited aggression by general arousal. *Journal of Personality and Social Psychology,* 1969, *11,* 289–293.

Geen, R., & Stonner, D. Context effects in observed violence. *Journal of Personality and Social Psychology,* 1973, *25,* 145–150.

Gergen, K. J. Social psychology as history. *Journal of Personality and Social Psychology,* 1973, *26,* 309–320.

Goldstein, J. H., Davis, R. W., & Herman, D. Escalation of aggression: Experimental studies. *Journal of Personality and Social Psychology,* 1975, *31,* 162–170.

Goranson, R. Media violence and aggressive behavior: A review of experimental research. In L. Berkowitz (Ed.) *Advances in experimental social psychology.* Vol. 5, New York: Academic Press, 1970.

Guyton, A. C. *Textbook of medical physiology.* Philadelphia: Saunders, 1966.

Heider, F. *The psychology of interpersonal relations.* New York: Wiley, 1958.

Hendrick, C. Social psychology and history: An analysis of the defense of traditional science. Unpublished manuscript, Kent State Univ., 1974.

Hitchcock, E., Laitinen, L. V., & Vaernet, K. *Psychosurgery.* Springfield, Illinois: Thomas, 1972.

Hokanson, J. E., & Burgess, M. M. The effects of three types of aggression on vascular processes. *Journal of Abnormal and Social Psychology,* 1962, *64,* 446–449.

Hokanson, J. E., Burgess, M. M., & Cohen, M. The effect of displaced aggression on systolic blood pressure. *Journal of Abnormal and Social Psychology,* 1963, *67,* 214–218.

Jacobs, P. A., Brunton, M., Melville, M. M., Brittain, R. P., & McClairmont, W. F. Aggressive behavior, mental subnormality, and the XYY males. *Nature,* 1965, *208,* 1351–1352.

Jones, E. E., & Davis, K. E. From acts to dispositions. In L. Berkowitz (Ed.), *Advances in experimental social psychology.* Vol. 2, New York: Academic Press, 1965. Pp. 219–266.

Joslyn, W. D. Androgen induced social dominance in infant female rhesus monkeys. *Journal of Child Psychology and Psychiatry,* 1973, *14,* 137–145.

Kelley, H. H. Attribution theory in social psychology. In D. Levine (Ed.), *Nebraska symposium on motivation.* Lincoln: Univ. of Nebraska Press, 1967.

Kelley, H. H. *Attribution in social interaction.* New York: General Learning Press, 1971.

Konecni, V. J. Annoyance, type and duration of postannoyance activity, and aggression: The "cathartic effect." *Journal of Experimental Psychology,* 1975, *104,* 76–102.

Laitinen, L. V., & Livingston, K. E. *Surgical approaches in psychiatry.* Baltimore: Univ. Park Press, 1973.

Lang, P. J., Rice, D. G., & Sternbach, R. A. The psychophysiology of emotion. In N. S. Greenfield & R. A. Sternbach (Eds.) *Handbook of psychophysiology.* New York: Holt, 1972.

Maccoby, E. E., & Jacklin, C. N. *The psychology of sex differences.* Stanford: Stanford Univ. Press, 1974.

Mark, V. H., & Ervin, F. R. *Violence and the brain.* New York: Harper, 1970.

McGuire, W. J. The yin and yang of progress in social psychology: Seven koan. *Journal of Personality and Social Psychology,* 1973, *26,* 446–456.

Miller, A. G. (Ed.) *The social psychology of psychological research.* New York: Free Press, 1972.

Moyer, K. E. A preliminary physiological model of aggressive behavior. In J. P. Scott & B. E. Eleftherion (Eds.), *The physiology of fighting and defeat.* Chicago: Univ. of Chicago Press, 1969. (a)

Moyer, K. E. Internal impulses to aggression. *Transactions of the New York Academy of Sciences,* 1969, *31,* 210–214. (b)

Moyer, K. E. The physiology of aggression and the implications for aggression control. In J. L. Singer (Ed.), *The control of aggression and violence.* New York: Academic Press, 1971. Pp. 61–92.

Mulvihill, D. J., & Tumin, M. M. Crimes of violence, Vol. 12. Staff report submitted to the National Commission on the Causes and Prevention of Violence. Washington, D.C.: U.S. Government Printing Office, 1969.

Orne, M. T. Hypnosis, motivation and the ecological validity of the psychological experiment. In W. J. Arnold & M. M. Page (Eds.), *Nebraska symposium on motivation.* Lincoln: Univ. of Nebraska Press, 1970.

Rose, R. M., Haladay, J. W., & Burnstein, L. S. Plasma testosterone, dominance rank, and aggressive behavior in male rhesus monkeys. *Nature,* 1971, *231,* 366–368.

Scarpetti, W. L. Autonomic concomitants of aggressive behavior in repressors and sensitizers: A social learning approach. *Journal of Personality and Social Psychology,* 1974, *30,* 772–781.

Schachter, S., & Singer, J. E. Cognitive, social and physiological determinants of emotional state. *Psychological Review,* 1962, *69,* 379–399.

Schill, T. R. Aggression and blood pressure responses of high- and low-guilt subjects following frustration. *Journal of Consulting and Clinical Psychology,* 1972, *38,* 461.

Schlenker, B. R. Social psychology and science. *Journal of Personality and Social Psychology,* 1974, *29,* 1–15.

Schuck, J., & Pisor, K. Evaluating an aggression experiment by the use of simulating subjects. *Journal of Personality and Social Psychology,* 1974, *29,* 181–186.

Shah, S. A. *Report on the XYY chromosomal abnormality.* Washington, D.C.: Government Printing Office, 1970.

Shuntich, R., J. & Taylor, S. P. The effects of alcohol on human physical aggression. *Journal of Experimental Research in Personality,* 1972, *6,* 34–38.

Shupe, L. M. Alcohol and crime: A study of the urine alcohol concentration found in 882 persons arrested during or immediately after the commission of a felony. *Journal of Criminal Law, Criminology and Police Science,* 1954, *44,* 661–664.

Stone, L. J., & Hokanson, J. E. Arousal reduction via self-punitive behavior. *Journal of Personality and Social Psychology,* 1969, *12,* 72–79.

Taylor, S. P., & Gammon, C. B. Effects of type and dose of alcohol on human aggression. Paper presented at the meeting of the American Psychological Association, New Orleans, September, 1974.

Tedeschi, R. E., Smith, R. C., & Brown, R. C. A reinterpretation of research on aggression. *Psychological Bulletin,* 1974, *81,* 540–562.

Teger, A. I., Katkin, E. S., & Pruitt, D. G. Effects of alcoholic beverages and their congener content on level and style of risk taking. *Journal of Personality and Social Psychology,* 1969, *11,* 170–176.

Tinklenberg, J. R., & Woodrow, K. M. Drug use among youthful assaultive and sexual offenders. In S. Frazier (Ed.), *Aggression.* Baltimore: Williams & Wilkins, 1974. Pp. 209–224.

Turner, C. W., Layton, J. F., & Simons, L. S. Naturalistic studies of aggressive behavior: Aggressive stimuli, victim visibility, and horn honking. *Journal of Personality and Social Psychology,* 1975, *31,* 1098–1107.

U.S. Commission on Marijuana and Drug Abuse. *Marijuana: A signal for misunderstand-*

ing. Washington, D.C.: U.S. Government Printing Office, 1972.

Valenstein, E. S. *Brain control*. New York: Wiley, 1973.

Violent Crime. Report of the National Commission on the Causes and Prevention of Violence. New York: George Braziller, 1969.

Walster, E., Berschied, E., & Walster, G. W. New directions in equity research. *Journal of Personality and Social Psychology*, 1973, *25*, 151–176.

Walster, E., & Walster, G. W. The year 2000: The future of small group research. Paper presented at conference on "Research Paradigms and Priorities in Social Psychology," Ottawa, Canada, 1974.

Weiss, W. Effects of the mass media of communication. In G. Lindzey & E. Aronson (Eds.), *Handbook of social psychology*. Vol. 5 (2nd ed.) Reading, Massachusetts: Addison-Wesley, 1969. Pp. 77–195.

Wenger, M. A., Jones, F. N., & Jones, M. H. *Physiological psychology*. New York: Holt, 1956.

Williams, J., Meyerson, L., Eron, L., & Semler, I. Peer rated aggression and aggressive responses elicited in an experimental situation. *Child Development*, 1967, *38*, 181–189.

Wolfgang, M. E., & Strohm, R. B. The relationship between alcohol and criminal homicide. *Quarterly Journal of Studies on Alcohol*, 1956, *17*, 411–425.

Zillmann, D. Excitation transfer in communication-mediated aggressive behavior. *Journal of Experimental Social Psychology*, 1971, *7*, 419–434.

Zillmann, D., & Bryant, J. Effect of residual excitation on the emotional responses to provocation and delayed aggressive behavior. *Journal of Personality and Social Psychology*, 1974, *30*, 782–791.

Zillmann, D., Katcher, A. H., & Milavsky, B. Excitation transfer from physical exercise to subsequent aggressive behavior. *Journal of Experimental Social Psychology*, 1972, *8*, 247–299.

Zimbardo, P. G. The human choice: Individuation, reason, and order versus deindividuation, impulse, and chaos. In D. Levine (Ed.), *Nebraska symposium on motivation*. Lincoln: Univ. of Nebraska Press, 1969.

Author Index

Numbers in italics refer to the pages on which the complete references are listed.

A

Adams, D. K., 75, *98*
Adorno, T. W., 49, *56*
Albert, R., 145, *164*
Alexander, A.A., 240, *257*
Alexander, K., 173, *191*
Alioto, J. T., 119, *127*, 206, 218, *231*
Alland, A., 177, *189*
Allport, G. W., 13, *32*
Anderson, N. H., 55, *56*
Andrews, F., 177, *190*
Angulo, E. J., 82, *95*, 247, 248, *257*
Applefield, J. M., 199, *233*
Aquinas, T., 11
Ardrey, R., 7, *8*, 100, 117, 126, *127*, 169, 177, *189*
Aristotle, 17, 99
Arms, R. L., 224, *232*
Aronfreed, J., 158, *164*
Aronson, E., 45, 46, 56, *58*
Atkins, A., 117, *127*

Ax, A. F., 109, *127*
Azrin, N. H., 7, *8*, 20, *32*, 174, *192*

B

Bachicha, D. L., 196, *230*
Bagley, A., 46, *59*
Bahr, A., 117, *127*
Baker, J. W., 106, *127*
Baker, N. J., 134, 154, *167*
Baker, R. K., 194, *230*
Baldwin, A. A., 38, *56*
Ball, R. L., 80, 81, *95*, 137, *164*
Ball, S. J., 194, *230*
Bandura, A., 1, 3, 4, *8*, 39, 55, *56*, 62, *94*, 120, *127*, 158, 160, 161, *164*, 170, *189*, 195, 196, 197, 198, 199, 205, 223, *230*, 241, *257*
Barnes, K., 145, *166*
Baron, R., 171, *189*
Baron, R. A., 5, *8*, 62, 68, 74, 75, 79, 80, 81, 83, 87, 88, *94*, *95*, 134, 136, 137, 145, 155,

261

Subject Index

A 6
B 7
C 8
D 9
E 0
F 1
G 2
H 3
I 4
J 5